Chicken Soup for the Soul®

Older & Wiser

Our 101 BEST STORIES

Chicken Soup for the Soul® Our 101 Best Stories:
Older & Wiser; Stories of Inspiration, Humor, and Wisdom about Life at a Certain Age
by Jack Canfield, Mark Victor Hansen & Amy Newmark

Published by Chicken Soup for the Soul Publishing, LLC   www.chickensoup.com

The publisher gratefully acknowledges the many publishers and individuals who granted Chicken Soup for the Soul permission to reprint the cited material.

Cover photos courtesy of iStockPhoto.com/mammamaart, and Photos.com.
Interior illustration courtesy of iStockPhoto.com/claudelle

Cover and Interior Design & Layout by Pneuma Books, LLC
For more info on Pneuma Books, visit www.pneumabooks.com

Distributed to the booktrade by Simon & Schuster. SAN: 200-2442

Publisher's Cataloging-in-Publication Data
(Prepared by The Donohue Group)

Chicken soup for the soul. Selections.
    Chicken soup for the soul : older & wiser : stories of inspiration, humor, and wisdom about life at a certain age / [compiled by] Jack Canfield [and] Mark Victor Hansen ; [edited by] Amy Newmark. -- [Large print ed.]

    p. ; cm. -- (Our 101 best stories)

    ISBN-13: 978-1-935096-17-7
    ISBN-10: 1-935096-17-6

1. Older people--Literary collections. 2. Older people--Conduct of life--Anecdotes. 3. Older people's writings. 4. Large type books. I. Canfield, Jack, 1944- II. Hansen, Mark Victor. III. Newmark, Amy. IV. Title.

PN6071.O5 C484 2008
810.8/09285   2008932009

PRINTED IN THE UNITED STATES OF AMERICA
on acid∞free paper
16 15 14 13 12 10 09 08   01 02 03 04 05 06 07 08

Chicken Soup for the Soul®

Older & Wiser

Our 101 BEST STORIES

Stories of Inspiration,
Humor, and Wisdom
about Life at a Certain Age

Jack Canfield
Mark Victor Hansen
Amy Newmark

CSS

Chicken Soup for the Soul Publishing, LLC
Cos Cob, CT

Contents

❸

~Making a Difference~

❹

~Across the Generations~

❺

~The Wisdom We've Earned~

❻
~Unexpected Friends~

❼
~Laugh Wrinkles~

8

~Final Gifts~

9

~Gratitude~

10

~Yes, I Can~

11

~Special Moments~

A Special Foreword

by Jack and Mark

For us, 101 has always been a magical number. It was the number of stories in the first *Chicken Soup for the Soul* book, and it is the number of stories and poems we have always aimed for in our books. We love the number 101 because it signifies a beginning, not an end. After 100, we start anew with 101.

We hope that when you finish reading one of our books, it is only a beginning for you too—a new outlook on life, a renewed sense of purpose, a strengthened resolve to deal with an issue that has been bothering you. Perhaps you will pick up the phone and share one of the stories with a friend or a loved one. Perhaps you will turn to your keyboard and express yourself by writing a Chicken Soup story of your own, to share with other readers who are just like you.

This volume contains our 101 best stories and poems for our dynamic older readers. We share this with you at a very special time for us, the fifteenth anniversary of our *Chicken Soup for the Soul* series. When we published our first book in 1993, we never dreamed that we had started what became a publishing phenomenon, one of the best-selling series of books in history.

We did not set out to sell more than one hundred million books, or to publish more than 150 titles. We set out to touch the heart of one person at a time, hoping that person would in turn touch another person, and so on down the line. Fifteen years later, we know that it has worked. Your letters and stories have poured in by the hundreds of thousands, affirming our life's work, and inspiring us to continue to make a difference in your lives.

On our fifteenth anniversary, we have new energy, new resolve, and new dreams. We have recommitted to our goal of 101 stories or poems per book, we have refreshed our cover designs and our interior layouts, and we have grown the Chicken Soup for the Soul team, with new friends and partners across the country in New England.

We know how it is to cross the magic 60 year mark and feel young at heart despite a few new wrinkles. We wouldn't trade away a bit of our wisdom and experience to get rid of all those life markers. We have earned them! In this new volume, we have selected our 101 best stories and poems about growing older and wiser from our rich fifteen year history. The stories that we have chosen will inspire you, teach you, and make you laugh. After all, there is nothing wrong with a few more smile lines.

We hope that you will enjoy reading these stories as much as we enjoyed selecting them for you, and that you will share them with your families and friends. We have identified the 35 *Chicken Soup for the Soul* books in which the stories originally appeared, in case you would like to continue reading about families and senior life among our other books. We hope you will also enjoy the additional books about families, pets, sports, and retirement years in "Our 101 Best Stories" series.

With our love, our thanks, and our respect,
~*Jack Canfield and Mark Victor Hansen*

Older & Wiser

Celebrating Life

The purpose of life, after all, is to live it,
to taste the experience to the utmost, to reach out eagerly
and without fear for newer and richer experience.
~Eleanor Roosevelt

The Odyssey

Attitudes are contagious. Are yours worth catching?
~Dennis and Wendy Mannering

One frosty Colorado morning, while I sipped coffee, my husband, John, said, "We need a lifestyle change. Let's go cruising." I listened dumbstruck, as he continued, "Leslie, what if all our savings and possessions were in one small briefcase? Imagine standing on a sidewalk with that briefcase dangling in your hand; where would you want to go? What would you do next?" Not taking him too seriously, I replied, "I guess I'd go to the beach, sit in a lounge chair and think about it first!"

John was obviously in the throes of a midlife crisis, and it was scaring me. In the ensuing weeks, I noticed his behavior changing. An avid technical reader, John was now reading things like *How to Survive Without a Salary* by Charles Long. My husband has always been an upbeat person, able to find new projects to keep himself motivated. Lately, John had been showing little interest in work and hobbies. His candle was burning low and dim. At fifty-four, he had enjoyed life as a university professor, but I could see he was ready for a metamorphosis, a new "lifestyle."

John wanted to be captain of his own ship, to sail with me from Florida to South America and back. "Let's rent a boat," I offered. But he insisted that we needed a lifestyle change. If we could come back too easily to our home and possessions, it wouldn't qualify as a true change.

In the back of my mind were the sad stories of two couples who had recently divorced, after years of good marriages. I pictured the ex-husbands, in their mid-fifties, riding new red motorcycles, young girlfriends aboard, off into the sunset. I wanted to blame their failed marriages on those red motorcycles. Could their wives have been the ones riding on those motorcycles instead? I wondered.

It was clear that John had to do something about his longings. It was also clear that I wanted to be part of whatever he did. So, I decided to invest in John's midlife-crisis recovery plan. "Okay, I will do this with you, but only for one or two years, max. What's two years in a whole lifetime?" I rationalized.

Weekly planning and budget meetings soon followed that cold January morning. We read about other people living the cruising lifestyle. In May, John requested sabbatical leave. In June it was approved, and I left my job soon after. We took two short trips down the East and West Coasts, shopping for a boat and a launch pad where we would begin our sailing odyssey.

In July, our home sold the first hour it was on the market. At that moment, it became utterly real to me that we were really going to do this "lifestyle" change! In a blur of garage sales and donations, we frantically got rid of STUFF that took us ninety-six combined years to accumulate.

Time was money now. For the first time as adults, we were unemployed and living off our savings and retirement monies. Decision-making got easier. We needed to buy a boat soon and start sailing before both our time and money dried up.

Homeless now after closing on our house, we put the proceeds into a beautiful near-new, forty-foot sailboat named *Sola Fide*, which means "faithful one" in Latin.

We drove our overstuffed ten-year-old compact car to Ft. Lauderdale, Florida, and rented a studio on a canal. With *Sola Fide* steps away, we began the sweaty process of outfitting her for ocean voyaging. Days turned into months as we hunted for marine gear and installed "homey" additions like a wind generator, a water maker, a bank of batteries, and a freezer cold plate. I was shocked at the costs of all these "necessities" and wondered if we would slip the dock lines before our money ran out.

Our big day finally arrived and we set sail. Our plan was to sail a loop from Florida to Venezuela and back, enjoying all the beautiful islands along the way.

We were novice cruisers with only limited sailing experience from brief chartering in the past. We picked up "just-in-time" cruising skills as we lived aboard our little vessel 24/7. Most of our sailing was during the daylight hours, with an occasional ocean passage in the blackness of night. I learned that you can't just stop your boat and anchor in 6,000 feet of water; you have to keep sailing until you reach a safe harbor.

There were dangers among all the pleasures. Occasionally we were challenged by heavy wind and sea. We met an unfortunate cruiser family that endured the loss of their boat. We also met cruisers who had gotten roughed up by modern pirates. John helped rescue cruisers who had run aground or who were dragging anchors.

Somehow our marriage survived this dramatic change of lifestyle. John took out a big "marriage-insurance policy": Thirty days into our trip, stressed-out over the steep learning curve, and getting a full dose of my ranting and wailing, John looked me in the eye and said, "Leslie, if you want to turn around at anytime, we can quit. Our marriage means more to me than this odyssey." Those were the most loving words I had ever heard. Knowing I had a parachute to safely escape with my husband, not without him, helped me endure the discomforts of this pioneer-like life. Curiosity also kept me going. I wanted to know everything this new way of life could teach me.

As we sailed the islands, we took time to enjoy the companionship of the locals and other cruisers, some of whom have become close friends. We had new adventures every day. When weather kept us at anchor, we got involved locally and in volunteer work, tutoring and reading with young children. One exciting day, we helped save dozens of beached pilot whales in Trinidad.

As our midlife odyssey approached the end of its second year, we sailed back up the islands to our Florida starting point. It was bittersweet to be home again. We were filled with new understanding and appreciation, and a renewed confidence that we could accomplish anything we set our minds to.

I am glad I responded positively to my husband's passionate desire to break out of our everyday lives. As we sailed, my own midlife voice spoke, having awaited this opportunity to be set free. It helped me rediscover myself. I learned that I am tough and resilient. Sometimes, we must step outside ourselves to learn who we really are. I am glad I experienced this radically different way of life. It was simple and freer than any I had ever known.

So where do you want to go? And what do you want to do now?

~Leslie J. Clark
Chicken Soup to Inspire a Woman's Soul

The Age of Mystique

Age is an issue of mind over matter.
If you don't mind, it doesn't matter.
~Mark Twain

On my fiftieth birthday, my older daughter gave me a pin that said "Fifty is nifty." I wore it to work that day, and what fun it was! All day, people kept saying things to me like, "Anita, you don't look fifty," or "Why, Anita, you can't be fifty," and "We know you can't be fifty."

It was wonderful. Now, I knew they were lying, and they knew I knew, but isn't that what friends and co-workers are for? To lie to you when you need it, in times of emergency, like divorce and death and turning fifty.

You know how it is with a lie, though. You hear it often enough, and you begin to think it's true. By the end of the day, I felt fabulous. I fairly floated home from work. In fact, on the way home, I thought: I really ought to dump my husband. After all, the geezer was fifty-one, way too old for a young-looking gal like me.

Arriving home, I had just shut the front door when the doorbell rang. It was a young girl from a florist shop, bringing birthday flowers from a friend. They were lovely. I stood in my doorway holding the flowers and admiring them, and the delivery girl stood there, waiting for a tip.

She noticed the pin on my jacket and said, "Oh, fifty, eh?"

"Yes," I answered, and waited. I could stand one last compliment before my birthday ended.

"Fifty," she repeated. "That's great! Birthday or anniversary?"

~Anita Cheek Milner
Chicken Soup for the Golden Soul

Forty Years in the Wilderness

Retirement has been a discovery of beauty for me.
I never had the time before to notice the beauty of my
grandkids, my wife, the tree outside my very own front door.
And, the beauty of time itself.
~Hartman Jule

For the first time in forty years, I'm not working. I didn't realize it until just recently, when, with nothing else to do at my desk one day, I penciled a few numbers on the side of a worksheet. There it was. Forty years.

Good grief, I thought. Isn't that the number of years the children of Israel wandered in the wilderness?

So I sat with my cup of Darjeeling, watching the rain hit the window, mentally conducting a review of where my life had been and where it might be going.

My forty years of work began when I turned fourteen and took a part-time job at the local Ben Franklin variety store. They knew and I knew that I should have been sixteen, but they needed me and I needed them. It was fun going to work after school... even more fun having money in my pocket on payday. During the next four years, I learned how to check inventory, price merchandise, attend the cash register and stock a candy counter. I prided myself on knowing the names of customers, decorating display windows and creating Easter baskets to sell in the spring-time. Although I was just a young girl, I was gaining skills that would stay with me forever.

From my days behind a counter at Ben Franklin, I moved swiftly through a lifetime of employment. I played the role of secretary, worked in schools and hospitals, spent time on the mission field and taught a diversity of classes, including kindergarten, needlework, cooking and drama. I manned phones and wrote payroll, co-owned a graphics business and opened a half-price card and gift shop. All in forty years.

My last job before retirement was difficult to leave behind. A Victorian tearoom in the heart of Duncanville, Texas, was the icing on the cake of my long career. Three years of hard work and pleasure mixed to perfection. It was an unforgettable day when I handed over the keys to the new owner. I took my time saying goodbye to familiar faces, favorite pieces of china and a parlor full of antique furnishings I had grown to love. Reluctantly, I handed over the copies of all my recipes. Then I walked one last time through the parlor, running my fingers along the gold fringe of the velvet drapes on the front window. It was an elegant tribute to four decades of labor.

Now, for the moment, there is nothing pressing in my life. No demands being made. No appointments to keep. No parties to plan. Recently, I finished reading my seventh book since leaving the workforce. Page by page, I fought getting up to go do something, but I overcame and read on. I've met new friends and traveled to faraway places, just sitting in my tapestry armchair.

My garden of herbs flourished on the porch this last

season. After years of neglect, now there is time. Time to water and cut back, check the soil and feed. I've enjoyed chive blossoms and fresh basil on salad, and stored away rosemary and thyme for winter soups.

Next month my sister and I are taking a trip together to San Antonio. It's her sixtieth birthday and we are celebrating by heading out of town. No rush. No fuss. No hurrying back to dive into stress again. We're planning to stroll down the Riverwalk and talk, sit in rockers at a log cabin bed-and-breakfast and sip on homemade lemonade in the afternoon.

Wandering in the wilderness for forty years has brought me into a new place. Friends often ask me if I will ever work again. "Maybe," I tell them. But for now I am enjoying the beauty of rest. I'm camping in the quiet of the day. Stillness is my neighbor. God is my peace.

~Charlotte A. Lanham
Chicken Soup to Inspire a Woman's Soul

Making the Rest the Best

On May 21, 1998, I commenced an adventure I spent seventy years preparing for—my eighth decade. I looked forward to it with great gusto, and I can already tell I have good news for you. Life begins at seventy!

I thought being sixty was incredible, but being seventy is almost incomprehensible. Other people aged, but I simply did not believe it would ever happen to me. Many, many years ago, the very idea that I would ever reach seventy was as remote as the thought that the year 2000 would arrive. The inevitable has finally arrived, though. Now that I have reached seventy, I can relax. People don't generally expect as much of me.

When I was in my sixties, people expected me to retire to a rocking chair on the front porch of a condo, "take it easy" and complain about all my aches and pains. They were always asking questions like, "Do you think you should be doing that at your age?" or "What are you going to do when you retire?" I never planned to retire at sixty, or sixty-two, or sixty-five, even though people expected me to. Fortunately, I didn't feel guilty when failing to meet their expectations. Now that I'm seventy, I still am doing all the fun things I enjoy, including playing tennis, climbing mountains and flying airplanes. I am considering retirement. But nobody asks me about it anymore.

Another benefit of being seventy is having lived long enough to accumulate more than a few gray hairs and smile lines. I go into this season of life with a rich reserve. And I'm not referring to my bank accounts. I'm referring to the reservoir of experiences I've gained. I fully intend to apply the lessons I've learned—first and foremost, to maintain a positive mental attitude. I also plan to keep an open mind to new ideas and to maintain a good sense of humor.

Over the years, my gratitude has grown for the many people I've met along the way—family and friends, as well as thousands of acquaintances. Some I've crossed paths with I like very much. Some I love. I wouldn't go so far as to say that I never met anyone I didn't like. But I am proud to say there were hardly any I simply couldn't stand.

I've always been accused of putting more on my plate than is possible for one human to handle. But my philosophy has always been to bite off more than I can chew—and then to promptly chew it. I have loved living this way. I'm realistic enough to know, however, that I will never be as vibrant as I was twenty, thirty or forty years ago. I am still in good health and capable of living a rich, full life—spiritually, emotionally and mentally. But now if I get carried away and promise to be three places at once, no one thinks badly of me. They just chalk it up to my being seventy.

Being seventy has other pleasant surprises. For example, everybody seems astonished that I'm still going strong. Some are amazed I can still walk without losing my balance and talk without forgetting what I'm saying. Since no one expects someone in their seventies to have perfectly good hearing, I can pretend I can't hear if I want!

Once you reach seventy, people offer to open restaurant

doors, help you with your jacket and save a place for you. If you're late, they know you'll arrive eventually. When you're over seventy, you don't need an excuse; people are just glad you make it. During an evening's conversation, people don't rudely interrupt you as often. They tend to treat you with respect just for having lived so long.

Being seventy is better than sixty, and it's significantly better than being fifty. When you're in your fifties, people hold you responsible for things over which you have very little control — the economy, social conditions, increasing crime, and the list goes on and on. Also, by the time you are seventy, your kids are old enough to recognize that you did the best you could as a parent and no longer hold you responsible for their problems. I am grateful my grandkids have taught my kids that important truth.

When you are seventy, you are given more choices. You can act either young or old. If you act too young, people say you're going through your second childhood. If you act too old, they think you're getting senile and smother you with kindness. You do have to guard against people expecting that you have all this time and nothing to do with it. Convincing them otherwise is sometimes a challenge. I keep telling people how busy I am, how I have goals enough to keep me busy until I'm one hundred, but I still have to say a lot of no's. I have noticed that I've had to say fewer since I put up a poster in my company headquarters office saying, "Retired — gone fishing, hiking, golfing, flying, cycling, snorkeling, swimming, reading, napping and smelling the roses... Meanwhile, have a nice day. Enjoy your work.... I've been there and done that."

Being seventy has reinforced a belief and practice I have held tenaciously to all my life. I don't have to be overly concerned about pleasing others. I don't have to wear suits, starched shirts or ties. I can wear tennis shoes, or no shoes, for that matter!

I can take a nap whenever I feel like it. I'm only sorry that I didn't start sooner. After all, Albert Einstein and Thomas Edison, so I've heard, took naps throughout the day all their lives and no one was bothered. People, in fact, just considered it part of their being geniuses.

Being seventy also gives me more perspective. I've learned not to sweat the small stuff. It's all small stuff. Time is very precious. It's too often wasted on hate, bitterness, holding grudges, or being unforgiving or vindictive.

Now that I've lived long enough to discern what is noble and what is not, I have recommitted myself to doing more good and also encouraging others to do more with their opportunities. I am convinced that doing good will keep my heart and mind strong and vibrant.

I do not know what the rest of my life will bring, but I am setting goals and planning for it to be a great adventure. I look forward to this new season of life, making the rest the best. I'm convinced right now that life begins at seventy. Of course, when I ask my older friends, they insist that life begins at eighty. I wonder if it really begins at ninety. I'll let you know when I get there.

~Paul J. Meyer
Chicken Soup for the Golden Soul

Surf's Up, Grama

My forty-five-year-old daughter, Sue Ellen, had been surfing for a couple of months, trying to entice me to go to the coast to try it. I kept putting her off, thinking, why would they want their almost seventy-year-old mother tagging along on this younger person's junket? "It will be a great girls' weekend out," Sue Ellen coaxed.

The plan intrigued me... and scared me half to death!

I kept being wishy-washy about the possibility, hoping Dad and I would follow through with our plans for a fall trip and I'd have a good excuse. When this didn't seem to materialize, however, I reluctantly penciled in the date on my calendar.

My forty-one-year-old daughter, Diana, and two grand-daughters, ages eighteen and twenty, were all psyched up to go as well. But Diana kept saying, "You're nuts to try this, Mom; even I'm afraid of getting hurt." Sue Ellen, on the other hand, was saying, "Go for it, Mom. You can do it, and you'll always be able to say that you surfed for your seventieth birthday."

Well, that did it. My better judgment took a back seat, and I was determined. My husband just rolled his eyes and said, "I hope you know what you're doing!"

In the weeks to follow, we all did our exercises and lifted weights to strengthen our wimpy muscles. One day when I stopped at Sue Ellen's, she motioned me into the dining room, where she had tape on her hardwood floors marking the foot placement on a virtual surfboard. She demonstrated the "pop up" procedure, where with one motion you pop up from a flat position on your stomach into a crouched position on the surfboard. Next thing I knew she had me on the floor doing a paddling motion with my hands and arms, then shouted, "Pop up!" Well, let me tell you, I felt like a newborn calf trying to stand!

The actual day arrived and, with gear and food packed in the car, we drove to Cannon Beach on the Oregon coast. We headed for the local surf shop to get outfitted—wetsuit, booties and gloves first. Next, a surfboard to suit one's size and ability. A short board is for the more experienced surfer. The long board gives a longer surface to manipulate, which was more my speed. This whole idea was becoming more of a reality every minute.

The surf coach we hired met us at the shop. Tony, a rugged, blond surfer type, was very laid back and comfortable to be with and seemed to enjoy our little group.

We followed him a few miles down the road to North Beach, which was in a more protected cove where the wind wasn't as strong and there were not as many rip tides with their strong undercurrents. We each unloaded our surfboards, strapped on a backpack, and hiked a mile or more down a trail, through the woods to the beach, pairing up to balance two surfboards between us.

It was a beautiful, warm, sunny weekend, and the area was crawling with funny-looking people in form-fitting wet suits. We donned ours there on the beach and draped all of our clothing over huge driftwood logs that had rolled in.

Tony was very safety conscious and spent a lot of time on the sand teaching us safety measures and surfing techniques. We learned how to lie on our boards, pop up to the crouch position and do a little two-shoe shuffle to balance and stand upright.

The waves were four to six feet high that first day, so I opted to stay on the beach and video the others. The second day, the waves had subsided to two to three feet high and I was ready. "You'll be up and surfing in no time!" said Tony.

He led us out through the surf and into the swells and held my surfboard while I got on. Lying on my stomach, I started paddling like mad. He gave me a push just as a big wave hit me. I remembered to pop up into my crouch position and I sailed like a bullet in a big whoosh of water toward the beach. I squealed with delight that I was still on my feet—that is, until the fin on the bottom of my board hit the sand, landing me right on my rump. I came up sputtering and coughing like a wounded pup, still leashed by the ankle to my board. Sue Ellen was on the beach filming me coming in. The girls and Tony were all clapping and cheering me on as I limped back to the beach, stifling my sobs of pain.

Gingerly, I perched myself between two logs so I wouldn't have to sit on my tailbone, which was steadily pulsating and throbbing. After collecting myself for a while, I thought the cold seawater would help, so I very slowly made my way across the beach and back into the water.

Standing sideways to the waves so as not to jar my posterior, the cold felt good on my bruised bottom. Just about then, Diana came sailing by on her board, thrilling to her latest ride in on a big wave... on her belly! "Diana," I said, "I can't bend over to get my board, but if you can get me headed right in the waves, I bet I can do that! I didn't come here to sit on a log all day."

I caught a few good waves belly-boarding, then was happy and proud to leave it at that. Tony said he was surprised that I'd gotten up the first time and stayed up that long; many of his students didn't even make it up the first time. A little praise did wonders for my bruised ego, if not for my bruised bottom.

After several hours of fun in the surf, it was time to leave. We trekked across the beach, up over the rocks on the bluff, and hiked the mile through the woods. It hurt to lift one leg up over the moguls, but with Sue Ellen giving me a pull from her end of the board, we got to the car and were mighty glad to be there. Those pillows for the ride back to Portland felt mighty good.

After about a week of a painful posterior, I checked in with the doctor. "Just badly bruised," he said. I've had a lot of fun telling the story, from my doctor who said, "You did this how?" to the nurse at the injury clinic who said, "At your age? Wish I dared to try that!"

A sensible senior perhaps I'm not, but in spite of having to sit on a pillow for a couple of weeks, I'm glad my good judgment temporarily took a back seat, that I took the challenge and had this fun "senior moment." I read somewhere that "Life is not a journey to the grave with the intention of arriving safely in a pretty and well-preserved body, but rather to skid in broadside, thoroughly used up, totally worn out and loudly proclaiming, 'Wow! What a ride!'"

It certainly was a ride to remember with daughters and granddaughters. They're each ready to ride the waves with gusto at the slightest mention of "Surf's up, Grama!"

~Pam Trask
Chicken Soup for the Grandma's Soul

A Perfect Moment

You can clutch the past so tightly to your chest that it leaves
your arms too full to embrace the present.
~Jan Glidewell

It was the weekend of my parents' sixtieth wedding anniversary party, and there was a lot to do. I had traveled from my home in Chicago, where I live, to my parents' home in northern New Jersey on Friday, and my two brothers, my sister-in-law and I had been working almost nonstop to put all of the final details in place. My brother Jerry had to call the caterer; his wife, Mary, had to buy the paper goods; I had to call the guests who hadn't responded to find out if they were coming; and my brother Rick had to pick up the cake. Along with these tasks, we had my parents' health needs to contend with. My parents were both in their eighties. My mother had suffered a stroke, and now needed help with many routine activities, and my father had been receiving chemotherapy for the leukemia that had recently been diagnosed.

It was stressful, to say the least. In addition to contending with the immediate tasks associated with the party, my brothers and I had stayed up late Saturday night discussing our parents' precarious health, and the challenges we would certainly face in the near future. We talked about it often, on the phone and whenever we got together, but there was never enough time. My parents' health needs changed in often sudden and unpredictable ways, so it was impossible to really plan for the future. We all worried about what the next few years, months, or even days might bring.

The party was scheduled for Sunday afternoon. It was to be an open house at my parents' home; more than fifty people were expected to show up and squeeze into the modest, three-bedroom ranch house. I woke up early on Sunday, already thinking of everything I had to do: set up chairs, move the dining room table, take my mother to get her hair and her nails done. I was feeling stressed before I even got out of bed.

My parents were still sleeping, and my brothers wouldn't be coming over for another couple of hours, so I decided to go for a run. Maybe that would help relieve my stress. I quickly pulled on my sweat pants and sweatshirt and a windbreaker, and stepped outside, quietly pulling the door closed behind me.

I jogged down the quiet street and up the next block, a long, winding street with many large, beautifully land-scaped homes. The last time I was here it was late summer, and the yards were an explosion of color, flowers and bushes of every kind spilling over the lawns and porches, and children's bicycles strewn in the driveways.

But now in the last weekend of March, it was chilly, gray and drizzling slightly. The ground was muddy, the grass sparse. I shivered and I pulled the hood of my wind-breaker over my head and ran a little faster as I crossed into the country club on the other side of the highway. My footsteps were the only sound, slapping on the damp pave-ment as I jogged down the road.

Usually, I enjoyed this route and the routine of running. But today, I was distracted. It was cold and the flowerbeds were still bare, and I had so much on my mind. I was completely engrossed in my thoughts, worrying about my parents' long-term needs and also about the things I still needed to do today to prepare for the party. I barely noticed my surroundings.

I was jogging along, head down, when I slipped. Suddenly, I was sprawled in the wet grass on the side of the road. I knew immediately that I wasn't hurt, but I was out of breath and my shoe was untied. As I tied my shoe, I looked up for the first time and noticed exactly where I was. I had jogged a little more than halfway around the lake that sits in the middle of the country club. When I was here last, in the summer, there were children splashing in the water, ducks quacking, bright flowers lining the road.

But today the lake was completely still. The trees, still leaf-less in early spring, stood out sharply against the gray sky, their trunks darkened by the mist. The ground along the edge of the lake was barren, with no hint of the riot of color that would burst from the soil in less than a month's time. And there was not another person to be seen, not a single car on the road, not even the cry of a bird or a duck to break the silence.

It was utterly pristine and perfect, and I thought it was the most beautiful thing I had ever seen. I sat there for several more minutes, just watching the stillness, listening to the silence.

Now that I wasn't running, I started to feel cold, so I reluctantly got up and started back towards my parents' house. But now I was acutely aware of what I was seeing, of where I was at that moment. I realized that I couldn't even remember the first half of my run. I had been so focused on the things that would come after, on everything I had to do, that I hadn't noticed whether there were buds on the forsythia bush at the entrance to the country club, or whether the house on the corner that had been half-built in the summer was finished yet, or whether Maynard, the elderly dog belonging to my parents' equally elderly neighbor, was lying in his usual spot on the front porch.

When I got back to the house, my parents were both up. My mother was sitting at the kitchen table in her bathrobe, reading the morning paper. My father was at the stove, making coffee. They looked up and greeted me as I came in.

"Hi, honey," my mother said, as she took my hand and squeezed it; her hands were soft and warm.

"How was your walk? Do you want some coffee?" my father asked, smiling.

It was late; I had been gone longer than I'd planned, and there was so much to do. I really should go take my shower, get dressed and get to work right away, I thought.

But it was warm in the kitchen, and the coffee smelled wonderful, and my parents were both there—it was an utterly perfect moment.

"I'd love some coffee," I said.

In the end, everything I needed to do for the party got done in time. And the party itself was wonderful. Celebrating sixty years of marriage is, of course, an amazing achievement. And for my parents, being able to share that celebration with their family and their oldest and closest friends was especially rewarding.

But for me, the best part of the whole day was that hour I spent sitting in the kitchen with my parents that morning, drinking coffee—just enjoying the moment, unburdened by the past or the future.

I know, of course, that I can't always have that luxury. As my parents grow older, the problems and the worries I have about them aren't likely to go away, and I'm going to have to continue to deal with them. But I think it's going to be a little easier now, because my focus has changed. Even though it's important to plan for the future, I'm going to make sure I'm not looking so far ahead all the time that I overlook the special and perfect moments that still happen, every day. I'm going to make sure I look for those moments, and savor them.

~Phyllis L. Nutkis
Chicken Soup to Inspire a Woman's Soul

The Postcard

The ambush came out of nowhere and everywhere. My platoon members and I were strung out and moving through the bush near Hiep Duc in the Que Son Valley of South Vietnam. It was August 20, 1969, and, as always, it was hot and wet.

All at once, the distinctive angry staccato of the enemies' AK-47 assault rifles filled the air. It was mixed with a different sound, that of a heavier machine gun. The incoming rounds slapped and tore through the foliage. Adding to the din were the shouts of the platoon sergeant to return fire. Company C of the 196th Light Infantry Brigade was in trouble.

Suddenly, it felt as if someone had smacked me — hard — with a baseball bat on the left thigh. I had been hit by one of the incoming rounds! I tried to scramble out of harm's way, but there was no escape from the withering fire. Then I heard the ear-splitting "ruuump!" of a grenade explosion, and the baseball bat smashed down hard again, this time pounding onto my right leg and foot.

My memory after that is of crawling — for what seemed like forever. I later calculated that over the course of six hours, I had dragged myself across two miles of ground. I did a lot of thinking and remembering in that time.

At one point during my slow and painful journey, it

occurred to me that I'd had the peculiar fortune to have been "drafted" twice. In January 1968, I was a late-round draft pick for the Pittsburgh Steelers, and in November of that year, the U.S. Army drafted me. In my weakened condition, I found this double-draft thing infinitely amusing.

But the joke soon faded, and my mind once again tried to grasp the reason that I was in Vietnam at all. The political reasons for the U.S. being there were easy to understand. The difficult part for a soldier like me to comprehend was my role in this conflict. I had been over all this in my mind many times before, and I always came back to an incident that had happened early on in my tour.

We had come across a village — not even a village, really, but just a couple of hooches inland. There was a family there — kids, an old man and an old lady. I saw that they didn't have anything — except for an old tin can. They had filled the tin can with water and put it on an open fire to boil. When I looked inside the can, I saw a buffalo hoof. That pathetic soup was their sustenance. I decided right then that if I could help these people take a step forward, then my time in the country would be worthwhile.

As it happened, my opportunity to follow through was cut short. My wounds got me evacuated to Tokyo, where the docs told me I had nearly lost my right foot and that I would never play football again. They informed me I was getting discharged with 40 percent disability.

This was not good news. Football was my whole life and dream — a dream that had started in Appleton, Wisconsin, at Xavier High School and matured at Notre Dame, where I had been voted the captain of the Fighting Irish in 1967. There wasn't anything else in my life I wanted to do. Football was something I identified with and that defined me.

It was a black time for me. Wounded and depressed, I

tried to contemplate a future without football. Then I received a postcard from Art Rooney, the owner of the Steelers. He had written only, "We'll see you when you get back."

Such simple words, but their impact was immediate. It was then that I determined that I would be back—I would fight this thing with everything I had. The first thing on the program was learning to walk again on what remained of my right foot.

With more patience and resolve than I knew I had, I succeeded. In 1970, I returned to the Steelers and was placed on injured reserve. By the following year, I was on the taxi squad. In 1973, I made special teams. That year, I began running. In 1974, I was still running—but now I wore the Steelers' number 20 jersey.

We won the Super Bowl that year. We won again in 1975, 1978 and 1979. Franco Harris and I ran and ran, setting some modest records along the way.

In 1980, I retired from football, having—against all probability—lived my dream. I have tried to thank providence for my exceptional second chance by serving as a board member of the Vietnam Veterans Memorial Fund and being involved with charities for disabled children. I've also done a lot of professional motivational speaking, hoping to inspire others to overcome any obstacles that may bar their way.

In my talks, I always tell people about Art Rooney, whose faith in me was contagious. As long as I live, I don't believe that I will ever experience more inspirational words than the simple sentence written on that long-ago postcard: "We'll see you when you get back."

~Rocky Bleier with David Eberhart
Chicken Soup for the Veteran's Soul

Realize Your Dreams

Each day comes bearing its own gifts. Untie the ribbons.
~Ruth Ann Schabacker

I had been working at a job I loved, an attendance coordinator at a high school, for eighteen years when I began to feel the stirrings of discontent. I had always been in a disciplinarian role and it was becoming uncomfortable. I felt as though I wasn't being true to myself in this role. I was ten years away from retirement and had decided to stick it out when the school district sent me to a weekend workshop. One of the classes, "Realizing Your Dreams," sounded intriguing, so I signed up for it.

After being introduced to the presenter, we were asked to close our eyes and think as far back as we could remember. What was it we loved to do most in the world? What had excited us and made us feel alive? We were to allow whatever came to our minds to be there, no matter how bizarre it might seem. The word "rhythm" came to my mind. I had loved it as a youngster. I had played the clarinet since third grade but had always wanted to be the kid behind the drums. However, during the fifties, girls usually played the flute, clarinet or piano. In high school, my dream had been to be in a rock band, but after years of playing the clarinet, learning to play the drums and joining a rock band seemed out of reach.

The presenter then gave us several exercises to take home. He said if we did the exercises religiously our "vision" would crystallize and manifest itself in our lives. At this point, I was thinking that drumming at the age of forty-five was probably a bit "out there," and maybe I should come up with something more suited to my age group. However, we were told to stick with our original idea, and start journaling, visualizing and acting like we had already reached our goal. It didn't matter, he said, that we had no idea at this moment exactly what the goal was... just do the exercises. He also said that doors would start opening in our lives, and we would need to recognize them as opportunities and walk through them—even if they felt uncomfortable at the time.

I don't know how many people in the class actually went home, did the exercises and realized a dream, but I decided I would try it. I bought myself a spiral notebook, and every morning I sat quietly and wrote a full page of "I am a drummer... I am a drummer... I am a drummer." I said this mantra to myself over and over during the day, and started to imagine myself drumming. All this seemed weird at the beginning, but it actually started to feel exciting and "right" after a couple of weeks.

After about two weeks of journaling and visualizing, my sister called to ask me if I knew about the large African drumming community in Seattle. I hadn't known about this, but I imagined that the community consisted of either Africans, which I am not, or hippies, which I am no longer. I did recognize this as a door opening, however, and decided to take a drumming class. The first six months found me in a group of people I judged to be very different from me. They were mostly younger, offbeat, not your mainstream types. Despite my discomfort, I found I loved the heart-pounding rhythms that were being generated. Soon after, I bought my first drum—it called to me; it had an energy that was powerful, yet simple and beautiful.

Several months later, I was at Seattle's Folklife Festival where I saw a group of children performing on African drums. It made the hairs stand up on my arms and brought tears to my eyes... this powerful sound coming from children! That was the crystallizing moment for me. I realized then and there that I wanted to take my educational experience and my love of drumming and teach children. I gathered my courage and spoke to the director, Kip, after the performance. He was excited to share his expertise and invited me to come to Port Townsend in the summer to help him teach a summer drumming camp. In August 1999, I boarded the Seattle to Port Townsend Ferry alone for my adventurous weekend. I pampered myself by staying in an old Victorian hotel. I spent my days learning that teaching drumming was not only fairly easy for me but also joyful and fulfilling. Kip was more than willing to let me instruct and give me information on starting my own business, purchasing drums and equipment, and lining up jobs. In the evenings, I walked on the beach, meditated, read, took in a movie and shopped at the local craft shops. I will always remember that weekend as a turning point in my life, spiritually as well as occupationally.

Back at home, I started fine-tuning my journaling: "I am a drumming teacher... I am a drumming teacher... I am a drumming teacher." My husband started introducing me as a drumming teacher, even though I still worked at the high school and only had one drum. I continued taking lessons and performing with my class; I started feeling a part of the Seattle drumming community. At this point, I knew I had to take this "game" I was playing to a different level, or it would always be just a game.

Just before the turn of the new millennium, at the age of forty-eight, I resigned from nineteen years at the high school, bought ten drums and a basketful of small percussion instruments, printed business cards, got a business license and made flyers describing my goals, spiritual intentions and drumming experience. I started calling parks departments, schools, Boys and Girls Clubs and YMCAs. I named my business "Heartbeats," because I loved with all my heart the journey I was embarking on. I was terrified but I did it. Now, four years later, I have a wonderful business where teaching drumming allows me to play instead of work.

In addition to teaching drumming, I also felt a great need to be a performer in a women's drumming group. I wanted our songs to be original compositions with a spirit-filled agenda. I wanted to be part of a group that played not only drums, but also other instruments to give it an unusual and interesting flavor. I started journaling these intentions and am now a member of OmBili Afro-Cuban Tribal Jazz all-women performing troupe.

I believe that we all can create whatever is in our hearts. We just need to visualize it, journal it, and feel what it is like to have accomplished it. It works for anything in life. Our imaginations are real and vibrant, and can be used to fill our lives with such joy.

~Margie Pasero
Chicken Soup to Inspire a Woman's Soul

A Matter of Life and Death

My mother's wedding ring and some of her other personal valuables were in my purse. Happy and grateful that my mother had come through heart surgery successfully, I was going to the hospital to pick her up. Carey, my happy-go-lucky two-year-old son, was with me in the car as I maneuvered through Houston's busiest freeway exchange. Then something happened that marked 1976 as the year that changed my life—a terrifying explosion. I remember it with every breath I take—literally.

Traffic came to a riveting halt. Stunned by the sudden shock of it all, I jumped out of the car with Carey right behind me. A strange stench choked me and stung my eyes, and then a huge cloud of toxic fumes enveloped Carey and me. I grabbed Carey and darted back into the car and closed the door. All the while, Carey was screaming, "Help me, Mommy. I hurt!" Frantic, I wrapped Carey in my suit jacket and lay on top of him, trying to protect him from the deadly fumes. Between passing out and throwing up, I tried to honk the horn in desperate hopes that someone would hear it and rescue us. Finally, after I hit the windshield wipers, someone pointed rescuers our way.

Later we found out that the highway holocaust had been caused by a truck pulling a large tank of anhydrous ammonia. The hitch broke, causing the trailer and tank to fall off the upper freeway and onto the lower freeway where I was driving. Fourteen people were killed instantly, and more than two hundred hospitalized. Carey and I were the only two survivors in the area where the explosion had ripped the freeway apart.

After the accident, Carey spent two-and-a-half months in the hospital, and I was there for more than a year. After that, live-in nurses stayed in my home for about two-and-a-half years. Carey and I both received around-the-clock love and attention from my husband. Before the accident, we all enjoyed a wonderful life. We climbed mountains, we went on trips and family outings together, and we even enjoyed our routine workaday life. But in 1976, all that changed. I was an invalid, blind, unable to breathe on my own and certainly not able to care for my two-year-old, my other children, nor my husband.

After a couple of years, I began getting better even though I still took antibiotics every day and breathing treatments three or four times daily. Then I'd suffer setbacks so serious the doctors would call all my family in to be with me while I died. But each time I miraculously rallied.

Different parts of my body gave out at different times. For example, I was blind a great deal of the time until I had a two-cornea transplant. Coping with blindness when I had enjoyed such an active life before the accident was an agonizing struggle, but my lungs—damaged from breathing the toxic fumes—posed the most life-threatening challenges.

The time had come when there was no longer a choice. I simply could not breathe on my own anymore. I was in the hospital for two months on a ventilator, but the doctors said they couldn't consider me for a lung transplant because I was in such poor condition.

I refused to give up hope. Too many people were praying for me. God had already worked numerous miracles in my life—just to be alive was the greatest one.

As I lay in the hospital teetering on a tightrope between life and death, I was told that a donor had been found.

I asked my husband Don to call our minister for me to talk to before I went into the operating room. My husband could not find our minister, so I asked him to find John Morgan, my brother's minister. When John came into my room, he said to me, "You are not going to believe this! Something has happened that I'm not going to tell you about until you wake up after your surgery." I was curious, of course, but I was simply too weak to interrogate him. John prayed with me that I would make it through surgery even though I was in critical condition.

After the surgery, when it looked like I was going to survive, my husband explained to me the miracle John had alluded to. "Last Sunday when we prayed in church for you, a young man and his family were there. His name was Jason. Later that day, Jason was shot and killed in a tragic act of violence. Jason is your donor."

Don filled in more details. "Jason's parents would not have even thought about Jason's being a donor if John had not prayed specifically for you that morning in church and mentioned your name." My husband continued, "Numerous people were on the waiting list—some for over a year. But Jason was the right size for you and the right blood type and had all the other technical compatibilities. Mickey, you were the only one right for Jason's lungs."

One day when I was still in the hospital recuperating

from the transplant, a man came into my intensive care room and asked Don, "Is Mickey Johnson your wife?"

Of course, my husband responded, "Yes." The man explained, "My father is in the hospital here, too, and I have come to see him." He then said, slowly and deliberately, "I was also Jason's schoolteacher." He continued, "I brought all these letters Jason's classmates wrote to your wife."

I cried as I read each letter. They were the most beautiful testimony to a teenager—or anybody—I had ever read. They talked about what a fine young man Jason was and how thrilled he would be that he was able to give life to me if he had to die. My heart almost broke with sadness for Jason's family. How could I ever thank him and his family for the joy that my own life had been extended because of his priceless gift?

I later found out that Jason was born in 1976, the same year as that freeway explosion. The same year that changed my life gave me life.

• • •

As a grandmother, I still have aches and pains, but they are merely reminders of the privilege of growing older. Like George Burns once said, "Growing older is not always golden, but it sure beats the alternative."

~Mickey Mann Johnson
Chicken Soup for the Golden Soul

Boys, Again

How old would you be if you didn't know how old you were?
~Satchel Paige

We first met when we were six years old. Jim and I became best friends, spending our summers together in a town on the south shore of Boston, where Jim lived year round and my family rented a house during July and August.

In those early years, we went barefoot almost the entire summer, the soles of our feet becoming tough as leather, our arms and legs dark as chocolate from the sun, our hair bleached yellow-white.

Jim and I learned to sail at the local yacht club before we were ten, competing against each other in the walnut-sized sailboats known as "rookies," treasuring the blue pennants for first place, red for second. The year we turned eleven, our parents sent us both off to the same boys' camp in New Hampshire, where we grew to love the overnight canoe trips, the campfire cookouts, the smell of pitch pine.

When we were fifteen, we were accepted at the camp as counselors-in-training, an important advance in grade and rank, the first of life's promotions. But life's work still seemed far away, and after a year of counseling, we committed our vacations to travel and adventure.

We spent a summer in Nova Scotia and Quebec, taking odd jobs and camping along the way in an old canvas sheepherders' tent. In the summer of 1956, Jim and I drove across the country and worked in a lumber camp in the state of Washington. We worked another summer in a boys' club in the slums of London, a far cry from the camp in New Hampshire.

The year after graduating from college, our last summer together, we drove to Central America, where we rode a narrow-gauged train through the jungles of Guatemala, stopping at villages with Mayan Indians selling their wares beside the track.

After that, we went our separate ways. Jim took a job as a teacher at a school in South Berwick, Maine. I became a journalist and lived in Boston. We both got married the same year and both had two children, a boy and a girl. The children grew up and two of them got married, starting families of their own.

We sent each other Christmas cards but found it difficult to stay in touch, our lives diverging. Our careers took us in different directions, gave us different experiences, involved us in entirely different communities of friends.

The years went by. The ambitions of youth were tested, cast off—some in success, some in failure. We aged. Jim's hair turned snow-white; I went bald. I developed back problems, Jim had a bout with skin cancer. We both turned sixty.

And then, miles apart, we both woke up one morning and knew it was time to retire. Separately, we came to the same conclusion in the same month. Both of us realized it was time to walk away from the jobs that had kept each of us engaged and excited for thirty-five years.

It was time to begin a new chapter of life.

I had heard about a research project in the badlands of Argentina—a team of paleontologists searching for the planet's oldest dinosaur fossils. And they were taking volunteers.

This Earthwatch project was more primitive than most. Volunteers brought their own tents and sleeping bags, lived in a barren area of the desert known as the Valley of the Moon. There was no electricity. No plumbing. No latrines. Just dinosaur fossils and occasional pit vipers.

On a whim, I called my friend of fifty-five years. We talked about our upcoming retirement, and I told him about the paleontology expedition. Then, on the spur of the moment, I asked him whether he would consider going on such a trip.

The answer was instantaneous and emphatic: Yes!

A few months later, just retired, Jim and I were pitching a tent along a dry riverbed at the foot of the Andes, pounding our stakes into the sandy soil with a large rock, the same way we had done as teenagers, traveling around the Gaspé Peninsula in Quebec.

Every day for the next two weeks, we hiked across the hardpack desert, searching for the fossilized remains of animals that had died there 240 million years earlier, dark purple bones in the white sand. We carried canteens of water and hunks of cheese in our knapsacks, just like the days we had hiked around the Grand Canyon. And in truth, the rugged landscape was very similar in both places—timeless and forbidding and very beautiful.

Late at night, lying in our sleeping bags, Jim and I looked up at the cold black sky, rimmed with stars, and talked about the time we had camped out in the Dakota badlands, far from any townships. We recalled how we woke up after midnight to hear a distant metallic sound, a faint clicking in the heavens, eerie and totally out of place in such a remote space. It wasn't until late the following day that we discovered the distant train track and figured out what that mysterious echo in the dark had been.

And as we had back then, Jim and I started to laugh. We couldn't stop. Our laughter rang across the desolate land and the years between us fell away, circles reconnected.

We were boys again.

~Timothy Leland
Chicken Soup for the Traveler's Soul

11

My Mother's Eyebrows

Do not be too timid and squeamish about your reactions.
All life is an experiment.
The more experiments you make, the better.
~Ralph Waldo Emerson

"Can you show me how to pluck my eyebrows?" she asked. I looked askance at my mother. It's not every day that a mother asks her high school freshman how to pluck eyebrows. She wasn't joking.

This request came from a mother whose adult life consisted of giving birth, raising eight children and keeping house as a dutiful wife trailing an Army officer from one installation to another. Surely, they had modeled Mrs. Cleaver after my mother, with her ever-present apron and no-nonsense approach to everything from child-rearing matters to baking homemade bread. On rare special occasions, Mom wore perfume and orange-red cream lipstick to accessorize sleeveless dresses and other Jackie O-inspired fashions when she and Dad stepped out for the evening.

In the ignorance of my youth, I believed that my mother was — year after year — forty-five years old. For some reason, I affixed that age to her persona. It just seemed right. She never got older than forty-five. To my young eyes, the age of forty-five bordered on geriatric.

It was with great pleasure that I showed my mother how to pluck eyebrows.

The changes were gradual. Not long after, Mom began contributing her bass voice to the Sweet Adelines; her Singer sewing machine—at one time reserved for spitting out summer outfits for me and my sister—began generating glittery gowns and other lush costumes. Fake eyelashes, tubs of facial cream, bottles of makeup and various shades of lipstick began to clutter the medicine cabinet and around the sink in her bathroom.

I remember the first time I saw Mom on stage; I almost didn't recognize her. The years had fallen away—she was no longer forty-five—and all assumptions about my mother were escorted quickly to the exit doors. Mom dazzled me with the way she swished around in costumes, smiling broadly to timed steps, carefully shaped eyebrows arching over false eyelashes and rouged cheeks.

This was not my mother.

Mom was... well, she was a woman!

My mother was a woman having the time of her life, and looking every bit as young as she was feeling.

We traipsed to countless Sweet Adelines shows in support of our mother. After all, she had spent nearly thirty years cheering each of her kids in school plays, church choirs, jazz bands, half time marches. Now it was her turn. She disappeared into a world of bus trips and workshops and competitions with the large chorus that sang barbershop-style, tirelessly honing scales and choreography. Loud, boisterous ladies with husbands to match came over to our house, filling our normally quiet lives with raucous laughter, songs and jokes. We grew to love these friends, revel in their good humor, idiosyncrasies and outlook on life.

When shows were held under the stars in the

amphitheater, we'd bring a cooler filled with sodas, cheese and crackers and kick back. After the biggest show of the year, my parents would attend the Sweet Adelines afterglow party and come home late with confetti in their hair. Year after year, confetti in their hair and flushed cheeks. Finally, when Mom made it to first row on the risers — reserved for the cream of the crop — it was a champagne moment.

Several years after Mom retired from the Adelines, she and my dad were paid a surprise visit on Valentine's Day by a quartet of familiar faces who crooned a medley of romantic songs to them — a surprise gift from the family. And then on my parents' fiftieth anniversary, we reserved a table for the ladies from the "good ol' days."

"C'mon, gang!" someone shouted. "Let's sing a song!"

And there she was again. Up there with her buddies, harmonizing with arms linked around each other's waists. Nostalgia welled up as I remembered the day she asked me how to tweeze eyebrows. I snuck a look at Dad. His beaming face mirrored the pride I felt, because Mom was proving it to us all over again — that age, after all, was just an attitude.

~Jennifer Oliver
Chicken Soup to Inspire a Woman's Soul

Older & Wiser

Chapter 2

Timeless Love

*Age does not protect you from love. But love, to some extent,
protects you from age.*
~Jeanne Moreau

12

A Fragment in Time

Love has no desire but to fulfill itself.
To melt and be like a running brook that sings its melody to the
night. To wake at dawn with a winged heart and give thanks
for another day of loving.
~Kahlil Gibran

The day was a total disaster from the moment I awoke. The dog had decided the cat was a most interesting chew toy, much to the cat's indignant cries, and if that was not enough, the toilet overflowed onto newly installed carpet. The cat, once again in a pickle as she lifted each paw in disgust and shook the water from it, looking at me accusingly as if I had made her life miserable on purpose.

As I entered the kitchen to get a cup of coffee, I heard a scratching sound coming from my cabinet. I slowly opened the door as quietly as I could, and sitting in the back munching on a box of Cheerios was the fattest mouse I had ever seen!

I sighed and closed the door, hoping he was enjoying his breakfast. After all, the Cheerios were ruined anyway—he might as well have the rest! Before tonight, I would have to find some way of coaxing him out of the house and back in the field where he belonged!

I had twelve people coming for dinner and had not

done the shopping. Time was slipping away, and my nerves were standing on end screaming, "Told you so!"

I locked the cat in the bedroom and scolded the dog, who looked at me with innocent eyes wondering what he did in the first place. Then I donned my coat and, totally frazzled, headed for the store.

There was a chill in the air as I pulled into the parking lot of the grocery store. The wind's icy fingers tugged at my coat as I hurried towards the door of the supermarket. I grabbed a buggy, and of course the wheels refused to go in the right direction, clattering through the aisles. Fine! I grumbled to myself. A perfect ending to an already perfect day. I decided that at least I would win the battle of the shopping cart. I shoved the cart next to the cashier's aisle and chose another that was more cooperative. Ahh, the sound of silence and smooth wheels; it didn't take much to bring a ray of sunlight into my life that day.

As I was standing in the produce section pinching the avocados, I heard that familiar annoying rattle of wheels, and I turned to the unfortunate person who'd obviously chosen my old buggy to say, "You have the shopping cart from hell!" What I saw changed the rest of my day into one I will never forget.

An elderly man with white hair and a face that was etched with wrinkles was pushing a hospital stretcher with one hand and pulling the basket from hell with another. He didn't notice the clatter or the wheels that went in different directions. He was busy guiding his wife, who lay upon the stretcher, closer to the produce so she could have a look.

She was a frail woman with gray at the temples and large blue eyes. Her hands and feet were twisted in odd directions and she could not raise her head but a tiny bit. He would pick up a piece of fruit and, with a sweet smile, hold it close to her, and she would nod her head and smile in return. They greeted everyone with a smile and a nod of their heads and didn't seem to mind that they were the subject of gawking and attention. Some people shook their heads in disgust that he would bring a stretcher into the grocery store; others whispered disapprovingly that they didn't belong.

I watched as he picked up a loaf of bread and touched her hand so softly. The connection between the two of them filled the space with so much love that it was palpable. I realized I was staring, as if to hold them in that moment of enchantment. Concerned that I was intruding, I forced my eyes to look away. I turned back to the avocado that was resting in my hand and noticed I had squeezed it a little too hard. I placed it back in the rack and moved to the dairy aisle, trying to catch another glimpse of this couple who seemed to be a magnet for my heart.

They had moved on to another part of the store, and I didn't see them again until I was finished with shopping and back in my car. I started the engine, and suddenly noticed that there, next to my car, were the elderly man and his wife. His vehicle had been parked next to mine, and as he put the groceries in the front of his van, his wife waited patiently on the stretcher.

He hurried to the back of the van, and a gust of cold wind blew the blanket off her frail body. He lovingly tucked it back around her as you would tuck in a child before bed, reached down and placed a kiss on her forehead. With a twisted hand, she reached up and touched his face. Then, they both turned to look at me and smiled. I returned the smile with tears rolling down my cheeks.

What tugged at my heart and brought tears to my eyes was not the condition either of them was in. It was the love and laughter they shared in going to the store together and being as they always had been... in love and needing each other.

The man placed the stretcher in the back of the van and made sure it was secure, and then he came around to the driver's side and stepped in. As they were leaving, he looked at me once again and smiled with a wave, and as he pulled out of the lot, I saw a small hand wave from the back of the van, and the most beautiful, vibrant blue eyes returned my gaze.

Sometimes in life one is struck with an astounding realization — that within a moment of time, which seems to move in slow motion, one can grasp the total beauty of life and love in its purest form. It plays before your eyes like an old black-and-white movie with only the sound of silence and the movement of the actors who, without words, will touch your heart. In that fragment of time, sitting in the parking lot, I felt the pure radiance of the profound, unconditional love of two perfect strangers who crossed my path on what I had thought was going to be a disastrous day.

I started for home with my car full of groceries and my heart full of hope. This couple had taught me a priceless lesson — that the little things don't matter, and the big things are just small hurdles when there is enough love.

~Victoria Robinson
Chicken Soup for the Romantic Soul

Never Say Never

Love is, above all, the gift of oneself.
~Jean Anouilh

"How would you like to accompany me to England for a week of sightseeing?" I stared at the e-mail in disbelief. It was from Mel, the widower I had been dating for six months.

I immediately replied, "Thank you for your generous offer, but I must respectfully decline. As much as I enjoy your company, I would not be comfortable traveling with a man I wasn't married to. Besides, I don't have a passport."

My dear husband of fifty-one years had died three years earlier. I learned to ease my grief by reading, writing, attending church functions and visiting my children and grandchildren. But as time passed, I missed belonging to a partnership.

Then friends invited me to a party where I met Mel. He was attractive, intelligent and had an engaging personality. To my surprise, he called two weeks later and invited me to join him for dinner.

I discovered being part of a couple again opened new vistas. Soon we were receiving invitations to parties and meeting each other's friends. After being in a desert of loneliness, I enjoyed the social oasis of dinners, concerts and theater.

We talked freely about our deceased spouses and how lucky we were to have found true love with them. Because we didn't think it was possible to find that level of love more than once in a lifetime, we both admitted our decisions to never marry again and decided to enjoy the companionship we found in each other.

Consequently, I was shocked at the invitation to travel together and questioned Mel's motives. Certain my response would sever our relationship, I was surprised when he phoned.

"I got your reply. Let's forget I asked about the trip."

Relieved, I mumbled, "Thanks for understanding."

"We are still going out tomorrow night, aren't we?"

"Sure." After all, he didn't seem to feel awkward about the situation, so why should I?

The following evening he held the car door open with one hand and handed me a legal looking paper with the other. "Just happened to be in the post office today and picked this up for you."

It was an application for a passport. What? Why, that sly man! Without comment, I tucked it into my purse and changed the subject. Nothing more was said, and we enjoyed the evening.

Amused he had bothered to get me an application, I filled out the papers, had my photo taken and doled out the $75.00 fee without telling him.

While attending a party with friends, we were invited to join their dance club. I was excited, but Mel resisted. "I played trumpet in a swing band during my youth so I never danced very much."

"If you're a musician, you've got rhythm," I reminded him. "If you've got rhythm, you can dance."

Although reluctant at first, Mel relented and agreed to take ballroom dance lessons—where he held me in his arms for the first time. With him holding me, I felt my heart melt... and immediately rued our platonic relationship. But I couldn't tell him lest he remind me about our "never marry again" agreement.

Then he began bringing candy and flowers, and I knew I was being courted. Although he was careful not to mention marriage, I sensed we were falling in love. Still, neither of us said a thing until the day he invited me to dinner at his house.

Fine china, crystal and sterling silver on a white linen tablecloth greeted me. Red roses graced the table. Before we sat down to eat, I confessed I had applied for and received my passport. When I showed it to him, his eyes sparkled and he flashed a mischievous grin.

He served a delicious rack of lamb with all the trimmings and we had a lively conversation as we ate. During dessert he said, "Sally, if I asked you to marry me, what would you say?"

"You haven't asked me yet." My startled response was quick. Awkward. Even a little coy.

"I think I just did."

Unprepared, I stammered, "Oh. Oh. P-p-probably."

He looked dejected, but didn't pursue the subject. I was so surprised I didn't know what to say. We cleared away dinner and cleaned up his kitchen, then he took me home.

Most of that night I lay awake pondering his proposal. I had been married to an extraordinary man once.

But Mel was wonderful, too. Was it possible to marry two extraordinary men in one lifetime?

The next morning, he called. "Last night I asked you to marry me and you said probably. How about a more definite answer," he urged. "Like yes?"

"But... what about our agreement?"

"Let's just forget it."

"Forget what?" I smiled into the phone, tingling with excitement.

"Let's fly to England for our honeymoon and never say never again."

~Sally Kelly-Engeman
Chicken Soup for the Bride's Soul

Whoever You Are, I Love You

I know God will not give me anything I can't handle.
I just wish that He didn't trust me so much.
~Mother Teresa

I never know who I am going to be when I visit my mother these days.

She has told me, on different days, even from one moment to the next, that I am her husband, her beloved brother-in-law, her grandmother. Then, on her good days, I am just Jim, or Jimmy, her son. Those are my good days, too.

It's confusing and frustrating for both of us. My mother doesn't have much to say to me anymore. She sits in silence, and I try to prod her into saying something. She searches for the right words and knows what she wants to say. I can see it in her blue eyes, still bright, and I know it hurts her when her search is fruitless.

"Why do I call you Mom?" I prodded her one day.

"Because you're my grandmother," she said.

"C'mon," I beseech her, "why do I call you Mom?"

She looks at me, a bit puzzled by my inquisition.

It's more than she can handle. Finally, she offers, "Whoever you are, I love you."

I've always known that.

My mother, Mary O'Brien, has resided the past five years in a nursing care center. After some bad falls, she didn't want to walk anymore for fear she'd fall again. She has been in bed or in a wheelchair ever since.

"I like it here," she tells me repeatedly. "They couldn't be nicer to me. I always try to make the best of it. I'm just getting old and rusty. It makes me feel better when you stop."

The feeling is mutual.

The admissions director kisses my mother whenever she sees her in the hallways. "She's one of my favorites." She asked my mother to identify me.

"That's Jim O'Brien, my son," she says, proudly.

"See, she knows," cried the director. "She fools you now and then."

I visited my mother on New Year's Eve, her ninety-fourth birthday. My wife, Kathie, came with me, and we brought birthday and Christmas gifts. I came back the next day to find Mom dressed in one of the new jerseys I had picked out for her. It was embroidered with cardinals on a fence in front of a home in a snow-covered field.

My mother's white hair was combed just right. She was sitting up in her wheelchair, looking lovely in her new outfit. She was smiling and more lucid than usual. She was making sense. I started to cry.

"What's wrong, honey?" she asked. I blamed it on the Christmas season, just getting overwhelmed by it all. She had a concerned look on her face. Once more, for a moment anyhow, she was definitely my mother.

I read her birthday and Christmas cards aloud to her. I

recognized the names of relatives and friends and felt grateful for their kindness. Thank God for such people.

"Whatever happened to me and all that stuff I once knew?" my mother asked, feeling bad about her lack of recall. "I'm a complete failure. I forget things I'm supposed to know. I love this place. I just don't love the way I am. Not knowing anything. Jimmy knows I used to be pretty sharp. Don't you, Jim?"

I smiled, delighted for her recognizing me.

Then she added, "I've been so lucky to have the dad I've had." As I prepared to leave, she looked my way. "I love you, Dad."

~Jim O'Brien
Chicken Soup for the Mother and Son Soul

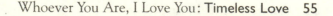

Loving Muriel

Seventeen summers ago, Muriel and I began our journey into the twilight. It's midnight now, at least for her, and sometimes I wonder when dawn will break. Even the dreaded Alzheimer's disease isn't supposed to attack so early and torment so long. Yet, in her silent world, Muriel is so content, so lovable. If she were to die, how I would miss her gentle, sweet presence. Yes, there are times when I get irritated, but not often. It doesn't make sense to get angry. And besides, perhaps God has been answering the prayer of my youth to mellow my spirit.

Once, though, I completely lost it. In the days when Muriel could still stand and walk and we had not resorted to diapers, sometimes there were "accidents." I was on my knees beside her, trying to clean up the mess as she stood, confused, by the toilet. It would have been easier if she weren't so insistent on helping. I got more and more frustrated. Suddenly, to make her stand still, I slapped her calf—as if that would do any good. It wasn't a hard slap, but she was startled. I was, too. Never in our forty-four years of marriage had I ever so much as touched her in anger or in rebuke of any kind. Never. I wasn't even tempted, in fact. But now, when she needed me most....

Sobbing, I pleaded with her to forgive me—no matter

that she didn't understand words any better than she could speak them. So I prayed and said how sorry I was. It took me days to get over it. Maybe I bottled those tears to quench the fires that might ignite again some day.

A young friend recently asked me, "Don't you ever get tired?"

"Tired? Every night. That's why I go to bed."

"No, I mean tired of..." and she tilted her head toward Muriel, who sat silently in her wheelchair, her vacant eyes saying, "No one at home just now." I responded to my friend, "Why, no, I don't get tired. I love to care for her. She's my precious."

Love is said to evaporate if the relationship is not mutual, if it's not physical, if the other person doesn't communicate or if one party doesn't carry his or her share of the load. When I hear the litany of essentials for a happy marriage, I count off what my beloved can no longer contribute, and then I contemplate how truly mysterious love is.

What some people find so hard to understand is that loving Muriel isn't hard. They wonder about my former loves—like my work. "Do you miss being president?" a university student asked as we sat in our little garden. I told him I'd never thought about it, but, on reflection, no. As exhilarating as my work had been, I enjoyed learning to cook and keep house. No, I'd never looked back.

But that night I did reflect on his question and prayed, "I like this assignment, and I have no regrets. But if a coach puts a man on the bench, he must not want him in the game. You needn't tell me, of course, but I'd like to know—why didn't you keep me in the game?"

I didn't sleep well that night and awoke contemplating the puzzle. Muriel was still mobile at that time, so we set out on our morning walk around the block. She wasn't too sure on her feet, so we went slowly and held hands as we always do. This day I heard footsteps behind me and looked back to see the familiar form of a local derelict behind us. He staggered past us, then turned and looked us up and down. "Tha's good. I likes 'at," he said. "That's real good. I likes it." He turned and headed back down the street, mumbling to himself over and over, "Tha's good. I likes it."

When Muriel and I reached our little garden and sat down, his words came back to me. God had spoken through an inebriated old derelict. "It is you who is whispering to my spirit, 'I likes it, tha's good,'" I said aloud. "I may be on the bench, but if you like it and say it's good, that's all that counts."

People ask me, "How do you do it?" Praise helps—Muriel is a joy to me, and life is good to both of us, in different ways. And we have family and friends who care for us lovingly.

Memories help, too. Muriel stocked the cupboard of my mind with the best of them. I often live again a special moment of love she planned or laugh at some remembered outburst of her irrepressible approach to life. Sometimes the happy doesn't bubble up with joy but rains down gently with tears. In the movie *Shadowlands*, when Joy Gresham reminds C. S. Lewis that their joy will soon end, that she will die, he replies that he doesn't want to think about it. Joy responds, "The pain is part of the happiness. That's the deal."

Muriel hasn't spoken a coherent word in months—years, if you mean a sentence, a conversation—though occasionally she tries, mumbling nonwords. Would I never hear that voice again?

Then came February 14, 1995.

Valentine's Day was always special at our house because that was the day in 1948 that Muriel accepted my marriage proposal. On the eve of Valentine's Day in 1995, I bathed Muriel, kissed her good night and whispered a prayer over her, "Dear Lord, you love sweet Muriel more than I, so please keep my beloved through the night; may she hear the angel choirs."

The next morning I was peddling on my exercise bike at the foot of her bed and reminiscing about some of our happy lovers' days long gone while Muriel slowly emerged from sleep. Finally, she popped awake and, as she often does, smiled at me. Then, for the first time in months she spoke, calling out to me in a voice as clear as a crystal chime, "Love... love... love."

I jumped from my cycle and ran to embrace her. "Honey, you really do love me, don't you?" Holding me with her eyes and patting my back, she responded with the only words she could find to say yes. "I'm nice," she said.

Tha's good. I likes it.

~Robertson McQuilkin
Chicken Soup for the Golden Soul

16

The Unlikely Best Man

Love is patient, love is kind.... It always protects, always trusts,
always hopes, always perseveres.
~1 Corinthians (13:4,7)

Day after day, I saw life at its loneliest—elderly men and women wasting away to nothing with no one to visit them. I was interning at a public healthcare facility, and the loneliness I witnessed was sad.

Then I met Sophia.

Despite her deteriorating physical condition, Sophia was an assertive little lady who proved to the entire nursing facility she was still full of vitality, humor and—most importantly—romance. She would often weave tales to the staff and fellow patients of her Romeo-and-Juliet-esque relationship with her husband Carl.

One of her favorites was the story of two hearts.

As young Depression-era lovers, Carl and Sophia were in love, yet extremely poor. But Carl didn't let that shake their love. On bended knee one Valentine's Day, he asked Sophia to marry him. Unable to afford an engagement ring, he presented her with a small brooch with two rhinestone-covered hearts.

"A woman needs two hearts," Carl said. "One to love,

care and live with; the other for the man of her dreams to steal."

They had been married thirty years when Carl died of a heart attack. On his deathbed, he gave her his last wish.

"Sophia, you deserve to be taken care of. I want you to move on and find yourself another husband."

Shaking her head in denial, Sophia cried until she couldn't speak. Carl grasped her hand.

"Don't worry. I'll be watching you from above. I'll send someone to take care of you." A few minutes later, he passed away.

Sophia's eyes brimmed with tears each time she repeated his last words. I'm not sure what pained her more — Carl's short life or that, after all these years, no one was sent to take his place in her lonely heart.

Then a new resident was admitted to the nursing home.

Like Sophia, John lost his spouse unexpectedly. The two clicked immediately and were often seen dining and visiting each other's floors. They were like two love-bitten teenagers, holding hands in the television lounge or headed out "on pass" for a date in the city.

Now, Sophia's eyes sparkled with refound youth. And the health of both drastically improved.

Sophia's ninetieth birthday was celebrated by all the residents at the facility with a special dinner cooked by the staff. When John was asked to give a speech, the twinkle in his eyes hinted he had something up his sleeve. Before Sophia could comprehend what was happening, he handed her a small jewelry box.

"Sophia, will you marry me?"

An emotional silence filled the room as she opened the box with shaky hands. Her mouth dropped and tears streamed when she revealed a ring with two heart-shaped diamonds.

"Every woman should have two hearts," John declared. "One is for me, and one is for Carl."

The couple married a month later. The nursing home chapel brimmed with staff, patients and local news crews elbowing each other to cover this sweet "December" romance. Gowned in scrubs, nurses served as bridesmaids. Sophia's daughter gave her away. And perched on a pedestal next to John was a large portrait.

A picture of Carl.

"The best man is supposed to give the couple his blessing," John said. "Carl gave his when he sent me to her."

~Jenn Dlugos
Chicken Soup for the Bride's Soul

17

Scenes from a Marriage

*The ultimate measure of a man is not where he stands in
moments of comfort and convenience,
but where he stands at times of challenge and controversy.*
~Martin Luther King Jr.

W e are standing in the kitchen glaring at one another. I remind my Valentine that he's officially taken over dishwasher duty, which means loading and unloading the old workhorse; that it's now 11:00 A.M.; and that, still, the clean dishes remain lodged inside while the dirty ones languish on the counter.

I avoid mentioning that in my dishwasher-loading/ unloading era, the deed was always done early and that the platters were always standing like sentries on the bottom shelf, not leaning precariously on one another. These are fighting words on a Sunday morning. We both know it. But somehow, seconds later, we burst into laughter at our own foolishness. It's Sunday — and Valentine's Day — and what difference does it really make in the long run that the dishwasher isn't unloaded or that the platters aren't in perfect order?

At this stage of our union, we finally understand the futility of dumb arguments and while we still have them, of course, we end them sooner than we used to.

Score one for very married Valentines. Forget the plump red satin heart-shaped boxes of rich chocolate. Forget the love poems penned in passion, the wild embraces, the waltzes under crystal chandeliers. For some of us, Valentine's Day, even in all its commercial, hucksterish glory, remains a reminder that, in ordinary life, it's the little stuff that counts.

The notes left on the kitchen table in haste, signed with nicknames only we recognize. The way he remembers to pick up the exotic cheese I love, even though it means going miles out of his way. The fact that when it's raining and we're going out, he pulls the car right to the kitchen door for a presumably liberated lady.

Yes, those trifles, friends, count dearly in this season when we're reminded that love changes everything, conquers all, and makes the world go 'round.

I agree with all of the above. But I also know better.

In the autumn of a long and committed marriage, we celebrate love in quirky, not just cosmic, ways. I make chocolate pudding the old-fashioned way, the cooking, stirring, scorch-the-pot method, when I detect a certain sag to my beloved's shoulders, a certain weariness in his walk. And the fuss feels both right and rewarding.

On mornings when we both awaken not like songbirds but like terminal grouches, we deftly avoid conversation. And yes, it's a loving, not hostile, gesture. And in the sleepless dark, when the demons come, I know that I can reach over to a man who is soundly sleeping, gently wake him, and find myself in the homeland of his arms.

We haven't waltzed under a chandelier of any description in years, but every now and then, when the mood is right, my Valentine and I will dance around the kitchen to the strains of the radio, preferably to an old Frank Sinatra ballad. It's so corny that it's embarrassing, but we don't care. And some of our best moments—moments that bind and bond us and make our hearts leap—have come when we've stood in a silent, dark room and watched a grand-child sleeping.

It may not be classic romance. It may not meet the rap-turous hype of magazines that speak of love as primal and wild, sensual and captivating. But for two late-middle-aged Valentines, those bedside vigils are an affirmation of loving long and well—loving right into the next generation.

So when the dishwasher eruptions come—and they always do—we rely on the best gifts of Valentinehood to get us though:

Humor.

Forgiveness.

Emotional generosity.

And a love that's old enough to have a burnished glow, but not too old to sparkle and to make two midlife Valentines enormously grateful for the gift of one another.

~Sally Friedman
Chicken Soup to Inspire a Woman's Soul

18

Real-Life Fairy Tale

I shall love you in December with the love I gave in May.
~John Alexander Joyce

"My first girl! My first girl!"
It was our forty-fifth high school reunion. Bob Grove's arms were extended as he headed toward me. It was only a moment before he had me in the biggest bear hug I had ever experienced.

His twin sister, a close friend of mine, had called and told me he was coming, so I was watching for him. We hadn't actually talked to each other since 1938—forty-seven years before. What a thrill to have such an exuberant greeting!

He had been my "first fellow," too. He had been in my geometry class, and he wore glasses. I had just started wearing mine, and I was extremely self-conscious. Although I was worried about people making comments about my appearance I told myself, At least he won't make fun of me. He'll be safe!

As our friendship had grown, he had carried my books from class to class, had come over to my house to play cards and had taken me to parties. But we had never even held hands.

His sister told me he was now single and retired, and

my husband had died over two years before, so we knew we were both unattached as we spent the rest of the evening together. He held my hand everywhere we went. By the end of the evening when it was time for me to go home (since I lived in town) he said, "Hey, wait up! I'll walk you to your car!"

He took my hand again and we headed for the parking lot. "Here's my car," I told him as I unlocked the door.

His hand had a tighter grip on mine as he pulled me back toward him, murmuring quietly, "When we were going together I was too shy to do this," and he kissed me gently on the lips.

I was taken by surprise, but enjoyed the feel of his warm lips on mine so much I returned the kiss before I hopped into my car.

Driving home I realized my heart was pounding, and it continued to do that all through the night—I could hardly sleep. And it is only the first day of the reunion, I kept thinking.

The next day we hung around together with old friends, then in the afternoon he asked, "Will you go with me to the dance tonight? I don't want to go alone. I want to sit with you!"

"Sounds good to me."

That night, while dressing for the big affair, I was looking forward to how great it would be to have his long arms around me. My two years as a widow had been devoid of any close, touching relationships, but I had adjusted well and hadn't been looking for a man. I couldn't believe how exciting it was to be with him. It's just a fling. He'll be flying away before long, I kept telling myself, hoping to calm down.

It wasn't long before he showed up dressed in his dark

blue suit, his Stetson hat and cowboy boots. He was still a cowboy at heart even though he was a retired mechanical engineer.

Music from a small band filled the air at the party. It was more fun than I had imagined. Then a booming voice came over the loudspeaker, "Breakfast will be at 9:30! No need to get up early!"

"Too bad I won't be able to go to the breakfast," Bob said.

"What? You mean you aren't staying?"

"Nope, my plane leaves at 10:30, so I will be gone."

"But the breakfast is the most fun of all. I can't believe you didn't plan to stay for it!" I was upset, and I'm sure it showed.

He looked straight at me and made me an offer. "If you'll promise to spend the day with me, I'll change my reservations."

"Of course I'll spend the day with you. I'd love to."

That meant we would have all day Sunday together, just the two of us.

When he drove me home, I invited him in. We chatted a while, but it was getting late and soon he was leaving. This time when he kissed me goodnight, I returned his kiss with enough enthusiasm that he acted pleased and surprised.

Next morning I was so happy I went around the house singing "Oh what a beautiful morning, oh what a beautiful day!"

After the breakfast, we took a drive out to our favorite desert vista, then returned to the hotel.

Sitting at a table in the bar was an old alum friend of ours. "Come on over and sit here," he said. "What's going on with you two anyway? You look so happy together."

Bob spoke up, "This is just the most fun I ever had!"

"Me, too," I chimed in, still excited over the way our day had gone.

"We decided to spend the day together," Bob explained. "I live in Corvallis, Oregon, fifteen hundred miles from here. No way can this last."

"What do you mean it can't last? Neither of you has any family to stand in your way. So what if you live fifteen hundred miles away? That's no excuse."

In those few minutes he convinced us to stop thinking of our fun times as a temporary situation. It hadn't taken much encouragement for us to feel closer from that moment on. It was a real "turning point" in our lives.

That night we had a late dinner and a romantic evening neither of us will ever forget.

Between phone calls and letter-writing, meeting each other in San Francisco three weeks later, and my going up to Corvallis to spend Thanksgiving with him (where we were snowbound for three days!), we made up for our lost years of togetherness.

We were married in March 1986, five months after we had re-met. Both of us were sixty-three years old.

At one time in my life, a long time before, I had wished that somewhere, sometime, I would find someone who would love me for the person I am, who would share my soul—a fantasy future. To think my wish came true!

It is still a thrill to be able to spend my "golden years" with someone so dear to me. We've been truly blessed to find each other again. There aren't many people our age (seventy-nine) who are so lucky!

~Norma Grove
Chicken Soup for the Romantic Soul

19

A Change of Heart

Aging forces us to decide what is important in life.
~Thomas Moore

Grandma got Grandpa out of bed and helped him to the kitchen for breakfast. After his meal, she led him to his armchair in the living room where he would rest while she cleaned the dishes. Every so often, she would check to see if he needed anything.

This was their daily routine after Grandpa's latest stroke.

Although once a very active man, his severely damaged left arm, difficulty walking and slurred speech now kept him housebound. For nearly a year he hadn't even been to church or to visit family.

Grandpa filled his hours with television. He watched the news and game shows while Grandma went about her day. They made a pact—he was not to leave his chair or his bed without her assistance.

"If you fell and I threw my back out trying to help you, who would take care of us?" Grandma would ask him. She was adamant about their taking care of themselves and living independently. The Brooklyn brownstone had been their first home and held wonderful memories. They weren't ready to leave it behind anytime soon.

Immigrants from Ireland, they met and married in America. Grandma was friendly, outgoing and unselfish; Grandpa was reserved, a man devoted to his family. But he wasn't big on giving gifts. While he wouldn't think twice about giving my grandma the shirt off his back, he subscribed to the belief that if you treated your wife well throughout the year, presents weren't necessary; so he rarely purchased gifts for her.

This had been a sore point in the early days of their marriage. But as years passed, Grandma realized what a good man he was. And, after all, anything she wanted she was free to buy herself.

It was a cold, gray February morning, a typical winter day in New York. As always, Grandma walked Grandpa to his chair.

"I'm going to take a shower now." She handed him the television remote. "If you need anything, I'll be back in a little while."

After her shower, she glanced towards the back of Grandpa's recliner but noticed that his cane was not leaning in its usual spot. Sensing something odd, she walked toward the recliner. He was gone. The closet door stood open and his hat and overcoat were missing. Fear ran down her spine.

Grandma threw a coat over her bathrobe and ran outside. He couldn't have gotten far; he could barely walk on his own.

Desperately, she scanned the block in both directions. Small mounds of snow and ice coated the sidewalks. Walking safely would be difficult for people who were steady on their feet, much less someone in Grandpa's condition.

Where could he be? Why would he leave the house all by himself?

Wringing her hands, she hardly felt the frigid air as

she watched traffic rush by. She recalled overhearing him tell one of their grandchildren recently that he felt he was a "burden." Until this last year, he had been strong and healthy; now he couldn't even perform the simplest of tasks.

As she stood alone on the street corner, guilt flooded her.

Just then, Grandpa walked around the bend of the corner. Head bowed, eyes focused on the sidewalk, he took small, cautious steps. His overcoat barely draped the shoulder of his bad arm; his cane and a package filled his good arm.

Desperate to reach him, Grandma raced down the block. Relieved to see that he was okay, she started to scold.

"I only left you alone for a short while. What did you need so badly that couldn't wait? I was so worried about you! What on earth was so important?"

Confused and curious, she reached into the brown bag. Before Grandpa had a chance to explain, she pulled out a heart-shaped box.

"It's Valentine's Day," Grandpa explained. "I thought you might like a box of chocolates."

A gift? All this worry for... candy?

"I haven't bought you a gift in a long, long time." His stroke-impaired words warmed the winter wind.

Tears flooded Grandma's eyes as she hugged his arm to her chest and led Grandpa back home. She shook her head slowly.

It just goes to show, she thought, it's never too late for romance.

~Denise Jacoby
Chicken Soup for the Bride's Soul

20

Love's Cross-Stitch

"**N**ow if you want to change your mind..." Del glanced from the road to read my expression, then faced back to the freeway traffic. "Remember, I'll understand if you'd just like to drive by the house. Not even get out. Or, at the front door, if you decide that's it for the first time, fine. The most important thing is that I care about you. More than any house or the things in it."

I smiled, nodding, hoping my eyes and the tiny muscle tugs around them wouldn't betray me. I didn't want to disappoint this man who was now the very center of my life. But how might I react when I saw for the first time the house he had lived in for the past twenty years, eighteen of them with his Lib?

I knew them both, but that was thirty-five years ago, when we lived in the same town. Lib and Del raised their two girls, then grew older in the house, the house which until now had been to me simply the address I wrote on envelopes of annual Christmas cards.

Then, a little over two years ago, when Lib was near the end, she had asked Del to write me. After her passing, I wrote to him. I shared with him a few of the helps that had served me when I lost my marriage mate of many years, assuring him I recognized our losses were not to be compared, yet believing them similar in a very real way. We corresponded for almost a year before he asked if he might come to see me.

Del signaled to take the off-ramp. I could still change my mind, but we would soon swing into a driveway somewhere to the right. I knew the area, though not in detail. He had driven the many miles to visit me countless times, but until now he had never suggested I visit him.

"Seeing me in your home could be difficult, Del," I warned. "Have you had many people in since you've been alone?"

He pulled to a stop at a light. "Neighbors. The girls, of course, and their families. The grandkids come over pretty often." He smiled at me.

"I mean outside of family and neighbors."

Still smiling, he shook his head no and pulled from the stop. "I want you to see my house. I've been looking forward to this evening. But the decision is still yours."

I tried to busy my mind on anything but the impending, immediate future. Crossing the bridge at the little creek woke the sleeping butterflies in my stomach; the house would be less than a block away. My heart banged against my chest. I hadn't felt this confused or just plain nervous since I was a teenager.

Del slowed for the turn onto Woodhurst, the street I had written on envelopes for years, then braked to a crawl. "Cold feet?"

"Clammy cold."

"Understandable," he said in the gentle, measured tone I'd grown to love. "But we've come a long way."

True. A long drive, and a remarkable length of time as friends. We had kindled from a resurrected, couples acquaintanceship a strong, sweet attachment. To enter Del's home now would ratify our closeness. To refuse would be to minimize our importance to one another.

I breathed in long, deep. "I'm ready, Del."

"Sure?"

"Sure." After all, I told myself, I must confront my fear. Too often I lectured to my daughter: How we handle our fears can determine the rest of our lives. Del and I were older, but we still had the rest of our lives.

The car turned into the drive of a modest, but freshly painted, tan house, the lawn around it cropped neatly; the shrubs near the entry were trimmed and welcoming.

He turned off the ignition and watched me. I smiled and took his hand. "Yes," I said.

Relief washed over him. He grasped my hand in both of his, then returned it to my lap and, like a boy, bounded out of the car.

Neither of us spoke as I walked into the living room, my knees loose-hinged, my mouth dry. My breath caught, and I felt suddenly light-headed. Del was at my side. "You okay?"

"I think so." I wanted to melt into his shoulders, feel his strength around me. But not now, not here.

He guided me to the dining room and said, "I'll just call the Chinese Palace. Shouldn't take them long to deliver. It's been too long since we ate." He slipped around the corner to the kitchen. How could I tell him nothing was going to help? Certainly not eating.

Alone now, I looked around the room. Pretty china in the hutch. I remembered one of the serving pieces from those long-ago dinner exchanges Lib and I used to do. A miniature tea set of rather coarse pottery was displayed at one end of the buffet. Probably belonged to the girls, but meant more to mother than daughters. On the opposite wall hung a lovely oil in a deep frame — a young girl sitting primly near a woodland stream. Lib's art selection. Here, there, her fancies, her expressions, all in affirmation of Lib.

Perhaps I might slip out while Del was still on the phone. I could take a cab to the bus station. I could be home by midnight. Later he would understand. He'd realize I simply wasn't ready to face the many Libs who still lived here. Or, I admitted to myself, I was still not prepared to confront my fear. Of what I wasn't sure. Fear of not measuring up to Lib? Fear that what Del and I felt for each other was less love than need? Did I merely need to feel loved? Did Del simply need a woman to fill the other chair at the table?

"Oh, and lots of rice. We like rice," he said around the corner, and his voice sent the usual prickles up my spine.

On the narrow wall between the hutch and the large window hung a framed sampler done in fine cross-stitch. I stepped closer to read the words: "To experience life? Or to be limited by the fear of it?"

Slowly, I read the sampler again. Lib's painstakingly crafted quote held meaning for her. But its message this evening was for me. Oddly, my breath evened.

Del rounded the corner, his eyebrows lifted in question. A glance took me in, and he smiled. "They'll deliver in a few minutes. Let's go see the rest of the house. Hungry?"

"Starved," I said honestly.

His hand slipped around my waist, and we walked down the hall. Side by side.

~Evelyn Gibb
Chicken Soup for the Golden Soul

21

A Husband for June Cleaver

My mother was the most conservative person I knew. She was my dearest friend, but if there were ever conflicts between mother and daughter, it usually had to do with her conservatism vs. my free spirit. Once, she was flabbergasted when she met me for lunch and I walked through the lobby of the St. Louis Marriott wearing shorts.

"Honey, you should have long pants on inside a hotel," she whispered worriedly to me. "Mom, I don't think anyone will faint over it," I teased.

She put June Cleaver in the shade. When I was small, my mother wore white gloves and a dress to her doctor's appointments. Even at seventy-four, she was the epitome of class and etiquette. So you can understand my surprise at her phone call that morning.

"You're going where, mom?"

"China Garden Buffet," she answered nonchalantly.

"You mean, a date?"

"Well, I think so, sweetie. Bill said he wanted to take me for Chinese and I told him I'd love to, but I insisted that we go Dutch, because since your Dad died, I don't expect people to be taking care of me."

"Right."

"Well, he said no," she explained. "He said he was going to pay, insisting that it was a date."

"A date?!" I shouted in shock.

"Well, that's what he said," she giggled.

I hadn't heard this kind of giddiness from my mother in twenty years.

My husband never understood why I worried about my mom after my dad died. "Honey, your mother went down the water slide at Water World. She's not an old lady, you know."

I knew that. But I still worried that being without my dad would destroy her unless I intervened. The responsibility of her widowhood weighed on me like a boulder that I couldn't lift off my shoulders. I was terrified that loneliness would eventually do her in.

"There's a condo development right near us. We could move her here to Colorado." I explained. "My grandmother started drinking when her husband died. I just can't leave her all alone."

The next morning, my mom called to tell me about her date. Suddenly she had to go answer her ringing doorbell. I could hear her talking to someone, thanking them and laughing.

"Oh sweetie, I just got the most beautiful bouquet of flowers."

"From whom?"

"From Bill. He's right here."

"He came over this morning?" I couldn't believe my ears.

"Yes! He picked them for me on his walk."

The following week, an envelope of photos arrived: pictures of mom at the Botanical Garden and sitting hand in hand with Bill on a riverboat beneath the St. Louis Arch. Then came the last picture.

"Oh my God, she's sitting on a giant turtle," I exclaimed.

"A turtle? Let me see," My husband said grabbing the photo. "It's a statue. I guess they went to the children's zoo. She looks like a little girl."

"I know," I said rolling my eyes.

I realized that Bill was the opposite of my father, who had been the company president and former ROTC sergeant. Bill had been a chaplain in the war and didn't think twice about joining his men by jumping out of an airplane behind enemy lines.

"To give them moral support," he said humbly.

He played the guitar, worked on houses for Habitat for Humanity and volunteered for six other organizations.

"We're going on a hike," my mom announced one day on the phone. "Bill needs my help because we're taking along four mentally retarded adults and we have to make sure they can stay on the trail."

I was so proud of her but I had to suppress my laughter. Was this really my mother doing all this?

Then she told me something that seemed to make the earth move.

"Bill asked me to marry him and I said yes." She gushed. "We thought we'd have a small, private ceremony the day after Christmas so you kids could all be here."

I flew in a month before the wedding to help with the arrangements and to help mom find a dress.

"May I help you?" the middle-aged saleswoman asked.

"We need a wedding dress," I smiled.

"And will you be needing a mother of the bride dress also?" she asked my mom.

"No, she is the bride," I said.

"Oh, how simply marvelous!"

My mother became the hit of Lord & Taylor. Every saleswoman over the age of sixty wanted to meet this septuagenarian who had beaten the odds and found true love again.

The day of her wedding, mom was getting dressed. "Look, new underwear!" She said holding up a pink and white striped bag.

"You went to Victoria's Secret, Mom?" I grabbed the bag laughing and pulled out the item.

"Well, I wanted something nice to get married in."

"Mom, I cannot believe that you, June Cleaver actually walked into a Victoria Secret store."

"Oh don't be silly," she said placing the bag on her dresser. "It's just a pretty bra."

The wedding was perfect, from the small ceremony in front of her pastor in the church vestibule, to the Mickey and Minnie Mouse atop their tiny wedding cake

The next morning, Mom and Bill came to see us with a few hours to kill before their flight. I noticed a bag in her hand.

"What's that?"

"Bob Evans," she laughed. "They have that all-you-can-eat breakfast bar and Bill loves their bacon."

"You went to a Bob Evans breakfast bar the morning after your wedding night?"

"Sure, why not?"

"They're very reasonable," Bill chimed in. "All you can eat for $5.99."

The next day she called from Disney World to tell me that they got on a shuttle bus full of cheerleaders from North Carolina who gave them a cheer on the bus when they found out she and Bill were newlyweds.

Then she went on to tell me that the wipers on the

rentcar kept squirting water and they had to drive it that way.

"We couldn't figure out how to turn it all off and it squirted the people next to us. I got the giggles so badly I almost wet my pants," she laughed.

"I wish my mother could have found a man," my friend Jody said, as I showed her the picture of my mom and Bill hugging Mickey Mouse at Disney World.

"She could if she wanted to," I said without hesitation.

I realized that it's not a lack of good men out there. My mom had the only real ingredient necessary to become a bride. She knew how to do more than love. She also knew how to receive it.

~Carla Riehl
Chicken Soup for the Bride's Soul

Older & Wiser

Chapter 3

Making a Difference

The cream of enjoyment in this life is always impromptu.
The chance walk; the unexpected visit; the unpremeditated
journey; the unsought conversation or acquaintance.
~Fanny Fern

22

Esmerelda's Song

Courage doesn't always roar. Sometimes courage is the little
voice at the end of the day that says I'll try again tomorrow.
~Mary Anne Radmacher

In my long athletic career as a gymnast, I had trained with the best. At Stanford University I coached the top Olympians and a nationally ranked team. But my favorite students were beginners—especially adult novices, filled with doubt about their abilities, but game enough to try.

Students of all ages and abilities would show up for my gymnastics classes—little boys with oversized shorts and mismatched socks; little girls with red pigtails and matching freckles; adolescents and adults who looked warily around at the apparatus, their fear mingled with excitement. Over the years I taught them—in a rooftop room at the Berkeley YMCA, in a fancy gym club in Atlanta and in a tiny studio in San Francisco—at Stanford, Berkeley and finally, Oberlin College.

There, I remember an amazing, heavyset young man named Darwin, blind from birth, who announced that he had his heart set on learning a front flip on the trampoline. Darwin's lack of balance or visual cues led me to doubt the likelihood of his learning even the basics of trampoline, much less a somersault. But I welcomed him to class and said we'd take it one step—or rather, one bounce—at a time. After many months of preparation and many failed attempts, on the last day of class Darwin Neuman accomplished a front somersault, to the cheers and tears of everyone in the class. I remember the mixture of surprise and delight on Darwin's face; I remember the moment as if it were yesterday.

I also remember other students, of course—one is a now-famous Broadway star. And over the years, many students have made me a believer by showing, again and again, the power of persistence.

But most of all, I remember Esme.

Her real name was Esmerelda Esperanza Garcia, but she asked me to call her Esme that first day of my ten-week course in basic gymnastics at Oberlin. Esme had no particular disabilities—she could see and hear and to all appearances was in good physical health—although she was a bit thin and frail for the rigors of bars and beam. As it turned out, I had never before met a teaching challenge like Esme. Something had brought her to me and to one of the more challenging physical education classes at Oberlin. She brought with her a set of psychological baggage that included her self-image as a klutz, and she seemed determined to demonstrate that each day. Esme didn't just fall behind everyone else—she was like a golfer who played entirely in the rough, never touching a fairway.

To fully appreciate what Esme faced, understand this: each term, as new students wandered into the gymnastics area and looked around, I would call them together and demonstrate a full exercise routine on the floor and on all the apparatus. These included a variety of swings, arm changes, handstands, cartwheels, and rolls and dance elements requiring flexibility, strength, coordination, balance, stamina and reflex speed. Then, as I watched the looks of incredulity, doubt or total disbelief on their faces, I would then predict that they would indeed be able to do every one of those routines by the term's end.

One of the greatest joys I experienced as a teacher was to help my students to do far more than they believed they could accomplish. So my courses became something more than mere skill learning; in transcending their limiting beliefs in this area of life, my students were more likely to excel in other areas as well. I believe that most students returned the second day on trust alone—on blind faith that "this guy might be able to deliver what he promises." So, beginning on the proverbial wing and a prayer, on hope and dreams and the challenge I'd set before them, they began.

In Esme's case, she had complete faith—negative faith. She was certain she could not even come close to what I had predicted, but at least she would learn something. Apparently intent on convincing me of her ineptitude, she told me stories of glasses of milk knocked over on the dinner table; of slips and falls, and of being the last-to-be-picked for every team in every sport at every school she attended. She was giving it another try because she had heard that I was a "miracle worker," and said she needed a miracle at that point in her life.

I'd like to say that a miracle happened—that Esme became the star of the class and went on to the Olympics, or some such thing, but that would be sheer fantasy. Esme trailed behind the class all the way to the end, and received a "B" for persistence, effort and yes, some discernable improvement.

But then she did something no student had ever done—Esme asked if she could take the same course over again. Normally, I would decline, because the class had a long waiting list, and new students should have an opportunity to participate. This time I made an exception.

By the third week of class, even with her head start, Esme was again behind half the class. But this meant she was even with, or ahead of the other half! — a new experience for her, and one that did not escape her notice. She was like a runner who glances back to see people behind her for the first time. This struck her with the force of revelation, and something wonderful happened — Esme was stuck in a handstand. Not permanently, but for a few wonderful seconds, her handstand was so straight, and so well balanced, she just hung up there, to my surprise and to her amazement. She came down beaming, and the entire class applauded.

A light went on inside Esmerelda Garcia on that day, in that moment.

After that, she started pleading with me to spend a little extra time to help her after class — with her cartwheel, her balance beam dismount, her hip circle on the uneven bars. She asked questions, tried, fell, asked more questions, tried again, her face focused with an intensity I'd only seen in world-class gymnasts and young children. Now it was do-or-die for Esmerelda Esperanza Garcia.

By the term's end, Esme got through every single routine, with only one minor fall and a few bobbles. The class members, who had come to know and help one another in their common endeavor, had come to know Esmerelda as well, and to respect her dedication. As she completed her last routine, they gave her a standing ovation. She laughed. Then she broke down in tears.

Who would have guessed that a two-unit physical education class could change someone's life?

My only bittersweet regret in teaching was that I hadn't learned more about each of my students—their lives outside the gymnasium. They showed up, were gymnasts for an hour and a half, two days a week, for ten weeks; then they left the gymnasium and went on with other classes, other lives.

As it happens, Oberlin College has one of the finest conservatories of music in the United States. And one of the many things I had not known about Esme was that she was a conservatory student, and that her specialty was voice.

In mid-April, after the last snowfall, as the first touch of spring warmed the air—about four months after Esme's triumphant completion of my class—I was walking through Tappan Square, the park directly across from the conservatory. I noticed an announcement sign—"Senior Recital: Vocalist…"—an announcement I would have passed by with barely a glance, until I saw the name of the vocalist: "Esmerelda Garcia."

That night I sat in a small audience of students, faculty and friends of Esme. I sat mesmerized by her voice, her skill, her charisma and her radiant singing. Again, her performance was rewarded with well-earned applause, which I joined enthusiastically.

I believe someone told her that I had attended, because when I returned home that evening, I found a note by my door. It read:

"Dear Dan, I was at an impasse in my singing and my life, and about to give up. Then I met you and learned what I could do." It was signed:

"With love and gratitude, Esme."

I gazed out into an evening made more beautiful by Esme's song. Memories of her voice mingled with images of her in the gymnasium, blending like the spring breeze through the blossoming apple trees. It felt good to be a teacher, good to be alive.

~Dan Millman
Chicken Soup to Inspire the Body & Soul

23

Matchless Moments

I have enjoyed many matchless moments in my life. But very few occurred while I was seven and eight years old. Diagnosed with polio, I was placed in a room with about thirty-five people, each in our own iron lung. I cried a lot because nobody, not even my mother and father, could visit me, much less talk to me or give me a hug. Contracting polio and possibly even spreading it to other people was a constant fear. Even the nurses avoided contact with us. One night, I lay in my own vomit all night because I was too sick and scared to ask for help.

When the doctor came to check on me the next morning, he pulled me out of the iron lung, placed me on the cold hardwood floor and began cleaning me off. He hugged me and told me God loved me. He began crying, and I cried with him. I'll never forget that experience. I was a terribly frightened, sick little boy, and it was one of the few matchless moments that year.

Finally, I was allowed to return home. After being there only a few days, a doctor and nurse came to the house to inform my parents that tests indicated I had tuberculosis. The choice was returning to the hospital or being quarantined in my home. I chose home. Being restricted to my bedroom was better than the iron lung, but being isolated from my friends and family was still very difficult. On Christmas, I remember my daddy knocking on my window. When I looked out on the fresh snow covering the ground, I saw that his footprints spelled the words, "I love you, Tommy." Another matchless moment I desperately needed.

By the time I returned to school a few years after being diagnosed with polio, I found I had forgotten much of what I had learned. Still, I was excited to be able to go back to school. But on my first day back, the teacher ordered me, "Tommy, come and sit right in the front." I was a big kid at a little desk, and I was embarrassed and didn't want everybody looking at me. Then the teacher said, "Let's see what all you've learned while you have been goofing off, while you've been sick or whatever your problem was." Then he told me to write the word "cat" on the blackboard. By then I was so scared I don't think I could have spelled my own name. I tried to talk with the teacher, but he wouldn't listen. Instead he ordered me out of the class, "You're misbehaving. Get out of here!"

I never went back to school, and I did not learn to read until my two sons were adults. Not knowing how to read and write put me at a distinct disadvantage for many years, and I was constantly plagued by it. But I worked hard and made a very good living. In fact, this once-illiterate sixty-ish-plus millionaire wrote a book about it. Going from an illiterate to the author of *The Millionaire's Secret: Miss Melba and Me* was another matchless moment in my life.

While many people my age were retiring, I dedicated myself to encouraging other illiterate adults to learn to read and write. And that's what I've been doing fervently since 1992. I have given over six hundred talks and have told many stories about how lives have been changed when illiterate adults have learned to read and to write. Encouraging those who can read and write to tutor those who cannot has also brought some matchless moments.

One of my favorite audiences to speak to about literacy is prisoners. Eighty percent of prisoners in the United States cannot read. My being able to offer encouragement to prisoners who have learned to read and write has provided some matchless moments for me—and hopefully some for them.

At a recent prison GED graduation this was true for one particular prisoner and for me. The graduates were hard-core criminals, so I was closely guarded everywhere I went. The prisoners were shackled, and fully armed guards stood inside and outside the large room where graduation was to take place. The graduates were seated to my right as I approached the podium. After the warden introduced me, he instructed under his breath, "Under no circumstances are you to hand over the microphone or get near one of these prisoners."

"No, sir, I won't," I said, assuming he meant the prisoners were dangerous. He made it sound as if one misguided yell over the public address system would incite a riot.

I congratulated the men, and the ceremonies continued with awards and diplomas presented. This hard-core group would never be released from prison, but it was obvious they desired a better life by being able to read about places they would never be able to visit.

During the question-and-answer session, one of the toughest-looking prisoners stood and asked if he could approach the podium. I glanced over at the warden, who shook his head no. I looked back at the young man. He had tears in his eyes but didn't seem to care. He knew this could be the last time he'd ever have any contact with the outside world. "But Mr. Harken, I just want to say something to my grandfather," he said.

Again, I looked at the warden. Again, he shook his head. When I turned back to the prisoner and saw the pleading look in his eyes, I couldn't stop myself from assuring him, "You bet! Come on over."

"Thank you, Mr. Harken," he said as he walked toward the podium. The little-boy expression on his face reflected gratitude and sincerity—and fright. I was convinced beyond a shadow of a doubt that he was harmless. His hand shook as he reached for the microphone, wiped his eyes and cleared his throat.

"I want all of you to know that my grandfather is the elderly gentleman over there wearing the old faded overalls. I'm sure he remembers back when I would make fun of him and of his clothes," the young man spoke from his heart.

"Grandpa, I will never get out of here because I didn't do things the way you advised me to," he said. "But I got this GED diploma because I wanted to show you I could do something right for a change. I love you, Grandpa. I'm sorry."

As his voice trailed off, I took the microphone back and told the grandfather to come up and give his grandson a big hug. I looked to the warden, then to the guards. There wasn't a dry eye in the place.

Another matchless moment! One I will never forget.

~Tom Harken
Chicken Soup for the Golden Soul

24

The Red Mahogany Piano

Why not go out on a limb? Isn't that where the fruit is?
~Frank Scully

Many years ago, when I was a young man in my twenties, I worked as a salesman for a St. Louis piano company. We sold our pianos all over the state by advertising in small-town newspapers and then when we had received sufficient replies, we would load our little trucks, drive into the area and sell the pianos to those who had replied.

Every time we would advertise in the cotton country of Southeast Missouri, we would receive a reply on a postcard that said, in effect, "Please bring me a new piano for my little granddaughter. It must be red mahogany. I can pay ten dollars a month with my egg money." The old lady scrawled on and on and on that postcard until she filled it up, then turned it over and even wrote on the front—around and around the edges until there was barely room for the address.

Of course, we could not sell a new piano for ten dollars a month. No finance company would carry a contract with payments that small, so we ignored her postcards.

One day, however, I happened to be in that area calling on other replies, and out of curiosity I decided to look the old lady up. I found pretty much what I expected; the old lady lived in a one-room sharecropper's cabin in the middle of a cotton field. The cabin had a dirt floor, and there were chickens in the house. Obviously, she could not have qualified to purchase anything on credit—no car, no phone, no real job, nothing but a roof over her head and not a very good one at that. I could see daylight through it in several places. Her little granddaughter was about ten, barefoot and wearing a feed-sack dress.

I explained to the old lady that we could not sell a new piano for ten dollars a month, and that she should stop writing to us every time she saw our ad. I drove away heartsick, but my advice had no effect—she still sent us the same postcard every six weeks. Always wanting a new piano, red mahogany, please, and swearing she would never miss a ten-dollar payment. It was sad.

A couple of years later, I owned my own piano company, and when I advertised in that area, the postcards started coming to me. For months, I ignored them—what else could I do?

But then, one day when I was in the area something came over me. I had a red mahogany piano on my little truck. Despite knowing that I was about to make a terrible business decision, I delivered the piano to her and told her I would carry the contract myself at ten dollars a month with no interest, and that would mean fifty-two payments. I took the new piano in the house and placed it where I thought the roof would be least likely to leak on it. I admonished her and the little girl to try to keep the chickens off it, and I left—sure I had just thrown away a new piano.

But the payments came in, all fifty-two of them as

agreed—sometimes with coins taped to a three- by five-inch card in the envelope. It was incredible!

So, I put the incident out of my mind for twenty years.

Then one day I was in Memphis on other business, and after dinner at the Holiday Inn on the Levee, I went into the lounge. As I was sitting at the bar having an after-dinner drink, I heard the most beautiful piano music behind me. I looked around, and there was a lovely young woman playing a very nice grand piano.

Being a pianist of some ability myself, I was stunned by her virtuosity, and I picked up my drink and moved to a table beside her where I could listen and watch. She smiled at me, asked for requests, and when she took a break she sat down at my table.

"Aren't you the man who sold my grandma a piano a long time ago?"

It didn't ring a bell, so I asked her to explain.

She started to tell me, and I suddenly remembered. My Lord, it was her! It was the little barefoot girl in the feed-sack dress!

She told me her name was Elise and that since her grandmother couldn't afford to pay for lessons, she had learned to play by listening to the radio. She said she had started to play in church where she and her grandmother had to walk over two miles, and that she had then played in school, had won many awards and a music scholarship. She had married an attorney in Memphis, and he had bought her that beautiful grand piano she was playing.

Something else entered my mind. "Elise," I asked, "it's a little dark in here. What color is that piano?"

"It's red mahogany," she said. "Why?"

I couldn't speak.

Did she understand the significance of the red mahogany? The unbelievable audacity of her grandmother insisting on a red mahogany piano when no one in his right mind would have sold her a piano of any kind? I don't know.

And then the marvelous accomplishment of that beautiful, terribly underprivileged child in the feed-sack dress? No, perhaps she didn't understand that, either.

But I did, and my throat tightened.

Finally, I found my voice. "I just wondered," I said. "I'm proud of you, but I have to go to my room."

And I did have to go to my room, because men don't like to be seen crying in public.

~Joe Edwards
Chicken Soup for the Grandparent's Soul

EDITORS' NOTE: In loving memory of our friend Joe Edwards—your stories live on in thousands of hearts you've touched.

25

Pay It Forward

A mother is the truest friend we have,
when trials heavy and sudden, fall upon us;
when adversity takes the place of prosperity;
when friends who rejoice with us in our sunshine desert us;
when trouble thickens around us, still will she cling to us, and
endeavor by her kind precepts and counsels to
dissipate the clouds of darkness,
and cause peace to return to our hearts.
~Washington Irving

I wasn't the first nineteen-year-old girl to have to tell her mother she was pregnant and not likely to be getting married then, or ever, to the baby's father. The confession brought a heavy sigh and probably more than a few private tears. Mom was not one for emotional displays. She was pragmatic. "What is your plan?" was her response to any number of emotional crises.

But in the spring of 1971, when my son made his appearance, she was fully engaged in a plan of her own. I would have to return to work full-time almost immediately, and she was firm: Nobody, nobody but Granny herself was taking care of this little boy. She was small and, at fifty-seven years of age, not terribly strong. Jason challenged her from 6:30 A.M. until 5:00 P.M. every weekday for three years. He was stubborn. She was patient. He jumped and climbed and ran as if he were made of springs rather than muscle and bone. She kept him safe. She taught him to knit and to hand sew. They cooked and baked. She always had supper ready when I arrived after work and would say, "You might as well eat here. I always make too much. What's the point of you going home and cooking, too?"

If she watched the clock or the window wishing for me to get there to rescue her, she never indicated it.

Jason was—and is—charming. He would flash his dimples at us, the sun glinting off golden hair, his crystal blue eyes dancing, and he'd have his way with us. He had two moms: a pretty young one and a pretty tired one. He was adored.

Thanks to my mother, Jason and I were able to spend our evenings and weekends cuddling, playing, getting by with only and exactly just enough, but as secure as two children with one guardian angel in a blanket and couch-cushion tent. He told his Granny one time, "My mom is magic. She can turn hamburger into all kinds of things." We were free of the stress that comes from weak support systems. My little guy and I had a solid one. We did a lot of growing up together.

When he was three, I married a wonderful man, and life took on all that happily-ever-after tone. Mom didn't need to do full-time care anymore, but she missed him and frequently asked to have him for a day. They would again cook, sew and sing together. "Would you like to swing on a star?" was her theme song. I would never deny her a chance to sing it to him.

Years passed, and we all grew up. Now Jason has two young daughters. His rock-and-roll mama is a grandma. My dimpled boy carries those babies into my house, one on each arm, both sheltered and secure. He moves with grace changing diapers and wiping spills as he coos and smiles with sheer delight over their every move.

I am not Granny, but Nanna. My house is now outfitted with a potty chair and a toddler bed. I trip over blocks and Playskool people again. The babies play with Fisher-Price toys that are over thirty years old and find them joyous. Of course, there are outrageous new toys all over the house and yard.

One recent weekend, my granddaughters came here so Jason could work an extra shift at his second job. When he got here to pick them up, he was exhausted and fell asleep in the chair with a baby on his chest.

I fixed supper and let him snooze. To me, they looked like two babies sleeping together. I woke him to eat and said, "No point in you going home to cook. I always make too much."

As he loaded the girls into his car that evening, bathed, pajama'ed and ready to tuck in, he hugged me. If there is a hug more precious than a son stooped to enfold his mom, I don't know what it would be.

"Mom, you don't know how much your help means to me." Those dimples, those still crystal-blue eyes that always smile.

"Oh, yes, I do. I do."

~Beadrin Youngdahl
Chicken Soup for the Mother and Son Soul

26

Magnolias

I have learned to use the word "impossible"
with the greatest caution.
~Wernher von Braun

I spent the week before my daughter's June wedding running last-minute trips to the caterer, florist, tuxedo shop
and the church about forty miles away. As happy as I was
that Patsy was marrying a good Christian young man, I felt
laden with responsibilities as I watched my budget dwindle...
so many details, so many bills and so little time. My son Jack
was away at college, but he said he would be there to walk
his younger sister down the aisle, taking the place of his dad,
who had died a few years before. He teased Patsy, saying he'd
wanted to give her away since she was about three years old!

To save money, I gathered blossoms from several
friends who had large magnolia trees. Their luscious,
creamy-white blooms and slick green leaves would make
beautiful arrangements against the rich dark wood inside
the church.

After the rehearsal dinner the night before the wedding,
we banked the podium area and choir loft with magnolias.
As we left just before midnight, I felt tired but satisfied this
would be the best wedding any bride had ever had! The

music, the ceremony, the reception—and especially the flowers—would be remembered for years.

The big day arrived—the busiest day of my life—and while her bridesmaids helped Patsy to dress, her fiancé, Tim, walked with me to the sanctuary to do a final check. When we opened the door and felt a rush of hot air, I almost fainted; and then I saw them—all the beautiful white flowers were black. Funeral black. An electrical storm during the night had knocked out the air conditioning system, and on that hot summer day, the flowers had wilted and died.

I panicked, knowing I didn't have time to drive back to our hometown, gather more flowers and return in time for the wedding.

Tim turned to me. "Edna, can you get more flowers? I'll throw away these dead ones and put fresh flowers in these arrangements."

I mumbled, "Sure," as he bebopped down the hall to put on his cuff links.

Alone in the large sanctuary, I looked up at the dark wooden beams in the arched ceiling. "Lord," I prayed, "please help me. I don't know anyone in this town. Help me find someone willing to give me flowers—in a hurry!" I scurried out praying for four things: the blessing of white magnolias, courage to find them in an unfamiliar yard, safety from any dog that may bite my leg and a nice person who would not get out a shotgun when I asked to cut his tree to shreds.

As I left the church, I saw magnolia trees in the distance. I approached a house... no dog in sight. I knocked on the door and an older man answered. So far, so good... no shotgun. When I stated my plea the man beamed, "I'd be happy to!"

He climbed a stepladder and cut large boughs and

handed them down to me. Minutes later, as I lifted the last armload into my car trunk, I said, "Sir, you've made the mother of a bride happy today."

"No, ma'am," he said. "You don't understand what's happening here."

"What?" I asked.

"You see, my wife of sixty-seven years died on Monday. On Tuesday I received friends at the funeral home, and on Wednesday..." He paused. I saw tears welling up in his eyes. "On Wednesday I buried her." He looked away. "On Thursday most of my out-of-town relatives went back home, and on Friday—yesterday—my children left."

I nodded.

"This morning," he continued, "I was sitting in my den crying out loud. I miss her so much. For the last sixteen years, as her health got worse, she needed me. But now nobody needs me. This morning I cried, 'Who needs an eighty-six-year-old worn-out man? Nobody!' I began to cry louder. 'Nobody needs me!' About that time, you knocked and said, 'Sir, I need you.'"

I stood with my mouth open.

He asked, "Are you an angel? The way the light shone around your head into my dark living room...."

I assured him I was no angel.

He smiled. "Do you know what I was thinking when I handed you those magnolias?"

"No."

"I decided I'm needed. My flowers are needed. Why, I might have a flower ministry! I could give them to everyone! Some caskets at the funeral home have no flowers. People need flowers at times like that, and I have lots of them. They're all over the backyard! I can give them to hospitals, churches—all sorts of places. You know what

I'm going to do? I'm going to serve the Lord until the day He calls me home!"

I drove back to the church, filled with wonder. On Patsy's wedding day, if anyone had asked me to encourage someone who was hurting, I would have said, "Forget it! It's my only daughter's wedding, for goodness sake! There is no way I can minister to anyone today."

But God found a way — through dead flowers.

~Edna Ellison
Chicken Soup for the Christian Soul 2

27

To Return Tomorrow

*It's so curious: one can resist tears and 'behave' very well in the
hardest hours of grief. But then someone makes you a friendly
sign behind a window, or one notices that a flower that was in
bud only yesterday has suddenly blossomed, or a letter slips
from a drawer... and everything collapses.*
~Colette

The phone rang on a dateless Friday night. John's family
requested a visit from the hospice nurse. They said he
wasn't able to make it to the bathroom, his weakness
had increased. I assured them I would visit in about forty-
five minutes, the time I needed to drive to their home. I was
not John's primary nurse, but I had made a few visits. This
sounded pretty routine. They needed support and an assessment. I would be home in a couple of hours.

John was in the room they had made for him on the
first floor next to the kitchen. It was the hub of activity
because he could see everywhere yet had privacy in his
recliner, his bed for several months now. John was thirty-
two years old in the final stages of testicular cancer.

"Hello, John," I greeted, making a visual assessment. I
listened to his mother, and then proceeded toward the blue
recliner with the footrest up. Gently I took his cool hand
in mine. Dull eyes and a different lusterless voice greeted

me back. Ashen skin with a fine transparency sat me down quickly to take vital signs. They concurred. John was near death, just as my years of experience told me when I entered the room.

Standing directly behind me was John's mother. "What is wrong, Susie?"

John was drifting, and I took her to the next room. Making eye contact, I said, "He is dying."

"You are wrong! He is not!" she screamed, then pivoted and leaped onto the day bed next to his chair. Leaning to his ear she said, "John, you can't leave me. I need you, John. Don't leave me." Tears streamed down her face as she stroked his head, "John."

I watched as John came back from the shadow of death's door unable to even lift his hand to hers. Their eyes met and he started in a garbled voice to recite Robert Frost's poem — "Whose woods these are...."

With each word he had a little bit more clarity as his spirit rose to the moment. When he completed the poem he looked into her eyes and told her it was time to leave, he was tired. "Mom, I love you, and I know we will meet again. I have fought very hard, but it is time for me to go. You will be okay."

"But I will miss our time together reciting poetry and scripture. John...."

"Mom, I love you." He drifted and never spoke again, although death didn't come for two more hours. Tears cascaded over both our cheeks. This was a moment I had never experienced in my long hospice career.

John's mother and I were the only ones to experience this resurrection of spirit to help a loved one come to grips with the final departure of her son.

Three days later a memorial service was held in an old

huge Presbyterian church close to the hospice office. The wooden pews were full from front to back with mourners. I sat alone. It was normal to attend funeral services, but this was unequaled. John's brother stood at the pulpit and read the entire poem "Stopping by Woods on a Snowy Evening" by Frost.

The tears that could not be repressed wet my clothes and embarrassed me. I was sobbing and I was the hospice nurse. Finally the service was over, and I returned to the office and sat in front of my boss, Carole.

"I am done in this career, Carole. I can't do it any more. There are no more tears. Today I cried for John, the experience I shared with John and his family, and all the other patients and families. I couldn't stop the tears."

Carole came around her desk and took my hands in hers. "You are grieving for many today. I think you will be okay but today you need to take care of yourself. Take the rest of the day off."

She gave me a solid hug and sent me home. I left the hospice office questioning if I could ever return to my present position. I found Carole's warmth and wisdom my healing salve. Rarely do employers see your needs and try so desperately to meet them.

Hospice has support groups for their staff, but it was giving me the time to heal that mattered most. In a few years I became a hospice director. This hospice experience was shared many times in telling the public what a difference hospice can make. John had given me a memory, and Carole had given me her wisdom.

~Susan Burkholder
Chicken Soup for the Working Woman's Soul

28

December Snow

If a friend is in trouble, don't annoy him by asking if there is
anything you can do.
Think up something appropriate and do it.
~Edgar Watson Howe

It was three days before Christmas, and I found myself riding in an old Chevy truck filled with rusting animal traps. We traveled down the two-lane country highway on that gray, frigid day, mostly in silence. I was too lost in my own pain and grief to take much notice of nature's gifts of winter.

My life was in complete turmoil. Just prior to that fateful holiday season, I thought I literally lived a storybook marriage with a husband who truly loved me. I was too blind to understand why, in the past few months, Jack had become cruel and unreasonable. It was only after he left me in September that I finally had to accept what I didn't want to believe: Jack had returned to a former love, a woman he had never really left.

I turned to my family for love and support, which they provided in abundance. However, the holidays were too much for me to bear. Christmas not only represents a time of love and togetherness, but Christmas Eve was my wedding anniversary. While others were singing carols and making merry, I would go behind closed doors to break down in tears. Although I found myself in that stage between grief and anger, I still could not bring myself to rail against the man I once believed was the love of my life.

My childhood friend Kathy lived in the house next door, and she had introduced me to Billy, a man several years our senior. Most of his education came not from books, but from life experiences. His red hair and beard had long since turned white, and he looked remarkably like Santa Claus. Unlike jolly Santa, Billy was very quiet, although he would watch you intently with piercing blue eyes. Silent Billy, a Vietnam veteran, was still haunted by memories. Before Kathy left to visit family for the holidays, she instructed Billy to "watch over Angie" while she was gone. Totally unaware of this request, I was surprised that winter afternoon to find Billy at the door.

"Darlin', you and me are going for a ride," he said with a strong Texas drawl.

Too startled to reply, I grabbed my coat and jumped into the old truck, wondering what life had planned for me next.

Billy turned off the main highway and onto a long country road that eventually took us to a small, heavily wooded park. In the summer, this little park was filled with visitors. Needless to say, now Billy and I silently sat in the parking lot alone, with only the sound of the cold wind blowing around the faded, old truck.

Finally, Billy turned and looked at me. "Darlin'," he began gruffly, "I have been watching you these past few days, and I recognize that you have been going through a war of your own. Years ago, when I returned from Vietnam, I was in bad shape, just like you are today. I couldn't do anything to help myself because I couldn't talk about the hell I'd just gone through. A very good friend recognized my deep pain, and he helped me through it. I want to pass that gift on to you."

Billy jumped out of the truck, walked around and opened my door. I followed him into the woods, too numb to be curious. Suddenly, Billy stopped, turned around to me and pointed to a large oak tree in front of us. "I'm gonna stand over there, and you are gonna talk to me. But when I go over to that tree, I'm not Billy anymore. I'm Jack, and you have permission to say anything to me that your heart desires. You can do this 'cause I am not gonna say a word back to you. I just want you to tell Jack how you feel. You will be perfectly safe here."

Without another word, Billy walked up to the tree, turned around and faced me.

My eyes welled with tears. I just couldn't do this. But Billy stood there, not making one move, not making one sound. Finally, I turned, closed my eyes and began talking to Jack. My words were soft, pleading for reason and understanding. After about ten minutes, I shook my head. Billy nodded, and I followed him back to the truck. Neither of us mentioned what had just taken place in the cold, lonely woods.

The next afternoon, Billy showed up again at my door. Again, we took the trip back to the oak. And again, I closed my eyes and started my pleas of reason. After a few minutes, the pleas became mixed with occasional words of frustration and anger. When I was spent, Billy took me back home. We did not speak of our secret.

The third day was very difficult, for it was the dreaded wedding anniversary. I was actually relieved to see Billy at my door that afternoon. I found myself walking ahead of Billy to our special spot in the woods.

Billy silently took his place in front of the tree. This time I stood in front of "Jack," looking him right in the eye. "How

dare you treat me the way you did, when I loved you so much."
I took a deep breath. "I was there for you all those times when
you said the world was against you. You knew I would do
anything for you, and you threw me away like garbage."

By then I was feeling very angry. My voice, filled with pent-up
emotion, became forceful and loud. I suddenly lost that desire to
tiptoe around the situation. Every word I screamed carried away
some of the incredible pain I had harbored for so long.

After several moments of release, I dropped to the
ground. Totally exhausted, I sobbed with a sense of rebirth.
Billy walked away from the tree, dropped to his knees and
held me. With tears running down his own rugged face,
the big Vietnam vet said in his soft drawl, "Darlin', for two
days, I stood here and listened to you plead your case, and
that told me how lost you had become. I also knew that
today would be the day that you would start to reclaim
yourself. Now that you and I both know what a good and
caring person you are, maybe you can start to see what
Jack allowed himself to lose. You deserve to restart your life
away from someone who willfully caused a beautiful young
woman such hurt and pain. I knew you could do it."

And with those words, the wind died and large snow-
flakes began to fall. I could actually feel my spirit being
cleansed and renewed.

Billy eventually moved back to his beloved Texas. A few
years later, I met and married a man whom I knew would
truly love and cherish me for the rest of our lives. Once again,
the holidays are a time of peace and happiness. And every
Christmas Eve, instead of memories of sadness, I smile and
remember my friend holding me in the soft December snow.

~Angie Rubel
Chicken Soup for the Soul Stories for a Better World

29

"Dog" and Mr. Evans

"She's famous, you know," the elderly man said humbly, half looking at the floor, while I examined his dog's swollen ear. But I could hear the pride in his voice.

A few moments earlier, just before entering the exam room, I had glanced over the chart for the patient in Room One. When I saw the patient's name, I thought, How original. A dog named Dog. Probably another backyard lawn ornament that's barely noticed and doesn't even get enough attention for someone to come up with an actual name for her. But then I also noticed she had been brought in for yearly exams and had received all our recommended vaccinations and preventative care. Perhaps this wasn't a neglected dog after all.

Inside the exam room, I met Mr. James Evans, eighty-four, and Dog, his eleven-year-old Weimaraner mix. I guess you could say they were pretty close to the same age. Mr. Evans had noticed the swelling and "dirty ears," and brought Dog right in to have her checked out.

As I continued the exam, he told me how he stumbled upon Dog's high intelligence when he started teaching her simple tasks. He taught her these mainly in case of an emergency since he had heart and other health problems. He noticed how quickly she caught on and began teaching her more tricks. Her most famous were counting and solving math problems. They started "showing off" for family and friends, then Mr. Evans began taking her to nursing homes, schools and other small groups to perform.

"The people seem to enjoy it," he said. "Everyone's always asking how she does it. I tell them I don't know, she hasn't told me yet," he laughed. "Maybe she can read my mind. I don't know... but she gets the answers wrong when I'm not concentrating."

When he first started telling me all this, I thought, Yeah, yeah, everybody thinks their dog is a genius. But I could now tell by the way his eyes lit up, and how Dog never took hers off him, that he wasn't boasting, but doing what he always did: sharing this special animal and her stories with others. He sensed that I was genuinely interested and told me he would bring a video of her next time. He readily agreed to my recommended preanesthetic blood testing and treatment of the ears.

Mr. Evans brought me the videotape the next time he brought Dog in, which was for her annual visit. Later that day, a few members of the staff and I watched it. Although it wasn't the best-quality tape, two things were evident: how much the small audiences enjoyed the performance and how Dog never took her eyes off her partner. Was she reading his mind? Or was she so adept at reading his body language that she was picking up on some subconscious cue he was giving her, something he didn't even know he was doing—and isn't that almost the same thing? However they did it, it was a result of both of them being completely in tune with and trusting each other.

Several months later, they were back in my exam room, both a little feebler. Mr. Evans wanted me to check those ears again. He thought she might be losing her hearing.

She was also having some trouble getting around. "But so am I," he chuckled as I carefully checked her over. Her ears were fine—just some wax, no infection—but her hips were arthritic.

The next time I saw them, Dog had to be carried into the exam room. Two years had passed since our first meeting. She was now thirteen and he was eighty-six. I dreaded this exam.

Before I even started, Mr. Evans looked straight at me with moist eyes and said, "Now, she's been too good to me for me to let her suffer. I would never let her down like that."

With that, I went on quietly with my exam. She was so weak. Laboring to breathe, her heartbeat was muffled and her eyes were dim. He agreed to leave her overnight so we could do more tests. He wanted to take the time to find out everything, but didn't want to allow her to be uncomfortable any longer if nothing could be done. I said I understood.

X-rays, EKG and blood work confirmed congestive heart failure, which had also caused liver disease. After treating her with heart medication, she was breathing a little easier and able to eat and drink. Something told me, though, that she was just holding on—holding on for him... for now. I prayed that she wouldn't die, not that night, not without him beside her.

I held my breath that morning as I entered the treatment room, trying to read my staff members' faces for the answer to the questions I didn't want to ask: How was Dog? Had she made it through the night? She was alive, but very weak. I had to call Mr. Evans. He seemed to already know what I had to report.

Mr. Evans patted her head as I injected the bright-pink

liquid, tears streaming down my face, my hands shaking. I glanced at my assistant, hoping to find a steady face. No luck. Her eyes were pools of water. Dog's leg, my hands, the syringe were now nothing but a blur. She took one last, deep, long breath.

Mr. Evans's son John carried out the large box. For the first time, James Evans looked old to me. I wondered how he would be without her.

Later that afternoon, John Evans called to let us know that his father had passed away—he had suffered a heart attack while Dog's grave was being dug. I couldn't believe the pain that hit my own heart. I don't know how long I stood, stunned, before taking another breath.

I felt responsible. I had ended Dog's life, and because of that, Mr. Evans's life had ended, too. But then I realized they wouldn't have wanted it any other way. The family knew this, too. They had Dog's body exhumed and cremated. And they placed her ashes with her best friend.

I am grateful to Dog and Mr. Evans. They did more for me as a vet than I did for them. For at those times when I feel discouraged, dealing with the aftermath of a person's neglect of a pet, I remember Dog and Mr. Evans, and my confidence in the bond is restored.

~Andrea B. Redd, D.V.M.
Chicken Soup for the Dog Lover's Soul

Never Too Late

Listen and you will learn.
~Shlomo Ibn Gabirol

It was an unusually busy day for the hospital staff on the sixth floor. Ten new patients were admitted and Nurse Susan spent the morning and afternoon checking them in. Her friend Sharron, an aide, prepared ten rooms for the patients and made sure they were comfortable. After they were finished she grabbed Sharron and said, "We deserve a break. Let's go eat."

Sitting across from each other in the noisy cafeteria, Susan noticed Sharron absently wiping the moisture off the outside of her glass with her thumbs. Her face reflected a weariness that came from more than just a busy day.

"You're pretty quiet. Are you tired, or is something wrong?" Susan asked.

Sharron hesitated. However, seeing the sincere concern in her friend's face, she confessed, "I can't do this the rest of my life, Susan. I have to find a higher-paying job to provide for my family. We barely get by. If it weren't for my parents keeping my kids, well, we wouldn't make it."

Susan noticed the bruises on Sharron's wrists peeking out from under her jacket.

"What about your husband?"

"We can't count on him. He can't seem to hold a job. He's got... problems."

"Sharron, you're so good with patients, and you love working here. Why don't you go to school and become a nurse? There's financial help available, and I'm sure your parents would agree to keep the kids while you are in class."

"It's too late for me, Susan; I'm too old for school. I've always wanted to be a nurse, that's why I took this job as an aide; at least I get to care for patients."

"How old are you?" Susan asked.

"Let's just say I'm thirty-something."

Susan pointed at the bruises on Sharron's wrists. "I'm familiar with 'problems' like these. Honey, it's never too late to become what you've dreamed of. Let me tell you how I know."

Susan began sharing a part of her life few knew about. It was something she normally didn't talk about, only when it helped someone else.

"I first married when I was thirteen years old and in the eighth grade."

Sharron gasped.

"My husband was twenty-two. I had no idea he was violently abusive. We were married six years and I had three sons. One night my husband beat me so savagely he knocked out all my front teeth. I grabbed the boys and left.

"At the divorce settlement, the judge gave our sons to my husband because I was only nineteen and he felt I couldn't provide for them. The shock of him taking my babies left me gasping for air. To make things worse, my ex took the boys and moved, cutting all contact I had with them.

"Just like the judge predicted, I struggled to make ends meet. I found work as a waitress, working for tips only. Many days my meals consisted of milk and crackers. The most difficult thing was the emptiness in my soul. I lived in a tiny one-room apartment and the loneliness would overwhelm me. I longed to play with my babies and hear them laugh."

She paused. Even after four decades, the memory was still painful. Sharron's eyes filled with tears as she reached out to comfort Susan. Now it didn't matter if the bruises showed.

Susan continued, "I soon discovered that waitresses with grim faces didn't get tips, so I hid behind a smiling mask and pressed on. I remarried and had a daughter. She became my reason for living, until she went to college. Then I was back where I started, not knowing what to do with myself—until the day my mother had surgery. I watched the nurses care for her and thought: I can do that. The problem was, I only had an eighth-grade education. Going back to high school seemed like a huge mountain to conquer. I decided to take small steps toward my goal. The first step was to get my GED. My daughter used to laugh at how our roles reversed. Now I was burning the midnight oil and asking her questions."

Susan paused and looked directly in Sharron's eyes. "I received my diploma when I was forty-six years old."

Tears streamed down Sharron's cheeks. Here was someone offering the key that might unlock the door in her dark life.

"The next step was to enroll in nursing school. For two long years I studied, cried and tried to quit. But my family wouldn't let me. I remember calling my daughter and yelling, 'Do you realize how many bones are in the human body, and I have to know them all! I can't do this, I'm forty-six years old!' But I did. Sharron, I can't tell you how wonderful it felt when I received my cap and pin."

Sharron's lunch was cold, and the ice had melted in her tea by the time Susan finished talking. Reaching across the table and taking Sharron's hands, Susan said, "You don't have to put up with abuse. Don't be a victim—take charge. You will be an excellent nurse. We will climb this mountain together."

Sharron wiped her mascara-stained face with her napkin. "I had no idea you suffered so much pain. You seem like someone who has always had it together."

"I guess I've developed an appreciation for the hardships of my life," Susan answered. "If I use them to help others, then I really haven't lost a thing. Sharron, promise me that you will go to school and become a nurse. Then help others by sharing your experiences."

Sharron promised. In a few years she became a registered nurse and worked alongside her friend until Susan retired. Sharron never forgot her colleague or the rest of her promise.

Now Sharron sits across the table taking the hands of those who are bruised in body and soul, telling them, "It's never too late. We will climb this mountain together."

~Linda Apple
Chicken Soup for the Working Woman's Soul

31

One More Task

*I don't think of all the misery but of the
beauty that still remains.*
~Anne Frank

Eve Jesson could have been bitter, but an inner
strength—and her faith—sustained her. She had
been widowed at seventy, after forty-three busy years
as a minister's wife. Then she had a stroke at age seventy-four,
which affected her entire left side: Her left hand and arm were
weak, and she walked haltingly with a four-pronged cane.
Nevertheless, her mental ability was sharp, and her independent spirit was strong.

Her daughter urged Mrs. Jesson to join their household, but she gently refused. "I don't think it works out
for the best," she said, "but I'd love to visit you often." She
sold her home, distributed her most precious possessions
among family members and moved into a nursing home
where I was a caregiver. She soon became a joy to all of us
on the staff. She was fastidious, thoughtful and friendly.
She took part in activities, helped arrange flowers and did
a bit of "mothering" here and there.

It was difficult for us to find her a suitable companion
to share the two-person bedroom. Many of our residents
had severe health or personality problems, or were mentally

infirm. With a quiet, gentle manner and the ability to do things for herself, Margaret Gravelle seemed like a more suitable roommate than many others. While Margaret's memory was vague, she knew she was ninety years old and had spent her life in nursing. Her only relative was her great-nephew.

Although Mrs. Jesson made few complaints about it, we knew Margaret woke her several times in the night when she was confused about sounds or the bathroom location. Mrs. Jesson had to remind Margaret of mealtimes and guide her to the dining room. Margaret could not grasp the notion that only one of the closets was hers and the other was for her roommate. One day, a nurse aide brought Margaret back into their room to change her blouse from the one of Mrs. Jesson's she was wearing, to one of her own.

"Well, she does have good taste," Mrs. Jesson said wryly. "That is my new silk blouse I got for my birthday."

A day came when we had arranged for the admission of a lady we thought would be a better companion for Mrs. Jesson. "I think we can provide a more suitable room-mate for you in a couple days," I told her. "We just have to arrange to move Margaret to a different room."

Later in the day, Mrs. Jesson came down to my desk. "Don't move Margaret," she said. "She really needs someone to look after her. She gets anxious in the night. She has no family and she is used to my being there.

"You know, I asked God many times why I had to go on living. When John died, I felt as if my life was finished too. But family, friends and faith all helped me. Then I had my stroke and I thought, why damage me so and let me go on living? Well, maybe he had work for me yet. Maybe I'm meant to look out for Margaret. I can give her some of the comfort my family gives me. Leave her in my room. It won't take that much effort to watch over her a bit."

Leaning on her cane, that gracious lady started back down the hall to her room to carry out the last loving task he had given her.

~Marian Lewis
Chicken Soup for the Girlfriend's Soul

Older & Wiser

Chapter
4

Across the Generations

I expect to pass through life but once.
If therefore, there be any kindness I can show,
or any good thing I can do to any fellow being,
let me do it now, and not defer or neglect it,
as I shall not pass this way again.
~William Penn

32

No Ordinary Auction

Do not complain about growing older —
many are denied the privilege.
~Robert Russell

I once attended an auction that was no ordinary auction. The public could bid on unclaimed items that people had left behind in safe-deposit boxes. These items were once deemed so important that people paid money to have them safeguarded in steel.

Diplomas, children's report cards, letters....

I remember how we shuffled along, past the coin collections and pocket watches and jewelry to documents and small items sealed in plastic bags.

Boy Scout patches, receipts from a Waikiki hotel, a child's crayon drawing of a bunny rabbit....

It was all unclaimed property, waiting to be auctioned; the forgotten or overlooked possessions of owners now dead.

Rosaries, letters, train tickets....

Each bag was a mystery, the clues doing more to arouse curiosity than to provide answers. I read the immigration papers of Udolf Matschiner, who arrived at Ellis Island in 1906. Did he find what he was looking for in America?

Two marbles, three stones, and a belt buckle....

Why these things? Did they represent some special memory, some special person?

Passports, telegrams, newspaper clippings...

A yellowed article from a 1959 Los Angeles newspaper was headlined "Vlahovich's Mother Sobs at Guilty Verdict." A mother's son had been convicted of murder. The mother wept, pleading with the judge to spare her son. "Take my blood," she screamed. "Kill me!" What happened? Did she watch her son die in San Quentin's electric chair?

Undeveloped film, birth certificates, marriage certificates....

The official business of life intermingled with the unofficial business of life — a lock of blond hair, a child's math paper and a poem called "Grandmother's Attic," typed on a typewriter with a sticky e.

It was as if those of us at the auction had been allowed entry into hundreds of grandmothers' attics, the attics of unknown people.

Diaries, photographs, the ink print of a newborn's feet....

In death's wake, most of the items spoke volumes about life. They also suggested a sense of finality, a realization that life on earth ends, and you can't take anything with you.

So what will we leave behind?

A six-by-twelve box full of mementos can speak volumes about what we valued. But it's only a whisper compared to the legacy of our lives themselves.

Amid our he-who-dies-with-the-most-toys-wins world, perhaps we should dare to leave....

An investment in other people.

An example of a life guided not by the capricious winds of culture, but rock-solid principles.

And an inspiration to our children and grandchildren to become all they have been designed to be.
Ah, heaven. The ultimate safe-deposit box.

~Bob Welch
Chicken Soup for the Golden Soul

33

The Dying Light

I learned to speak as I learned to skate or cycle:
by doggedly making a fool of myself until I got used to it.
~George Bernard Shaw

I line up the six-foot putt. All is quiet, save for a few people talking quietly in the distance. Slowly, I take the putter back and stroke the ball. For a split-second, the ball rolls toward the hole, then slides decidedly off to the right, like a car exiting a freeway long before its destination.

"Maybe you'd like to try something else," says the young salesman, watching from beside the artificial-turf putting green.

For an instant, our eyes meet. I am standing in one of the West Coast's largest golf shops, and a young man twenty-five years my junior is telling me — behind his veneer of entrepreneurial etiquette — that I cannot putt.

After thirty-two years of golf frustration, it's time, I've decided, to face the reality that I can no longer blame my ineptness on my irons or woods. Instead, I've decided to blame it on my putter. So here I am shopping for a new one. After nine years, I am kissing my Northwestern Tour model goodbye for a younger, sleeker model.

I feel so cheap; alas, I am a desperate man. At forty-five, my golf game is going through a midlife crisis. And so emerges a belief, a hope, a desperate clinging to the idea that I can somehow buy my way back to respectability.

Long a believer that the swing, not the equipment, makes the golfer, I've scoffed at friends who plunk down hundreds of dollars to find "new and improved" clubs to help them once again hit the drives of their youth. I've chided them for seeing some pro win a tournament, then rushing out to buy the replica of the putter he used; after Jack Nicklaus's stunning Masters win in 1986, who can forget that rush on putters whose heads were roughly the size of bricks? The golfer makes the club, I've long insisted — not the other way around.

But in recent years, my game has gone so far south that even my putter talks with a twang. Blame it on a schedule where golf now makes only a rare guest appearance. After months of not playing, I usually prepare for a round like I prepare for a yearly dental checkup: by flossing the night before — i.e., hitting a bucket of balls — and hoping I can fool the hygienist. Of course, it never works — in the dental chair or on the golf course.

Blame it on a number of other excuses; the bottom line is that some sales kid who didn't even start shaving until after the invention of the Big Bertha driver is now trying to help save my golf game.

I look up at the kid with one of those don't-you-think-I-know-what-I-need looks on my face, then put my pride on a leash. "Sure, let's try something else."

"If you'd like, you can go out on our real putting green and test them," says the young salesman.

The kid is nice — he's only trying to help, after all — but something about this situation just doesn't seem right. I take three putters, a couple of balls, and start walking toward the outdoor putting green.

"Uh, I'll need you to leave your driver's license," he says.

"I'll only be, like, two hundred feet away," I say.

"Store policy."

You gotta be kidding. What's he think I'm going to do—take three putters and a couple of Titleists and hop the first plane to Mexico?

"Seriously?" I say, thinking that my slight balking will probably waive the mandate.

"Sorry."

I look at the young man incredulously and say the only thing that's left to say.

"But I'm your father. Doesn't that count for something?"

"Sorry, store policy."

I pull out my driver's license and hand it to the kid who I once taught to drive. The kid I once taught to play golf. The kid who I haven't beaten on a golf course since he was a sophomore in high school.

I love this kid. I'm proud that, at age twenty, he's found himself a job that he likes and is good at. I think it's wonderful that he has developed into a near-scratch golfer who has shot 69, won back-to-back men's club championships, and posted an 84 at night, using a glow-in-the-dark ball.

But deep inside I have this tiny dream: to beat him just one last time, at anything: golf, home-run derby, or h-o-r-s-e on the backyard hoop. Like Nicklaus coming back to win the Masters at age forty-seven, I'd like one last hurrah to remind the world I'm still around.

It's not a vindictive thing at all. It's just a little pride thing. Not a chest-beating thing, but Pride Lite. Father-son pride. It's wanting to be the hero one last time. It's wanting to still be considered significant, like when you give your son a bit of advice about life itself and he tries it and it works and you think: I'm still needed. I still matter.

And one more thing: Weird as this may sound, fathers want their son's approval. In Ryan's journal, I wrote this about the first time we played golf together as a team. He was sixteen:

Going to the 18th, the two teams were all even. I nailed a 152-yard 7-iron to within two feet of the cup, sunk the putt for birdie and we won! But I was so nervous standing over that putt, more nervous than you'll ever know. (Until now.) Why? Because I wanted so badly to prove to you that I wasn't just this hacker of a dad. That I could pull through. That I could produce under pressure. Because I want you to be the same kind of guy, whether the venue is golf, marriage, work, whatever. I want you to pull through when you need to. Withstand the pressure.

"Do you wanna try one of these putters?" he asks, snapping me back to reality. "This is like the putter you bought me when I beat you for the first time."

I remember the day. He was fifteen. I shot 88. He shot 86. Though I'd done all I could to prevent it, I was glad he'd won, proud to have been outdueled by my own son. I wrote a mock newspaper article—"Ryan stuns Dad for first win!"—and made good on a promise to buy him the putter of his choice.

Since then, it's been his show. I've watched proudly from the edges of the fairway and learned what it must be like for a kid to grow up with high-achieving parents, because whenever I play now, people expect me to be good because Ryan is. And I'm not.

Not long after Ryan won his second men's club championship at a Eugene public course, I teed up my opening drive at the same place and promptly hit it out of bounds. It was like Einstein's father flunking Algebra I.

"So," said the starter, "you're Ryan Welch's father, huh?" As if he really wanted to say, "So much for that axiom about the acorn not falling far from the tree, huh?"

For the most part, I've accepted this role reversal. Twice now, Ryan has had me caddie for him in tournaments that brought together all the winners of club championships from around the state. And I've considered it one of the highest honors a father could be accorded: to be able to carry on my back the clubs of a son I used to carry in my arms.

But deep down, the instinct quietly gnaws at me to prove myself—to nobody else but myself.

~Bob Welch
Chicken Soup for the Golfer's Soul, The 2nd Round

34

Reconnecting

My son Kent and I always had a great bond. Our communications were cemented by his sharing grade-school notes on the refrigerator, long journal entries crammed on the back of postcards during climbs and treks, late-night e-mails that ended with, "Mom, I think I need a woman," and phone calls about interesting females, all of whom were apparently forgotten as soon as he met Janet. The minute he told me, "Mom, she's a park ranger, she paints her toenails and wears a toe ring," I knew that this attractive young woman was a good match for him.

They planned a June wedding in California, unaware that his parents' marriage had unraveled back home in Kansas. I was the one to tell both of the children, living far away, in a letter. My daughter came and worked through communication with both her father and me. Kent did not respond. I finally reached him by phone and was met by a vehement, "I don't want to hear about it, Mom!"

I managed to stay outwardly calm while we finished the conversation as quickly as possible. Asking about their wedding plans was painful and confusing for me, so I ventured, "How's work?" A one-word answer, "Fine," exhausted that subject. Weather was about the only topic that didn't evoke some reference to family or the chasm that loomed between us.

From that day, we exchanged civil calls and e-mails about mundane happenings and family news, but I had no clue what he was really thinking.

Each time I would start to write feelings once easily expressed and received, his denied anger echoed in my head. In fear that I would say something to turn him against his father—or further against me—I would hit delete, not send.

The grief was almost as heavy as with the divorce itself. I had also lost my son.

Months later, I awakened with the conviction that I must speak from the heart. I wrote an e-mail and hit send:

Dear Kent,

It came to me this morning that you're possibly having as much of a struggle coming to some kind of clarity over this divorce as I am....

I told him how wounded I felt at first, how I came to realize that the marriage couldn't be "fixed," that I would miss my in-laws until they got comfortable enough with my being outside the clan to reestablish friendship ties, and assured him that neither his dad nor I wished the other ill after thirty-six years.

I don't see a single thing you or your sister did or didn't do as affecting our decision to divorce. Dad assured me that he loves you both just as much as ever. I do, too, and always will.

Ramblings from an aging mom or, maybe, insights from within a cracked cocoon when I'd like to see from the perspective of a butterfly.

A three-page answer came immediately. Kent's old voice was there, honestly telling me what he thought and felt. He recounted his fiancée's quizzical look when he spoke of his parents' "perfectly balanced marriage," of Mr. Sequential vs. Mrs. Random, taciturn vs. gregarious personalities, nightly TV vs. frequent travel, retiree vs. second-career seeker, stock market vs. spiritual reader. Our breakup had rocked Kent to the core. He was about to commit to a marriage when most of his friends scorned the convention, and his role models had just chopped it all off at their clay ankles. He was anxious about how we'd handle the upcoming wedding.

He wrote that our superficial communication had taken its toll on him, too, but it had given him time to decide what he did and did not want from married life. He would work to keep common interests alive in his marriage and thought he might actually be a better husband from what he had learned from us. Above all, he loved us both.

The sweet relief I felt is difficult to describe. I read his letter over and over, grateful for the healing passage of time that brought insight and courage (or desperation?), that helped me stick my neck out vulnerably, and risk that helped us both to grow. Mostly, I felt thankful for the mother-son bond, mended.

~Virginia Fortner
Chicken Soup for the Mother and Son Soul

35

Somewhere, Babe Ruth Is Smiling

They were two chairs from Yankee Stadium, number fifteen and number twenty-two, and they sat in the basement of his grandparents' home for years, unnoticed. Now and then, family members would come upon them and be told the story of how they were purchased. It seems when Yankee Stadium was rebuilt in the early seventies, thousands of these chairs were sold at a modest price. Fans sitting in number fifteen and number twenty-two watched the likes of Babe Ruth, Mickey Mantle and Lou Gehrig as they made baseball history. Perhaps one of them even caught a ball hit by one of the all-time baseball greats.

Someone approached my son-in-law about buying the chairs. A generous offer was made, and the family met in the basement to make a decision.

Grandson Ryan, a nine-year-old Little Leaguer just returning from a baseball game and wearing Lou Gehrig's number four on his uniform, protested.

"I don't believe you're selling those chairs," he said. "You can't give them to someone else." He approached his grandfather, the original owner of the chairs, with puzzled young eyes. "Why are you going to do that now?"

His parents, being much wiser about such things, explained that they could all make a healthy profit if they sold them. And now there was a buyer.

"You don't understand," Ryan was told as he persisted. Of course, the grown-ups understood better. They were older. They were wiser. And they were certainly more realistic about financial matters. Everyone would benefit from the money received.

The chairs were lifted from the dust and cobwebs that had gathered about them and placed in the center of the basement. They were chipped and worn. There were no fans sitting in them now, no cheers throughout the stadium surrounding them, no baseball greats to look down at with wonder. And yet they held a majesty that silenced even the adults for a few thoughtful moments.

The debate concentrated on whether to keep the chairs until they gathered more value or sell them now. But while the conversation continued, the Little Leaguer with the number four on his shirt sat down in seat number twenty-two. And while the family decided that it was the best thing that could have happened to them, and that the money sure would come in handy, and that a bird in the hand was worth two in the bush, while all of this was coming about in the basement, the Little Leaguer began to cry. He didn't usually cry in front of an audience. It made everyone uncomfortable.

"I think we'd better go upstairs," his father said. The discussion was over. The decision made. The chairs would be sold.

But his son didn't move. It was as if Ryan were glued to the chair. "I can't get up," he said. It seemed he couldn't, even if he tried.

It was his grandfather who approached the boy. "Would you explain to me why you are so upset?" he asked.

Grown-up words came from Ryan's mouth when he spoke, as if they were delivered from somewhere else. "The people sitting in these seats got to see them all, the great ones, Gehrig and Mantle and Ruth. Right from this seat." His young hands caressed the chair. "Sitting here, I know just what they felt like," Ryan said. "What a great feeling."

Of course, everyone knew the wise thing to do, and the realistic thing to do. And the prudent thing to do. But no one wanted to remove this young baseball player from his chair, especially his grandfather who remembered what it was like to be that young and in love with baseball.

It was Ryan's chair now. Everybody in the basement realized it. And they finally understood what he was trying to tell them. There wasn't enough money in the world to buy seat number twenty-two now that Ryan had found it, and there wasn't enough money in the world to equal the look on Ryan's face when he threw his arms around his grandfather to thank him.

That night a nine-year-old boy wearing a number four on his baseball shirt took home Yankee Stadium seat twenty-two.

And somewhere, Babe Ruth was smiling.

~Harriet May Savitz
Chicken Soup for the Grandparent's Soul

EDITORS' NOTE: In loving memory of our friend Harriet May Savitz — your stories live on in thousands of hearts you've touched with your many contributions to Chicken Soup for the Soul.

Always a Mother

*Is there anything more precious, more steadfast,
more constant or enduring than a mother's love?*
~Author Unknown

To watch her worry and fret as she waited for news of how her little girl came through brain surgery was almost more than I could bear. Through her tears she recounted stories of her little girl and voiced her longing to be right there with her. As she continually checked her watch, counting down the time that the doctor said surgery should take, I tried to think of comforting things to say. My words did not seem appropriate for she was in a place I had never been. How could I understand her vigil, the agony that waiting was causing her?

Finally, the telephone rang. Marie had come through surgery fine and would recover with time. The look of relief flooded her face as her body visibly released its grip on her nerves. At last, this eighty-six year old mother could relax, knowing her seventy-year-old "little girl" was going to be fine.

~ Elizabeth Vinson
Chicken Soup for the Mother & Daughter Soul

A Gift Through the Generations

My grandmother was of average height, with hazel eyes and salt-and-pepper hair that framed a round face. She had lots of laugh lines and a smile that said she had plenty of love to give. When you hugged her, there was plenty to hang on to. I know because I hugged her a lot.

She wasn't beautiful by today's definition. She didn't turn heads when she walked into a room. If you saw her on the street, you would probably have walked by her without a second glance. There are millions of overweight grandmothers in the world — mine would have blended right in.

But if you did walk by her, if you didn't notice her, you would have been missing someone special.

When I was growing up, going over to my grandmother's was always a special occasion. Although there was little money for new furniture or fancy knickknacks, the house was filled with food and love, in equal amounts. Even now when I think of her, more than thirty years after her death, I find it hard to separate my memories of her from the food she made.

Mostly, I remember her baking. The kitchen table would be covered with flour and she would be up to her arms in dough, her short, nimble fingers able to turn the most mundane ingredients into light, flaky treats from the old country. While my contribution to the baking was often no more than carrying ingredients from the fridge to the table, I took my role as her assistant very seriously.

I don't think I ever felt as close to her as I did then, when it was just the two of us in the kitchen. The older grandchildren would be out shopping or at the movies, too old or too sophisticated to want to spend time with a grandmother who wasn't up on the latest fashion or music group.

Not me. I was exactly where I wanted to be — in a cramped kitchen helping my grandmother. While she measured and kneaded, whipped and stirred, she talked to me. Not about the big world out there, but about the little world in which we lived. The day-to-day stuff: school, food and family.

Mostly what she did was to make me feel loved and wanted. In that kitchen, while I was with her, I was the most important person in her life.

I didn't inherit my grandmother's culinary talents, but I did inherit her eyes, her sense of humor and, unfortunately, her build. For the longest time, I saw that as a curse. Instead of being tall and slender, I was short and dumpy. More peasant stock than royalty.

I blamed my excess padding on both my grandmother and my mother. They were the ones who gave me one hip that's a good inch lower than the other one.

Hips that in the old country would be considered good childbearing hips, but which in this country are too wide.

During my teens and into my twenties, every time I

looked in the mirror, I saw only my defects. I was too short, too round-faced, too wide in the hips, too this and too that. There was nothing about my body that I liked.

It was all their fault.

Now, when I look back, I can see how much time and energy I wasted blaming them for passing on their less-than-perfect physical traits. Because I was so focused on what I saw as their negative traits, I forgot the thing that mattered most — their real beauty.

I would look at the last picture ever taken of my grandmother and would feel how much I missed her. But I was missing more than her. I was missing my heritage. Luckily, as I got older, and maybe a little bit wiser, I began to understand and to reach out for it.

My mother is now older than my grandmother was when she died. Over the years, my mother has begun to look more and more like my grandmother. Her hair is starting to go salt-and-pepper and she has begun to put on a little more weight around the middle. There are also more lines on her face than there used to be.

The family resemblance is becoming stronger and stronger with each passing year.

In watching my mother grow more like my grandmother, I am rediscovering just how beautiful my grandmother was and how beautiful my mother is. And in rediscovering their beauty, I am also discovering mine. No, not the textbook definition of beauty, but my own definition. One that is right for me.

I no longer complain quite as much when my mother visits and brings me boxes of food. I now understand that, like her mother before her, my mother sees food as love. While she doesn't bake quite as well as my grandmother did—no one ever will—my mother bakes love into every-thing she makes.

As I get older, the family resemblance is coming out more and more in me, too. The hazel eyes, the laugh lines, the hair with the first gray ones appearing and, yes, the figure with the full hips and expanding middle. Only now I don't see them as a curse, but as a blessing.

All of these things form a bond between me, my mother, my grandmother and all their mothers who came before them. I only have to look in the mirror to see that I belong to a long line of very special women.

Of course, I expect to get more and more beautiful as I get older, with each laugh line and each gray hair tying me more closely to those who have come before me.

After all, in my family, beauty is a family tradition.

~Harriet Cooper
Chicken Soup to Inspire a Woman's Soul

38

He Was a Hero, Like All Grandfathers

My grandfather didn't only provide a guide to living; he lived
life fully and modeled for me how to do it—
mostly with love and kindness.
~McAllister Dodds

A while ago, a legend entered my life in the most common of ways, disguised as a grandfather. His name was familiar, and I knew what he did long before I met him in a sticky, half-empty middle school gym. We were watching a basketball game. I was there to see my son, and he was there to see his grandson. They play on the same team—a pretty good team, like a lot of other pretty good teams that play in gyms across the city every Saturday afternoon. Their fans are vocal and intimately tied to the players. Mother. Fathers. Siblings with nothing better to do. Sometimes grandparents. I saw him every week.

His past made him extraordinary, and periodically I would watch as people stopped to shake his hand. I assumed that he had gotten used to that, as well as to the deference and muffled whispers that followed him wherever he went, a long time ago. I wondered if that made life harder or easier, but as I watched him I decided that he had gotten used to that, too, and it was clear that although he enjoyed it, he had given it a place. A nice place, to be sure, but certainly somewhere below watching his grandson.

Over the years, his grandson and my son became friends. They did things that any other middle school friends do. Movies. Football. Basketball. But interspersed with the routine, there was always the reminder of the legend.

"Mom, can I go to the Hall of Fame luncheon with Jeb and his grandpa?"

And visits to Jeb's house were followed by, "We went to Jeb's grandpa's house. He has a really cool trophy room."

"I imagine he does," I would reply.

"No, this is really cool. He has a copy of his Hall of Fame bust."

I don't know why, but each time the reminder came, it took me by surprise.

Last week after school, for no other reason except that he likes to draw, my son came home and drew a copy of an autographed publicity shot Jeb's grandpa had given him. He worked on it for hours. He finally brought it over.

"It's very good," I said and for the first time I really looked at the photo. It had been taken about forty years ago. I compared the photo and the drawing. "You've done the body perfectly," I said.

And he had. He had copied in detail the body of the athlete kicking a football. But the face in the photo and the face in the drawing didn't match. The face John drew was not the face of forty years ago. The face in the drawing was the mature face that he knew. John had drawn the face of the grandpa.

"But it's not the best I've done," he said.

"Well it's not a perfect copy, but it's very good," I replied. "You should give it to him."

The next morning my alarm went off at five, and, as is my routine, I lay in bed and listened to the radio's news broadcast. The broadcaster was talking about The Toe.

I knew before they said it why The Toe was the lead story. Legends become lead stories when they are gone.

I listened for a while and went downstairs. The drawing was sitting on the kitchen table. "Lou Groza," it said, "Hall of Fame, '74."

When John came home from the funeral, he mentioned a passage that had been read. It was titled, "Little Eyes Upon You."

"And what did it say?" I asked.

"It said that older people should watch the steps they take because little kids are watching. Because to little kids, older people are heroes."

Older people. Not legendary sport stars. Ordinary grandpas and grandmas and aunts and uncles and fathers and mothers.

This time the grandpa and legend just happened to be the same man.

I was wrong about the drawing. It was perfect.

~Sue Vitou
Chicken Soup for the Grandparent's Soul

39

The Healing

I t happened hundreds of miles away on my grandmother's
porch. I went there to recuperate from the surgery that
had taken away my uterus, ovaries and so many years of
monthly battles with my body that I thought of it more as
an adversary than part of my being. I had read all about the
depression and mood swings and reduced libido that would
follow, but no one mentioned the emotional barrenness that
had descended upon me and left me helpless. I did what I had
always done when I felt lost: I went home to be healed by the
sun and the sea and my grandmother's hands.

There was the plane and then there were her arms taking me in and letting me rest my head and heavy heart. The
first day, she threw away the pills and prescriptions in my
bag. She called her friend Yeya from across the road, and
Cecilia from over the rise and Aurelia from the botánica.
They consulted with each other, and together they decided
on my new remedios. Every day abuela went into her garden and collected herbs. Then it began — the endless baths
in lengua de perro to reduce the swelling and calm the
nerves, gallons of genjibre tea to calm the vomiting, higuera
to fight infection and flor de virgen to lift the sadness.

But the most important part of my recovery had nothing to do with herbs. The most important remedio, it

turned out, was community. "I don't care what the doctorcitos said. That girl living alone up there in the cold... no wonder she got sick. She needs warmth on the inside and on the outside." And all the ladies agreed.

A cot was set out for me on the porch, and every day, as my grandmother went about her chores, her white-haired friends hobbled up the hill and across the road. After they had washed the breakfast dishes, they would twist their hair into buns, put on their gold earrings and come to sit with me. They brought secret ointments warmed by the sun and applied the balm all over my body. As I lay there too tired and pained to care, I surrendered myself to their hands—wrinkled hands that missed holding babies and soothing toddlers. They brought me their love in the folds of those wrinkles and kneaded it into my body. And while their hands worked, they gave me the gift of their stories that lived under their nails, between their fingers, in their hair. They told me of their lives and the lives of others—everyone in the town. They shared their dreams with me and their disappointments. They celebrated their joys and whispered their failures.

I looked at them with their limp aprons and their cracked feet in oversized men's slippers. I watched their mouths and listened to the words floating out through ill-fitting dentures or swollen gums. The days grew into weeks, and still I listened. They filled my days and my emptiness with their teeming lives. My grandmother told them I was writing down their stories, and they smiled behind cupped hands and brought me more, trusting that I would be gentle with their tales. They brought them in their pockets, their teacups, their photo albums, their treasure boxes. They brought them in lockets and broken picture frames and yellowed newspapers. They must have rummaged in the bottom of their drawers, under the beds, between the old dresses, in the back of the wardrobes. They brought me huge, leather-bound Bibles and yellowed christening gowns and pressed flowers. They brought me the pieces of their lives and bade me make them a quilt of words. When the world was moving too fast for them, they asked me to stop time.

It took a community to heal me, a community of old women bringing me the many stages of their lives. And now that those ladies are long gone, all that is left of their world is their stories. They told me stories I had never heard and stories each of them knew by heart. As they spoke, they suddenly turned into a group of young girls playing in the creek, young women sending their men to war, mothers-of-the-bride letting go of their no-longer-little girls, old women sitting before their husbands' coffins wondering what life held in store in the empty days ahead. Their stories made me realize that my life, just like theirs, would be lived in stages, and that this was only one of them. Their stories were gifts from their hearts, remedios that helped me recognize my own humanity in theirs, gave me strength, and restored my mind and heart.

The strength and hope I heard in the stories of these ancianitas inspired me to be a writer, so that I could share their lives and their wisdom with others, long after they were gone. I am forever grateful.

~Dahlma Llanos Figueroa
Chicken Soup for the Latino Soul

40

Choosing Life

Many years ago, my grandfather gave me a silver wine goblet so small that it holds no more than a thimbleful of wine. Exquisitely engraved into its bowl is a bow with long ribbon streamers. It was made in Russia long ago. He gave it to me during one of the many afternoons when we sat together at the kitchen table in my parents' home memorizing phrases from his old books and discussing the nature of life. I was quite young then, no more than five or six, and when I became restless, he would revive my attention by bringing out the sacramental Concord grape wine he kept in the back of the refrigerator. He would fill my little beribboned wineglass with Manischewitz and then put a splash of wine into his own, a big silver ceremonial cup, generations old. Then we would offer a toast together. At the time, the only other celebration I knew was singing "Happy Birthday" and blowing out the candles. I loved this even better.

My grandfather had taught me the toast we used. It was a single Hebrew word, "L'Chaim" (pronounced le CHI yeem), which he told me meant "To life!" He always said it with great enthusiasm. "Is it to a happy life, Grandpa?" I had asked him once. He had shaken his head no. "It is just 'To life!' Neshume-le," he told me.

At first, this did not make a lot of sense to me, and I struggled to understand his meaning. "Is it like a prayer?" I asked uncertainly.

"Ah no, Neshume-le," he told me. "We pray for the things we don't have. We already have life."

"But then why do we say this before we drink the wine?" He smiled at me fondly. "Grandpa!" I said, suddenly suspicious. "Did you make it up?" He chuckled and assured me that he had not. For thousands of years, all over the world, people have said this same word to each other before drinking wine together. It was a Jewish tradition.

I puzzled about this last for some time. "Is it written in the Bible, Grandpa?" I asked at last. "No, Neshume-le," he said, "it is written in people's hearts." Seeing the confusion on my face, he told me that "L'Chaim!" meant that no matter what difficulty life brings, no matter how hard or painful or unfair life is, life is holy and worthy of celebration. "Even the wine is sweet to remind us that life itself is a blessing."

It has been almost fifty-five years since I last heard my grandfather's voice, but I remember the joy with which he toasted Life and the twinkle in his eye as he said "L'Chaim!" It has always seemed remarkable to me that such a toast could be offered for generations by a people for whom life has not been easy. But perhaps it can only be said by such people, and only those who have lost and suffered can truly understand its power.

"L'Chaim!" is a way of living life. As I've grown older, it seems less and less about celebrating life and more about the wisdom of choosing life. In the many years that I have been counseling people with cancer, I have seen people choose life again and again, despite loss and pain and difficulty. The same immutable joy I saw in my grandfather's eyes is there in them all.

~Rachel Naomi Remen, M.D.
Chicken Soup for the Jewish Soul

Chapter
5

Older & Wiser

The Wisdom We've Earned

*One of the most courageous things you can do is identify
yourself, know who you are, what you believe in,
and where you want to go.
~Sheila Murray Bethel*

41

Awakening

Sometimes the heart sees what is invisible to the eye.
~ Jackson Brown Jr.

There were so many admissions that night that I had begun to lose count — and my temper. A seasoned intern, I had learned well the art of the quick, efficient work-up. Short-cutting had become a way of life. Morning was coming and, with it, my day off. All I wanted was to be done. My beeper sounded. I answered it. I heard the tired voice of my resident say, "Another hit, some ninety-year-old 'gomer' with cancer." Swearing under my breath, I headed to the room. An elderly man sat quietly in his bed. Acting put upon, I abruptly launched into my programmed litany of questions, not really expecting much in the way of answers. To my surprise, his voice was clear and full, and his answers were articulate and concise. In the midst of my memorized review of systems, I asked if he had ever lived or worked outside the country.

"Yes," he replied. "I lived in Europe for seven years after the war." Surprised by his answer, I inquired if he had been a soldier there.

"No," he said. "I was a lawyer. I was one of the prosecuting attorneys at the Nuremberg trials."

My pen hit the floor. I blinked.

"The Nuremberg trials?" He nodded, stating that he later remained in Europe to help rebuild the German legal system

Right, I thought to myself, some old man's delusion. My beeper went off twice. I finished the examination quickly, hurried off to morning sign-out and handed over the beeper.

Officially free, I started out the door but suddenly paused, remembering the old man, his voice, his eyes. I walked over to the phone and called my brother, a law student, who was taking a course on legal history. I asked him if the man's name appeared in any of his books. After a few minutes, his voice returned.

"Actually, it says here that he was one of the prosecution's leading attorneys at the Nuremberg trials." I don't remember making my way back to his room, but I know I felt humbled, small and insignificant. I knocked. When he bid me enter, I sat in the very seat I had occupied a short time before and quietly said, "Sir, if you would not mind, I am off-duty now and would very much like to hear about Nuremberg and what you did there. And I apologize for having been so curt with you previously." He smiled, staring at me.

"No, I don't mind." Slowly, with great effort at times, he told me of the immense wreckage of Europe, the untold human suffering of the war. He spoke of the camps, those immense factories of death, the sight of the piles of bodies that made him retch. The trials, the bargaining, the punishments. He said that the war criminals themselves had been a sorry-looking bunch. Aside from the rude awakening of having lost the war, they could not quite understand the significance of the court's quiet and determined justice or of the prosecution's hard work and thorough attention to detail. The Nazis had never done things that way. So moved had he been by the suffering he encountered there that he had stayed on to help build a system of laws that would prevent such atrocities from happening again. Like a child I sat, silent, drinking in every word. This was history before me. Four hours passed. I thanked him and shook his hand, and went home to sleep.

The next morning began early, and as usual I was busy. It was late before I could return to see the old man. When I did, his room was empty. He had died during the night.

I walked outside into the evening air and caught the smell of the spring flowers. I thought of the man and felt despair mixed with joy. Suddenly my life seemed richer and more meaningful, my patients more complex and mysterious than before. I realized that the beauty and horror of this world were mixed in a way that is sometimes beyond understanding. The man's effect on me did not end there. Despite the grueling call schedule, the overwhelming workload and the emotional stress of internship, something had changed within me. I began to notice colors, shapes and smells that added magic to everyday life. I learned that the gray-haired patients that I had once called "gomers" were people with stories to tell and things to teach. After nearly two decades I still look to the night, remember that man, and reflect on the chance and privilege we have to share in the lives of others, if only we take the time to listen.

~Blair P. Grubb, M.D.
Chicken Soup for the Jewish Soul

42

One Hour a Week

What we love to do we find time to do.
~John L. Spalding

Willliam waits for me in front of Room 210, hands holding something behind his back, head tilted away as I approach. "I don't feel like reading today," he announces, avoiding eye contact. He is almost ten, handsome and polite, with dark brown eyes as big as pennies. And he's on to me. As the year has passed, he's figured out that I'm a pushover.

"How about one book?" I suggest, "In our favorite spot? Then we can play your game." Negotiations complete, he pulls the board game front and center, and we walk down five steps to a white window seat to begin reading *Frog and Toad Together*. Suddenly, he stops.

"Too many pages. I can't read that many pages."

"How about if you read one, then I read one. I'll start."

"No," says William. "I'll start."

And so it goes. Once a week for one hour, going on three years, William and I meet with the assigned task of improving his literacy. Mostly we goof around. On his high-energy days, we whip through easy readers. I celebrate every new word he masters with a cheerleader-like frenzy. "Wonderful! Great! You are a reader, William!" He fires back with enthusiasm of his own: "How many books can we read today? Ten? Twelve? Let's read eighteen!"

Sometimes we just play games — Trouble or Mancala. He plays to win, and does. Sometimes, we sneak into the school cafeteria, scouring it for a Popsicle or a bag of salty chips. Other days are a chore. He's distracted, annoyed even, watching his buddies swat each other's heads as they march down the hall to the Media Center while he's stuck with me. "William," I tease, "where are you?" On those days, I feel defeated. But I'm never sorry I came.

Once William came to school with a family crisis embedded in his face. As we sat together on the white bench, he shed his bravado and tucked wet eyes into my shoulder and I would have held him there forever. But he is, after all, nine years old. The storm passed quickly. He sat up, wiped his eyes and asked, "Can we play Trouble?"

A teacher I know stopped me in the hall one day to ask if I would be returning the following year. "Of course," I told her. "Well, good," she said. "William needs you." I wanted to correct her: Actually, I need William.

I am forty-three years old, with a full-time job I like and three neat kids who, so far, still like me. But sometimes I catch myself letting work problems distract me from them at home, when I open the mail instead of focusing on a detail of their day, or rush through their bedtime rituals so I can crawl into bed with a book.

Sixteen years into marriage, I'm a decent spouse. But the most romantic getaway we have these days is to the wholesale club to buy in bulk. At work, where I manage nine creative people, most days go well. But last week I missed a deadline and screwed up an administrative detail and got some facts wrong in a meeting and wondered why they ever hired me.

I have friends I adore who complete my world. But we can never seem to find time for lunch anymore, and one is battling depression and my words, meant to comfort, come out trite and patronizing. "Hang in there," I tell her. "It will get better." Dear God.

My world is safe and solid and good, except when the wheels come off unexpectedly and I feel as though I will drown in self-doubt. When I say something stupid, or feel envy, or bark at my kids because I'm tired, or forget to call my mother, or call my mother and feel ten years old again, or go to work with graham crackers ground into my shoulder and my sweater buttoned wrong.

But I have one hour.

One hour a week when I have no self-doubt. When I walk down a noisy elementary school hallway covered with children's art and my respite awaits me.

"When will you come back?" William asks.

"Next Wednesday, silly. I always come on Wednesday."

"I wish you could come on Mondays instead," he says. "Then I wouldn't have to wait so long for you."

One hour a week I am granted the greatest reward possible: The comfort of knowing that I am absolutely in the right place, doing the right thing.

My life will catch up to me soon enough. But for the moment, it will just have to wait.

~Gail Rosenblum
Chicken Soup for the Working Woman's Soul

God Has a Plan

I t was the day after Christmas. The snow on the rooftop had the requisite number of hoof prints, and all was cozy as we slept inside our warm flannel sheets. But when the phone rang at 4:30 A.M., any sense of comfort flew up the chimney. I became ice cold, and my heart started pounding. Phone calls that early in the morning are never good.

My brother, Jim, was on the line. "What medication is Mom on?"

"Just some high blood pressure medicine, I think. Why?"

"She's having a heart attack."

Our mother? Having a heart attack? It couldn't be happening. She was the healthiest eighty-four-year-old lady you could imagine. She ate heart-healthy salmon eight out of seven days a week and never touched anything deep-fried. Physically fit, she didn't know that twenty-five-pound vacuum cleaners are perfectly happy in closets. She thought hers should be exercised regularly, hoisting it up and down several flights of stairs.

Four years earlier, when she was a mere spring chicken, age eighty, she noticed a leak on the ceiling in the house where she lived with our father for forty-eight years. She hired a handyman to fix it. He was up on the rooftop when a thunderstorm began rumbling. Mom donned a well-worn jacket, climbed out the second-story window at the top of the stairs, shimmied over to the handyman's side of the roof and began helping him nail down the shingles. When a neighbor saw this, he shouted up to her, "Do your children know what you're doing?"

"No," she scolded him, "and don't you tell them!"

We eventually found out and tried to reason her out of such future activities. Getting on the rooftop, a la Dancer and Prancer, was reasonable, as she defiantly explained. "The handyman is sixty-five years old and has health problems. I didn't want him to get sick when it started raining."

Two years later, we asked Mom to consider living with one of us kids. She decided to move three hundred miles to be near me and my family, but "Only if I can have my own house." We agreed, with the stipulation that she stay off the roof. We bought her a house with no inside access to the roof—just in case.

As she settled in, she declared, "It's about time I start a new chapter in my life. The good Lord has a plan to provide for us. He never gives me anything I can't handle with His help." Then she warned, "Just promise me you won't tell anyone here my age. I don't want my new friends to think I'm old."

It didn't matter. Her actions at her Monday-Wednesday-Friday exercise class at church fooled them anyway.

So when the phone rang that December 26th, I was baffled why this wonder woman was having a heart attack. But, as she trusted, the good Lord provided a plan. My brother had heard Mom taking aspirin in the bathroom outside his bedroom door. He was wide awake when she said, "I think I'm having a heart attack." Instead of being in her own home where volunteer fire and ambulance services would have taken her to a hospital twenty minutes away, she was at my brother's, where the paramedics arrived in just three minutes.

Faster than Santa can swoop down the chimney, the emergency crew strapped her to the gurney and transported her to a hospital rated to have the best cardiac care in western Chicago just ten minutes away. She was in surgery before you could sing, "Grandma Got Run Over by a Reindeer."

Mom is wise beyond her eighty-four years: "God has the right plan, even when we can't see it." A plan to help push heavy Hoovers, scale rooftops and save my mom at Christmas time.

~Jean Palmer Heck
Chicken Soup for the Christian Soul 2

44

First Love

The heart of a mother is a deep abyss at the bottom of which
you will always find forgiveness.
~Honoré de Balzac

As far back as I can remember, I was the loud, adventurous and mischievous daughter; she was the quiet, traditional and ladylike mother. I always blamed our problems on our age difference. She was thirty-eight when I was born, and at that time, in the late '60s, that was old to have a baby. Though I was never embarrassed that I had the oldest parents in my group of friends, I felt that their advanced age accounted for their being so strict and conservative.

It was inevitable that the "loud" daughter and the "quiet" mother would clash. In my early teens, we argued a lot and it created an ever-growing wedge between us. One major problem was how strict she was when it came to boys and dating. We argued until we were blue in the face about when I would be allowed to date. Finally, the magic number was determined... sixteen.

In no time I was sixteen and dating. She didn't talk to me about it directly, but I could tell my mother was very concerned. I couldn't understand why. Didn't she realize I was a responsible, intelligent girl who would never date a jerk? I assumed it was due to her "old-fashioned" ways.

She was a strict "older mom" who just didn't understand today's world.

Then toward the end of my first year of dating, I met him. He was a great guy. My parents liked him instantly, though I could still see a look of concern on my mother's face. Was she ever going to trust me? My boyfriend and I were in love and after going together steadily for a year, I started college. Anyone who has experienced first love and then a sudden separation knows the chances of staying together are slim to none. When we broke up, so did my heart. I was devastated. This eighteen-year-old know-it-all suddenly didn't know what to do. I immediately ran to my "mommy" and cried on her shoulder like a baby.

Did she lecture me? Did she say, "I told you so"? Not once. Instead, she slept with me in my bed, held my hand and even kissed me on the forehead just like when I was a little girl. She never made me feel stupid or ashamed. She listened to my sad story and watched silently as the tears rolled down my face.

After a while, although I was feeling better, I was still very confused and didn't quite understand what had just happened to me. I was very angry, and I expressed my concerns to my mother. I was surprised at the tone of my voice. It had a harder edge. I wasn't so trusting or naïve; I felt older and more tired.

My mother gently explained the reasons she had been so concerned during my courtship, opening up to me like she never had before. She had always been so conservative with me about sharing her emotions that I sometimes wondered if she had ever been a teenager. Now, she told me about her first love and how she'd felt when it was over. Her heart had been broken, and the tears hadn't stopped for weeks. When it was all said and done, she'd felt just as hopeless as I was feeling. She told me that in time her pain went away, becoming only a faint memory. She assured me that one day I would meet the man I would marry, and when I thought of my first heartbreak, I would smile. I would forget the pain and only remember the love.

I was surprised, shocked and relieved all at once. Surprised that my father wasn't my mother's first love. Shocked that she had actually shared this story with me. And relieved that my mother was not only a mom, but also a woman who had experienced the same kind of pain I had... and survived. It was then that my mother became my best friend.

After that, I shared all the challenges and problems in my life with her. College, dating, career and of course, more heartbreaks. But none ever seemed as serious as the first. I loved how close we were. Even my friends commented on our relationship. It made us both very happy and proud.

Then one day, many years later, I met him: my future husband. The first thing I did was call my mom and tell her all about him. During the phone conversation she asked me if I remembered my first heartbreak. Giggling, I answered yes, wondering why she'd asked.

I could hear the tenderness in her voice as she responded, "Are you smiling?"

~Sophia Valles Bligh
Chicken Soup for Every Mom's Soul

45

Nana's Mysterious Panache

Other things may change us,
but we start and end with family.
~Anthony Brandt

She was grand! But Nana adamantly disclaimed the title, explaining, "No one is grander than your own mother."

Picture Rosalind Russell's portrayal of Auntie Mame and you get a glimpse of my grandmother. Strong and independent, she drove the first car in town, wore pants when that was still scandalous, and she never minded a bawdy joke. Nana vivaciously dashed through life, lighting up the lives of everyone she met. I wondered why the slings and arrows of life never seemed to overwhelm her.

Domestic chores, even the making of lard soap, were performed effortlessly and cheerfully. I'd watch as she scurried about, emptying ashtrays into the silent butler. How unique that was! Yet, upon seeing a bored child, she'd immediately drop her towel and sit down to teach a game of solitaire.

Basking in the warmth of her sunny presence, I'd

watch as the last hairpin was pinned in her brightly hennaed hair.

"Want to walk to the grocer's with me, Honeypot?"

"Oh, yes." I was always proud to walk with her. Tall and slender, and dressed so impeccably (she was the only grandmother who wore spike-heeled shoes—an important distinction to me), Nana energetically marched along, calling out, "Hello there, Little Miss Pumpkin. Bunny Boy, how's your lovely mama today?" as neighborhood kids waved and shouted, "Hi, Mrs. K." They sensed here was a woman who knew—and believed—in kids.

Deliverymen and visitors always lingered at Nana's gracious home. Laughing and chattering, she discussed politics or recipes with equal enthusiasm; her gold cigarette holder waving through the air, punctuating the discourse with grace. Framed by a strong, square jaw and prominent cheekbones, her wonderful smile—wrinkles danced as she spoke, and sparkling green eyes watched for signs of trouble. The surly became cheerful; crudeness was treated with gentility. Nana gave strength to the sorrowful, calm to the hysterical, and everyone left feeling touched by her love. Why, I pondered, did she never seem cranky?

Widowed at age fifty-two, she invited me for sleepovers more often. Mornings, waking to her raspy voice singing in the kitchen, brought new adventures in food.

"Your breakfast is served, my queen." Pretending to be my lady-in-waiting, Nana pulled out the chair with a flourish. Elegantly set, my place held a juicy, ripe mango and a boiled egg standing in a delicate little cup. Fine crystal and bone china were used daily, never stored away.

Some evenings, after the dinner table was cleared, Nana would throw a sweater over her shoulders and go out into the night. Finally, I asked, "Nana, where are you going... can I come?"

"No, darling," she'd chuckle. "This is my alone time." I sensed an air of mystery in this.

One evening, after Nana had slipped out, I climbed out the bedroom window and followed her — at a distance; Nancy Drew stories had taught me well. Nana walked swiftly down two lamplit blocks and went inside the neighborhood church (churches never closed back then). I hid behind a massive pillar as Nana knelt down in the pew; no prayer book in her hand. After a few moments, she bent her head. When she finally looked up, I saw, in the glimmer of dozens of candles, her face shining with tears. Nana was crying! She stared at the altar. Slowly, ever so slowly, the corners of her mouth began to curve upward. The gentle curve grew and grew. At last, that unique and wonderful smile returned. A moment longer she sat, then, as though consummating a business deal, she briskly arose, genuflected once, and bustled away.

Once back snug in bed, I contemplated what I'd just learned. Bring my sorrows to church. Leave them there. In the face of adversity, put on a smile; before long, it will be genuine. Nana had struggles just like the rest of us; she just refused to succumb to them.

~Lynne Zielinski
Chicken Soup for the Grandparent's Soul

46

Divorce, of Course

Anyone can be passionate, but it takes real lovers to be silly.
~Rose Franken

As most public-course golfers know, it is not uncommon for a weekend round to take five or six hours, if you can even get a starting time on your favorite local course. The volume of people who cannot play mid-week, coupled with those looking for a respite from yard work or the spouse, causes a flood of players filling every available tee time. Slow play is inevitable because of the varying capability of weekend golfers. As a result, you will hear complaining, more-than-occasional cries of "Fore" and frustrated players waiting on every tee.

Marching into this fray one weekend, I joined a threesome following a group of older women. My playing companions were male, somewhat grayer than I, and seemed unusually anxious about playing behind the women. They muttered while the women teed off, they muttered while waiting for the fairway to clear and they muttered continuously until they reached the green. I could only make out a few words here and there, mostly about slow play.

After several holes, which seemed to take forever, one of the men asked me if I was married (I am), and if my wife played golf (she does not). I returned the conversation by asking the same questions.

The first gentleman waived a disdaining hand and said, "No more, and thank God." I was not certain which question he was answering.

The second man smiled and said, "Divorced, and she does." I just smiled back.

The third man looked intently down the fairway at the women ahead of us and then turned and spoke. "I was married to the woman in the blue pants, up there in the fairway. George was married to the woman in yellow, and Dave to the one in white. My wife hit the ball farther than I could, and she putted better. Asked her for a divorce last year, after thirty-seven years of marriage."

"Is it just a coincidence that they are in the group ahead?" I asked.

"No," the third man (I can't recall his name) replied, "we've been doing this every weekend for two years."

"You mean you arrange this, even though you are divorced because of golf? But why, if it frustrates you?"

"Frustrates us? What do you mean?" George asked.

"Well, you're muttering on every hole, complaining about how slow the round is. Why would you want to play behind them?"

They smiled at each other, then looked back to me. "Son," George started, "we're not frustrated. We've got new clubs, good health for our age and a regular game every Saturday."

"You see," the third man continued, "our playing golf left them home alone. So, after George's wife divorced him three years ago, and then Dave's, the women took up the game with my ex. They enjoyed it so much, it changed their attitude. In fact, they became like girls again, and George and Dave have been dating them ever since."

"But you said you were divorced last year."

"Sure. It improved George and Dave's sex life, so I convinced my wife to divorce so we could have the same thing. And it worked. Couldn't be happier."

"But the complaining I hear, what's that?"

George and Dave smiled again. "Slow play!" Dave said. "The sooner we get done with this round, the sooner we get to date night."

~Gordon W. Youngs
Chicken Soup for the Golfer's Soul

47

The One Who Got Away

The greatest happiness of life
is the conviction that we are loved—
loved for ourselves, or rather, loved in spite of ourselves.
~Victor Hugo

I think every woman has one—that ex-beau who niggles his way back to consciousness after a family fight, a bout of stretching the weekly paycheck or even after the oaf you really married leaves his dirty socks smack in the middle of the living room floor.

You know the guy I'm talking about. And who cares if you can list fifteen reasons that you're glad you didn't marry him?

So what if he talked too much—or was too shy, too arrogant, too possessive? So what if he gambled and his relatives borrowed money? This man would never do a strip tease on the rug and he'd have too much couth to yell if you forgot his mother's birthday or spent ten bucks over budget on bedroom drapes. Best of all, he would understand and cherish your finer emotions.

Even knowing you really wouldn't want him doesn't make the man less desirable in times of marital stress. Believe me. Like the fish that got away, the guy I almost married has had moments of near perfection.

The only problem with my romantic past is that, after twenty years, I was fated to meet "him" again at a wedding.

I knew he'd be coming, and let me tell you, there's nothing like knowing you'll meet an old boyfriend to make you feel young again. Or regress to adolescence.

After buying two dresses, both of which looked ugly, I had a row with my husband over the expense. I got a perm — row number two — at which point, my hair frizzed and looked terrible. I hadn't been vain enough to wear a girdle for fifteen years, and the one I found in the attic was two sizes too small. Talk about depression!

More than anything, I was positive I would (a) break out in zits, (b) catch a red-nosed cold or (c) come down with the plague the morning of the big event.

Unfortunately, no disaster occurred and, tightly girdled, I tottered off on heels I usually have sense enough not to wear. I also wore enough makeup to have supplied Detroit.

The makeup might have caused row number three had I been listening to my husband on the way to the church. I was too busy worrying about the wrinkles that even creams couldn't hide. What if my dream man didn't recognize, after all, what really were laugh lines in disguise?

The amount of time I'd "hogged the bathroom" (that much of my husband's complaints got through) made us late and the church was packed. Craning my neck and missing half the ceremony, I couldn't spot my old flame. Tension grew until finally, at the reception, there he was!

He was blue-veined, pudgy, short. So short that he never met my eyes when we talked. He was too busy trying to hide the thin spots of hair — not quite as robustly auburn as I recalled — by tilting his head back and staring at some illusive spot six inches above me.

The man — my ideal! — was prudish, opinionated, a bigot. The sort of yo-yo who'd not only shed socks in the living room, but wear two pairs a day so he could shed them in the kitchen, too. How could I have imagined he would understand me?

I walked away from that reception deeply thankful to be married to a fine, tall man who had hair and lacked racial opinions. By the time my husband and I arrived home, I'd forgotten all about my dream man. And as I shed the girdle and sluiced the makeup from my face, I vowed to tell my real man much more often how much I appreciated him, flaws and all!

~Margaret Shauers
Chicken Soup for the Romantic Soul

Input and Outcome

I was frightened, terribly frightened. In my situation, who wouldn't be? The last time I'd gone under a surgeon's knife I had nearly bled to death. Now I was about to do it again. This time, they would open my abdomen to determine whether I had cancer.

I'd done a lot of reading since my first horrific experience. This time I would not be a passive patient lying helpless on a table. This time I had a plan.

Surgery was scheduled for 8 A.M. Tuesday at a major Los Angeles hospital. I was told to check in on Monday afternoon. That night, the anesthesiologist visited me in my room—the usual procedure for a brief, pre-surgery meeting. I could hear the anxiety in my voice as I questioned him: "Doctor, last time I had surgery, I felt horribly nauseous afterwards. Could you give me a different anesthesia this time?" He agreed and said he would if possible.

I added, "I've read a book called *Healing Now*, by Bobbie Probstein, which proposes that even when someone is totally sedated, their subconscious mind records what's being said, and that those words take on the power of hypnotic suggestions. I believe this is true and respectfully ask that you repeat the following statements to me: 'Sheri, you are allowing perfect surgery. You're doing fine! Keep up the good work! You have the ability to heal perfectly. You will give us a clear field (as little blood as possible at the surgical site). Your healing will begin immediately!' Would you be willing to read me these statements?"

He made a few brief notes on my hospital record, looked at me strangely and said, "Are you serious about this stuff?"

"I'm absolutely serious about it. And I'll only accept an anesthesiologist who will cooperate with this. Are you willing?"

He looked away and twiddled the pen in his fingers. He started to say something, apparently thought better of it and looked at me without saying a word.

"Doctor, whether or not you happen to agree with my view, I'm the one under the knife. And it's my strong belief that saying these positive things will help. They certainly can't hurt. This is my body and my health. I need your assurance, your word that you'll do what I'm suggesting, even if you do it just to reassure or humor me. I know the surgeon doesn't have time, and you'll be standing at my head, keeping track of my vital signs."

"All right," he said. "I'll do it. I've never said things like this in surgery before, and I don't agree with your belief that an anesthetized patient can hear anything. But if you feel that strongly about it," he said, a wry grin on his face, "you have my promise I'll do what you want."

"Thank you! Oh, one more thing, please. I don't want any negative talk from anyone while I'm under, no matter what you may find. Okay?"

"Okay."

He then asked me to repeat what I wanted him to say, wrote it down and left the room. The nurse came in a few minutes later. "You're lucky to have that doctor tomorrow morning," she said. "He's the head anesthesiologist for this hospital. He's very good."

When I awoke after surgery, I had no idea what day or time it was. I wanted to get up and move around, with a little watchful help. I felt surprisingly good. It suddenly dawned on me that I wasn't nauseous at all, and I vividly remembered the uncontrollable sickness from the time before, and the fear that the stitches wouldn't hold.

My surgeon came in later that day. "You're doing great!" he said. "You exceeded my expectations. Given the procedure I performed, you've come through in better shape than anyone I can remember. I understand the staff is delighted, too; you've been up sooner and getting around with far more ease than most patients. And I've been saving the best news for last: Your results are all negative. In this case," he added quickly, "negative is good—absolutely no sign of a malignancy."

The next day the anesthesiologist dropped by, a big smile on his face. "Well, I'm impressed. You did so well and had little bleeding, so I'm going to repeat the same positive suggestions for all my patients from now on."

"Oh, I'm delighted, Doctor. Thank you for doing what I requested." I was thrilled beyond words. "What anesthesia did you use instead of the other one? I didn't have a problem this time."

"The truth is, Sheri, I used the same one, because it's the best there is." He laughed out loud. "I didn't give you anything to prevent nausea because I didn't want your system to have to deal with an additional drug—I just kept saying, over and over: you will have no nausea."

Our partnership had clearly worked.

Now I appreciate that I have the power of choice in my medical care—even when I'm apparently unconscious.

I read somewhere that the quietest and most compliant patients don't do as well in their healing as those who are more assertive. So I believe in taking matters into my own hands, working with my medical team rather than just letting them work on me. Why not go for the best results possible? I may sound a little odd, but who cares what people think? It's my body, my health and my life.

And after my second surgery, I have a newfound appreciation for the combined powers of my body, mind and spirit. What a team they make!

~Sheri Borax
Chicken Soup to Inspire the Body & Soul

Ripples of Reflection

I t had been years since I'd fished with my father. Yet as I stood on the secluded bank of a beautiful lake in Rocky Mountain National Park, memories flooded back.

Dad had taught me how to fish — how to tie on a swivel, select which bobber to use, when to fly-fish and when to bait up for the bottom.

As I cast my line, the reflection of Glacier Basin blurred. I pulled my bobber slowly toward me, the ripples reminding me of the day Daddy taught me how to find the best spots. It was a deep, dark pool on a river, near a large boulder.

"Put your line right there."

"Why?"

"Because there's a big one waiting for your fly."

"How do you know?"

"Just try it."

My fly landed in the exact spot he had pointed to and disappeared beneath the water. I never questioned Daddy again.

While mulling this memory, I realized that he not only taught me how to fish, but how to live. In the deep, dark pool of boyfriends, he seemed to know which one would make a good husband, and he was right. With every casting lesson, he was teaching me patience and choices.

"Don't land your line over there."

"Why?"

"It's grassy under the surface. You'll lose your bait."

He could have been saying, "Don't choose that route for your life. It's dangerous."

With my two sons now grown and living their own lives, my husband Jim and I are enjoying our empty nest. Yet as I stood on the secluded bank of a beautiful lake in Rocky Mountain National Park, I became that little girl again.

"You're my long-legged fisherman."

"Oh, Daddy."

"I'm proud of you, daughter."

"Because I can fish?"

"Because you've grown into the woman I hoped you would."

A couple walking by asked if I'd caught anything.

"Nuthin'," I replied, with tears streaming down my cheeks.

In confusion the man said, "Don't worry, we've talked to everyone around the lake and they aren't catching anything either." They walked away quickly, most likely thinking that I was a bit too unstable to be fishing alone.

It didn't matter. If I had caught a fish that day, it would have interrupted the wonderful time I was having with my father.

~Kathleen Kovach
Chicken Soup for the Fisherman's Soul

Older & Wiser

Unexpected Friends

*From quiet houses and first beginnings,
out to the undiscovered ends, there's nothing worth the wear
of winning, but laughter and the love of friends.
~Hilaire Belloc*

An Anonymous Rose

The manner of giving shows the character of the giver,
more than the gift itself.
~John Casper Lavater

"Happy Valentine's Day," one of the other teachers called to me as we left the school building and walked to the parking lot.

"Thanks, the same to you."

She giggled as I returned the greeting. "This will be the most romantic Valentine's Day ever. Burt and I were looking at diamond rings, and he asked what kind I wanted. I'm sure he's going to propose tonight."

"Congratulations," I said. "Although I should congratulate the groom and say 'best wishes' to you."

"Maybe you better save it, in case I misread the signs." Even though she smiled, I saw the panic in her eyes.

"There's no school on Saturday and I can't wait until Monday," I said. "Call me tomorrow with the happy news."

"Okay. If you don't hear from me, you'll know the news was bad."

"It'll be good," I assured her with a thumbs-up sign.

I watched the young teacher burn rubber as she took off. She was so in love and so eager to start her romantic evening, I felt for her.

"Dear Lord," I whispered, "please make this a happy day for her to remember, not a disappointment. May she receive the proposal and the ring she wants, and may their love last forever." Then I added, "Please help me through the pain of remembering my own special Valentine's Day."

Ray and I had dated for years and were deeply in love, but a lot of obstacles kept us from marrying. Finally, the time was right, and, though we couldn't have a big wedding, we wanted it to be special.

"Let's get married on Valentine's Day," I told Ray. "Even with your absentmindedness, you won't forget our anniversary."

Miraculously, Ray never had a problem remembering our anniversary. Of course, the valentine cards I always scattered over the house for weeks ahead might have helped.

For our twelfth anniversary, we invited our two closest couple friends to dinner, and Ray brought me a dozen long-stemmed red roses. "One for each perfect year," he'd written on the mushy valentine enclosed.

That was the last anniversary we ever celebrated. Ray died eight months later.

The date I chose, so he would remember, became a day I would come to wish to forget. But I never could. Worst of all, now I was alone on Valentine's Day every year.

My children were grown and married. My actor buddy was rehearsing a new play, and I could no longer count on Mary, my frequent companion. There was no romance on the horizon, no small grandchild to give me a handmade, crayon-drawn paper heart. Because I was a reading specialist and didn't have a regular class, I had no handful of "teacher" cards.

Thoughts of going home to a lonely, empty house were

so depressing, I stopped at the mall. Nothing captured my attention, and I wandered around in a daze. Enticing smells wafted to me as I passed a large restaurant, which reminded me that I was hungry, but I didn't have the guts to go in by myself. I considered going to the movies, but again, I couldn't face going alone.

Feeling there was no place left to go, I went home. The house was dark as I pulled into the driveway, but the automatic light came on as I approached the house. I gathered the mail from my mailbox, and clutching it in one hand, opened the storm door with the other.

On the step between the doors was a long, slender package wrapped in green tissue: I could hardly wait to open the wrapping.

Once inside the house, I unwrapped the paper to reveal a single perfect, long-stemmed red rose. Its beauty and sweet scent reminded me of the dozen red roses Ray had given me so long ago. I tore through the wrappings looking for the card, but there wasn't one. I looked for a clue to the sender's identity, but came up empty-handed.

After a while, I called my son and daughter, but neither of them knew anything about the rose. "You must have a secret admirer," my son said. "There's a guy out there who's interested in you."

My daughter's explanation was less encouraging. "The florist may have delivered it to the wrong house."

"There was no address on the package," I told her. "It must have been left in person."

"Then it was probably a neighbor—someone who wanted to thank you for a favor."

The possibility sounded logical, and I racked my brain trying to decide if I had done anything special for one of my neighbors. When nothing came to mind, I began to mull over my son's suggestion. I had to admit, the idea of a secret admirer intrigued me. Being a romantic at heart and having a writer's imagination, I spent the rest of the evening weaving all kinds of plots around the idea. In fact, I became so absorbed, I didn't remember this was a day I'd wanted to forget.

I never did learn who brought me the rose, but I knew it had to be a good friend. A friend who cheered me by letting me know someone cared, yet wise enough to give me something to wonder about.

Since then, starting with the young teacher who didn't get the hoped-for proposal, I've given an anonymous rose to many friends in pain. I hope each one has brought as much comfort as the one that I received brought me.

~Polly Moran
Chicken Soup for the Girlfriend's Soul

51

Greta and Pearl: Two Seniors

W hen the phone rang and the gentleman on the other end said he wanted to place his dog, an eleven-year-old German Shepherd named Greta, I winced. He had sold his house, was moving to a temporary apartment and would soon be leaving the country. As the director of Southwest German Shepherd Rescue, I agreed to see and evaluate the dog with a note of realistic caution to the owner: he'd better start thinking about a contingency plan.

Greta sure was a nice old gal. We put her information on our web site right away and did receive a couple of inquiries, but no one wanted to deal with the little annoyances that sometimes come with an aging dog.

Rescue organizations function within a large cooperative network. One day I received an e-mail from a woman named Suzanne who ran another rescue group. She said that she had an elderly woman, Pearl, looking for an older, large German shepherd. I suggested that Suzanne visit our web site, where she could view the two senior-citizen canines currently in our rescue program. About a week later, Suzanne e-mailed me Pearl's phone number and advised that, although the woman was eighty-six years old, she felt that it would be worthwhile to pursue the adoption.

I immediately phoned Pearl and told her all about Greta. I explained that she was on medication, and Pearl laughed and said they could take their pills together. I made it clear that the average life span of a German shepherd is between ten and twelve years, but many reach thirteen to fifteen years of age. I also asked about her mobility and ability to care for such a dog. Pearl was undaunted and informed me that, in her younger days, she'd run a Great Dane rescue program. She told me that she would make arrangements for Greta to live with her granddaughter, on her forty-acre ranch, should anything happen to her (Pearl). Further, Pearl said that she was still driving her car, and if need be, was able to make trips to the vet.

I explained our policies and advised that I would be paying her a home visit.

We don't usually place German Shepherds in apartments for a number of reasons; however in this case, it seemed appropriate. Greta didn't need a lot of exercise — what she needed was a lot of TLC, a sense of security and a devoted companion who was around all the time. And Pearl's needs were exactly the same.

After meeting Pearl and her husband, Bert, and checking out what would be Greta's new home, I agreed to introduce them. We arranged to meet at a nearby park. The meeting went so well that Greta went home with them on the spot.

Every time I made a follow-up call, I held my breath. And each time, Pearl told me everything was going great. I asked that she periodically contact me with updates. Whenever I heard Pearl's voice on the other end of the phone, I found myself waiting for the other shoe to drop.

During one call, Pearl told me that Greta had a bath and had gone to the vet for a checkup. She had her tested for every disease known to man or beast, and apart from a sluggish thyroid, Greta was in fine shape. In subsequent conversations, Pearl related that Greta shadowed her everywhere. She spoke about how Greta would place her body across Pearl's if she sensed any unsteadiness. The next call was to tell me: "If I were to have molded a dog from clay and given it life, it would have been Greta. I cannot imagine life without her." I assured Pearl that I was certain Greta felt the same.

We were into week five of Pearl and Greta's union when I received a phone call from a very distraught Pearl. The management of her apartment complex had informed her that, despite the fact that she was permitted to have pets weighing up to a hundred pounds (which we had verified), certain specific breeds were excluded: Rottweilers, German Shepherds, Dobermans, chows and pit bulls. There was no mention of this restriction in her lease, nor had Pearl ever been made aware of this policy. Nonetheless, Greta would have to go.

I assured Pearl that we would fight all the way to court if necessary. She informed me that she would rather live in her car than part with her new companion, yet I could sense the panic associated with the possibility of being uprooted at nearly eighty-seven years of age — with an ailing husband, to boot. I advised Pearl that I would need a few days to do some research. I had to read the Landlord/ Tenant Act and familiarize myself with that aspect of the law.

In the meantime, I suggested that Pearl obtain a letter from her doctor stating that she needed Greta for her psychological and physical well-being, that Greta assisted both her and her husband with balance issues and provided them with a sense of security. Pearl's husband, Bert, was going blind as a result of his diabetes and spent a good deal of time sleeping, leaving Pearl lonely and depressed. That is, until Greta came along. Both she and Greta had become reignited. This was truly a mutually beneficial relationship.

I put in a call to the cofounder of REACH (Restoring and Extending Ability with Canine Helpers). I asked if she thought getting an eleven-year-old German Shepherd certified as a service dog was feasible. In essence, she said that as long as the dog could fulfill Pearl's needs as outlined by her doctor, and provided Greta could pass the Level One Assistance dog test, "Yes, assuming you feel that Greta's temperament is sound enough." I asked her to start the process and told her I'd get back to her.

I checked with Pearl to verify she had her doctor's letter and to let her know that a small army would be marching into her home in a few days. She had no other information and no preparation.

One week after that distraught call from Pearl, the certified REACH evaluator (with clipboard and score sheet in hand), an additional temperament tester, two strangers to the dog and family, two children and one female German Shepherd unknown to both Greta and Pearl arrived at their home. It was a cool day but I was sweating. I had no idea how the obedience aspect of the evaluation would go. I did not know how much control Pearl would need or have over Greta as Greta faced strange dogs inside her home territory, unfamiliar kids bumping into her, food temptations while being called and so on. I was confident that Greta would be fine with everything else.

Forty-five minutes later, the score sheets were given to

the REACH evaluator. Greta had passed with flying colors! At the tender age of eleven, Greta became a Certified Level One Assistance Dog, and Pearl became the proudest lady in Arizona. As they were presented with their official certificate and Greta's badge, Pearl held out her arms to the entire room, proclaiming, "I love you!"

As the "team" was pulling out of the parking lot, we saw Pearl, with the letter and certificate in hand, and Greta, with her badge hanging from her collar, heading in the direction of the manager's office. I phoned her that evening to ask her how it went. Upon seeing their credentials, the manager had said, "Well, I guess she can go just about anywhere now," to which Pearl had crowed triumphantly, "You got that right!"

~Stefany Smith
Chicken Soup for the Dog Lover's Soul

52

I Found My Best Friend After Forty Years

Friendship is the golden thread
that ties the heart of all the world.
~John Evelyn

Joyce Duffey and I grew up in a small Arizona mining town during the 1930s and 1940s. She was my best friend and the sister I never had. When we weren't watching Shirley Temple movies at the theater, we were taking piano and dancing lessons. After swims at the city pool in the summer, we'd split an ice-cold Popsicle down the middle. At my house, we'd play with dolls for hours on end and sneak cookie dough my mother had left in the refrigerator. I went horseback riding with Joyce and her dad, and she came on my family's picnics. Joyce's mother had died when she was six, so when we reached adolescence, we both learned the facts of life from my mother. And together, we discovered what was really important: makeup, hairstyles and clothes!

So it was difficult for us to part in 1944, when my family moved 350 miles away. Wartime gas rationing made travel unlikely, and we could only write letters from the time we were separated, at fourteen, through our college years—until we finally were reunited at my wedding, when Joyce, of course, was one of my bridesmaids. After her own marriage, I saw her one more time, when I went to California in the 1950s for my grandmother's funeral.

I never dreamed I would lose touch with her completely. But we both had small children and were so busy with our growing families and many moves across the country that we let our letter-writing lapse. Finally, a Christmas card I sent to Joyce was returned with "address unknown" stamped across the envelope. Her father, too, had died by then, and I had no idea how to find her.

My family and I eventually settled back in Arizona, and as the years went by, I thought of Joyce often. I wanted to share with her my joy and pride as my children grew up, married and made me a grandmother. And I needed, so much, to share my sorrow when I had to put my mother in a nursing home and when first my brother, and then my father, died. Those milestones made me aware of the importance of old ties—and the gap in my heart that only a friend like Joyce could fill.

One day, as I sat reading the newspaper in the spring of 1992, I saw an article about teenage gangs. Next to it was the photo of a social worker named Kevin Starrs. That's a coincidence, I thought. Joyce's married name was Starrs, and her husband was a social worker. The young man in the photo did resemble Joyce and her dad. Then I chided myself for jumping to conclusions: There must be thousands of people named Starrs. Still, I decided it wouldn't hurt to write Kevin a letter, telling him about my childhood friend and how those coincidences compelled me to contact him.

He phoned me the minute he heard from me. "Mrs. Conder," he said, "Joyce Duffey Starrs is my mother!" I must have yelled loudly enough to be heard in South

Dakota—where, Kevin told me, Joyce was living. He was as excited as I was, and I could hear in his voice his love for his mother. After he gave me her phone number and I gave him mine, he added, "You know, three of us children live nearby. My mother visited us here in Phoenix several months ago."

My eyes welled up with tears. "She was here—only a few miles from me—and I didn't even know it?"

I promised Kevin I'd call Joyce that very evening. I didn't have to wait that long. Ten minutes later my phone rang.

"Margie?" Even after forty years, I recognized the voice instantly. As soon as Kevin had hung up from our conversation, he'd called his sister, who'd telephoned their mother and gave her my number.

We laughed and cried, and got caught up on each other's lives. It turned out that Joyce had lived in northern Arizona—so close to me—for a number of the years when we each thought we would never hear from the other again. In the weeks that followed, we talked frequently on the phone and exchanged long letters with photos of our spouses, our children, our grandchildren and ourselves. There were so many things to tell each other!

That summer Joyce flew to Phoenix. When she called me from her daughter's home, I hurried there, excited and nervous. Would we have that same feeling, that bond, we'd had as children? But there was no need to worry. She was waiting for me at the front door, and I could still see that fourteen-year-old in her sweet grin.

"You look just the same!" we said simultaneously, as if we both were blind to wrinkles, added pounds and gray hair. We fell into each other's arms.

The next week was filled with hours of catching up,

reminiscing and sharing confidences. We giggled like little girls as we pored over old photos. Together, we revisited our hometown, which now looked so small, and other favorite spots where we'd spent time together. The best part of our reunion, though, was meeting each other's children and grandchildren. Joyce had an emotional reunion at the nursing home with my mother, who, though she can no longer speak, smiled with such happiness that we knew she recognized my long-lost playmate.

The empty place I'd had in my heart for forty years has been filled to overflowing with our renewed friendship. Old friends really are the best friends. And there's one more thing Joyce and I now know for sure: We won't lose each other again!

~Marjorie Conder
Chicken Soup for the Girlfriend's Soul

53

The Little Dog
That Nobody Wanted

An animal's eyes have the power to speak a great language.
~Martin Buber

When Dad found Tippy — or rather, Tippy found Dad — it was a hot day in my southern Missouri hometown, in the summer of 1979.

For most of his life, Dad had never cared too much for pets, but the sight of that skinny, mange-infested pup seemed to open a door in his heart. Then that little lost pup slipped ever so meekly through the door.

That morning, Dad had been visiting with customers in the electronics shop where he had landed a part-time job after retirement. Suddenly a terrified, yelping stray puppy bolted through the door.

"I've lived many a year," Dad said that evening as he stepped into the house, "but I've never seen anything so pitiful as this." In his arms he cradled a cardboard box, and inside the box was a tiny wayfarer from an unimaginable hell.

Dad couldn't hold back the tears any longer. "I just couldn't put her back out on the streets. Look at her... we've got to do something to help her. She was just crying and crying and so scared," Dad said as Mom took the box from his arms. "Look at those open sores. Who could be so cruel as to let her get in this condition?"

Mom peered down into the box and was repulsed by what she saw. "Oh, she's too far gone," she told my dad, shaking her head in disbelief. "Let's just have the vet put her out of her misery."

No bigger than a teakettle, the wretched little terrier was being consumed by disease and starvation. Lifeless marble eyes bulged sadly atop a thin pointed nose; bony long legs curled around each other like limp spaghetti on a plate.

"I'm awfully sorry," the vet told Dad the next day. "There's really nothing I can do to help her now. She's too far gone."

But Dad insisted.

"Well, okay—if you want to try, here are some pills and some medicated cream to rub on her mange sores. But don't get your hopes up. I doubt if she makes it through the weekend."

Dad wrapped the sick, homeless pup back into the old bath towel and carried her to the car. That afternoon, he carried her gently out under the maple trees in the backyard and began the medication treatments.

"Every day your father totes that poor, miserable little creature out under the trees and massages the ointment into her skin," Mom said. "Those oozing sores cover her entire body. He can't even tell what color she's supposed to be—all her hair has been eaten away by the mange and infection."

"I won't keep her if she gets better," he promised Mom. "I'll find a good home for her if the medicine works." Mom was not too happy about helping a dirty, uncomely runt with no fur and spaghetti legs.

"I don't think we'll have to worry," Mom sighed. "But don't feel bad when the medicine doesn't work. At least you tried."

Nevertheless, every day, out in the shade of the big maple trees, Dad faithfully doctored the pup with no hair and bony legs, the little lost dog that nobody wanted.

For the first few days after the stray pup entered Dad's life, there was slim hope for her survival. Disease and starvation had taken the little dog down a cruel path. It seemed only a miracle could help.

For seemingly endless days, Mom watched through the kitchen window as Dad continued to cart the little dog in the box out under the maple trees, where he doctored the wounds of neglect.

No one remembers exactly how long it took to see a glint of hope in my dad's countenance—and in the marble eyes of that pup. But slowly, with timidity and reserve, the pup began to trust my dad, and the first waggle of her skinny tail brought intense joy to my father.

Mom never wanted any part of that rescue effort, for she was not interested in bringing a dog into the house and their lives. But when she saw her husband's face the first time that pup showed an ounce of playfulness, she knew that Dad was struck with more than compassion.

Dad came from a rugged hill family who farmed the rocky ridges of the Ozark Mountains. He knew little joy as a child and worked hard at manual jobs as an adult. Reaching down to rescue that weak, mangy pup seemed to mend his wounded spirit, especially when he succeeded at beating the odds by nursing Tippy back to health.

"Just look at her!" Mom smiled. "You've really done it! She's growing her hair back and she's starting to play a little bit. No one thought she'd even live another day, but you stood by her and believed that she could make it."

As the pup continued healing, she began showing her true colors—except they weren't the prettiest of colors in the prettiest of patterns. A white patch here and there, a crowd of hazy black spots around the snout and chest, mottled white blotches against a black torso. And because of the white tip on her tail, she was given a common name for a common dog: Tippy.

"Now, honey, I've tried to find her a good home but nobody needs a little dog right now," Dad lamented. "I've asked around everywhere. I promise, I've tried real hard." Mom knew he was trying about as hard as a man choosing between a lawn mower and a good hammock on a hot summer afternoon.

"Well, I don't know who would want her," Mom said. "Even with her hair grown in and all those sores gone, she's still kind of ugly and gangly."

A few weeks later, after unsuccessfully trying to trade her off on someone, Dad said, "Now, I know she's not a cute little dog, but I guess she'll have to do. Nobody else wants her."

There. He'd said it. And Mom knew the little lost dog that nobody wanted had curled up to stay.

She would have to sleep out in the laundry room, not in the house, Mom scolded. Dad and Tippy complied with the rules, and their singular friendship sprouted and blossomed in comforting ways—for they came to need each other during Dad's worst of times.

"That pup saw your dad through all his pain and cancer for the next three years," Mom recalled. "Sometimes I think God sent that little dog to be with your dad in the end."

After Dad died, Mom went out to the laundry room

one day and gazed down at the quiet little creature curled up obediently in her cardboard box bed.

"Hmmm... okay, Tippy," she said softly. "Maybe it won't hurt having you come inside the house just once in awhile. It's awfully lonesome in there." At that moment, Mom felt connected to the homely little dog, as if Dad's hands were still reaching down to help them both in time of need.

In the following months, Tippy and Mom became soulmates of sorts. The cardboard-box bed was brought in from the laundry room to Mom's bedroom, where it stayed for the next fourteen years.

"As long as I had that little dog," Mom said, "it was like a part of your dad was still here. She brought life back into the house."

Eventually, the rigors of time and age took their toll on Mom's little friend; blindness and painful joints set in. With overwhelming sadness and regret, Mom asked my brother to help take Tippy for her final trip to the vet.

"I reached down to cradle her head in my hands," Mom said, "and she leaned her face against mine as if to say thanks for all we had done for her."

Tippy lived seventeen years after that fateful journey of terror through traffic, rundown warehouses, pain and suffering to find my dad. And looking back over the years, it seems to me now that the true miracle was not in the healing forces of Dad's loving hands and kindness toward the little lost dog that nobody wanted—but in the difference they made in each other's lives.

~Jan K. Stewart Bass
Chicken Soup for the Pet Lover's Soul

54

A Friendly Act of Kindness

There are three things that grow more precious with age:
old wood to burn, old books to read and old friends to enjoy.
~Henry Ford

Beverly and I have been best friends for years, and, like a well-worn sweater, our friendship has hung in there, through thick and thin. After her divorce three years ago, she moved several states away. We keep in touch through cards, letters and weekly telephone calls. Her call last Saturday night changed both our lives.

When the phone rang, I could almost predict who'd be on the other end. I picked up the receiver and said, "Hello?"

"Hello, yourself," a meek voice answered.

"Beverly, how are you doing?" Silence.

"I found a lump in my breast," she whispered, at last.

A chill ran down my spine. "Are you sure?" I imagined the usual bright stars in her eyes flickering, then fading in reflection of her terror.

"Have you seen the doctor?" I bit my lower lip.

"Yes. The biopsy report came back positive. It's malignant," she sobbed. "I'm scheduled for surgery on Tuesday."

I tried to reassure her, but I knew she was terrified, and so was I. I did my best to hide my own fears. We chit-chatted some more, struggling to avoid the subject. After we hung up, I told my husband, who agreed I should book a flight. After all, I couldn't let Bev face her uncertain future alone.

The next two days and nights dragged. Monday morning finally arrived, and I drove the long trek to the nearest airport. Even with the heavy traffic to distract me, my thoughts kept returning to Bev. I prayed the whole way. The old belief, "C=D" (cancer equals death), kept creeping into my mind. I'd lost my mother to that disease seven years ago.

When I arrived, I wrote down where I parked and wheeled my bags to an open elevator. Exiting on the ticketing floor, I waited in line for about twenty minutes until it was my turn to step up to the counter and hand my identification to a tall brunette.

Her fingers tapped the computer keys for a moment. She studied the screen. When she looked up and handed my identification back, she said, "I'm sorry to inform you this flight is currently overbooked. If you can come back tomorrow morning, we can accommodate you on another flight."

"But," I stammered, "I have to get on this flight. This is not just a vacation trip or anything like that. My best friend is having surgery—she needs me." A tear formed and trickled down my cheek.

"I'm sorry. Everyone showed up, which is usually not the case. Even the standby passengers aren't getting on."

"But I made a reservation."

"Yes, just two days ago. That's why you've been bumped." She shrugged her shoulders and said, "Next."

I trudged away from the counter and plopped into a vacant seat to assess my situation. All the while tears streaked my face. I fished in my purse for a tissue, dabbed my cheeks and blew my nose. The loudspeaker announced the first boarding call for rows twenty to thirty. I watched several people rise and hurry to obtain a place in line. I swallowed hard. A sinking feeling in my chest turned into a knot as it reached my stomach. Defeated, I sighed and bent down to gather my bags.

"Perhaps I can help you," a soft voice said. "I couldn't help overhearing your conversation with the reservationist."

I glanced up and saw an older woman with smiling blue eyes gazing at me. The early morning sunbeams streaming in through the large airport windows illuminated her ivory complexion. Soft silver-gray hair framed her face. I wiped away a tear and asked, "How?"

"Well, I have a ticket and am assigned seat 7B. I'd be honored if you would take my place." She waved the ticket and boarding pass at me. Her intense eyes seemed to beckon me to take it.

Tempted, I hesitated for a moment, wondering what the catch was.

"I couldn't take your seat. Aren't you anxious to get to your destination?"

Her smile faded. "There's no one waiting for me at the other end. I live alone. Staying here one more day won't make a difference. My daughter will come and take me back to her house. Won't my grandchildren be surprised?"

I could almost taste her loneliness. I said, "It would mean so much to me. But I'd never be able to repay you. Are you sure?"

Her eyes sparkled. "Don't be silly. Go to your friend." She handed me the ticket.

Humbled by her kindness, I accepted. We strolled to the counter together and made the necessary changes. Because of her compassion, I would be able to be with Beverly and to give her my love and support. Gratitude flooded my soul.

I turned to this generous mystery lady and extended my hand. She took it, squeezing back, and said, "Someday you'll see a woman in distress and you'll do the same." With a wink, she released my hand.

My trip was a success. Everything went well with Beverly: The surgeon assured us both that he'd removed all of the cancer.

To this day, I often think of that special woman who sacrificed convenience for friendship. I will never forget her act of kindness. I hope when it's my turn, I can give as freely as she did and pass on her legacy of kindness.

~Suzanne A. Baginskie
Chicken Soup for the Girlfriend's Soul

55

To Infinity

In 1974, when we were fourteen years old, Ralph and I became close friends. We used to sit in his front yard and eat cookies and talk for hours. Ralph had a girlfriend and I had a boyfriend, but I thought he was one of the nicest boys at our school.

A few years after graduation, I received an invitation to Ralph's wedding. I arrived alone and waiting outside was Ralph, receiving me with the kind and welcoming smile I had always known. We talked a while, and for some reason I turned and went back to my car and went home. We lost touch for several years. At our ten-year class reunion I looked up and, once again, there was that familiar smile. It was Ralph. "What happened to you?" I asked. "I've been getting divorced," he said with a twinkle in his eye. "Where have you been?"

"I've been getting married," I responded. We sat and reminisced all evening, promising to keep in touch. We contacted one another a couple of times a year and kept each other up on what was going on in our lives, but never saw each other until eight years later. My marriage ended and I found myself living alone in an apartment with my little daughter. Ralph called and asked, "Is there anything

I can do for you? Is your car running okay? Does your daughter need anything? Do you have enough money?"

I told him, "I need to see my old friend. It's been too many years." So we met for a beer and, once again, sat and went over old times. The hours flew by and next thing we knew we were asked to leave. The restaurant had closed.

We got together a couple of more times and found ourselves talking until the sun came up. As Ralph left, I found myself sad watching him go. One evening, I invited Ralph over to have pizza and watch a video. He came over and brought photo albums. As we went through the albums, I felt compelled to tell him that I felt I might be falling in love with him. Mortified with myself, I went in the bathroom and tried to figure out how I could escape from a second-story-apartment bathroom without being discovered! I was afraid I had just destroyed a precious friendship. I had stepped on hallowed ground.

When I returned, Ralph was sitting there with a Cheshire-cat smile on his face. "Lisa, I have loved you for twenty years. You have been the standard I have judged all women by. I don't want to let this opportunity slip past me." I told him that I was afraid that if it didn't work out, we would lose this priceless friendship that we had carried through the years. We agreed our friendship wouldn't be broken and that we had the potential here for something rare and priceless.

Sure enough, we were married nine months later. Engraved in our wedding rings are the words "to infinity." With my daughter, we became a family.

One day we came across his high school yearbook and decided to look up what I had written to him all those years ago. It was so many years back that I'd forgotten.

There was my handwriting. A full page long. And there

I had written: "Ralph, You are the nicest boy I have ever met. I know we will be friends for the rest of our lives... in fact, I love you so much that I think when we grow up we should just get MARRIED."

Who'da thought all those years ago as we sat in his front yard eating cookies that those two young kids really would be friends... and lovers forever... to infinity.

~Lisa Ferris Terzich
Chicken Soup for the Romantic Soul

56

Picked Just for You

Flowers are love's truest language.
~Park Benjamin

"I'll call you right back, Marge," I told my friend on the phone. "Someone's at the door. Probably another salesman."

On our street we get salespeople of all kinds—remodeling, newspapers, entertainment discount cards, you name it—plus eager children with Girl Scout cookies, boxes of candy, gift wrapping packages and Easter eggs, all in the name of charity for more schools and clubs than I can keep straight.

This time my door opened to two little girls. I had met Alyssa, six, a couple of weeks before. Since then, she'd waved to me every time she struggled past my house on a pair of inline skates almost as big as she. Like most of the children on our street, she called me "Grandma Bonnie."

Now Alyssa smiled. "Hello, Grandma Bonnie!" she chirped. "This is my little sister, Ariana. She's three." To her very nervous sister, "It's okay, honey. She's nice people. You'll like her."

The three-year-old held a "bouquet" in one hand, and the other gripped a tiny notebook and huge broken crayon. "Go on," her big sister urged, "tell her."

Ariana looked at me solemnly. "I want to help raise money for my preschool," she said, holding out her flowers. "So I'm selling these for one dollar a bunch."

I had a hard time hiding my grin. I understood her notebook and crayon—a substitute for the record-keeping forms and pens she'd seen the older children lug door-to-door with their wares. She couldn't, of course, even print her own name, much less a receipt.

As for the bouquet, it consisted of seven scraggly oxalis blossoms. Now if you're a gardener, you're probably already cringing. If you're not, let me explain. Oxalis is a weed, a madly determined, clover-like plant that's almost impossible to get rid of. Worse than dandelions! Obviously Ariana had plucked these despised but thriving flowers from her own yard or a neighbor's—or maybe even mine.

Her big sister smiled. "Aren't they lovely, Grandma Bonnie? And they only cost a dollar for the whole bunch. It's all for Ariana's preschool."

Now maybe I was being played for the world's biggest sucker, but the girls' initiative did tickle me. "All right," I agreed, "one dollar coming up."

Alyssa tucked the bill in her sister's skirt pocket. Then Ariana handed me my purchase. "Uh," I suggested, "why don't you just keep the flowers and the money both? Then you could sell the flowers to someone else."

Both girls stared at me, horrified. "Oh, no, Grandma Bonnie!" Ariana cried. "We picked them just for you. See, they're beautiful!"

And so they were. Seven slender stems soon graced the bud vase by my kitchen window. A week later, they were still crowned with a tassel of perfectly shaped lemon-yellow bells of joy—twice as many as when my little neighbor handed them to me with dozens of new buds yet to open. What a bargain!

I had called these tiny plants "weeds"—disgusting, worthless things with no right to exist. But in their innocent hearts, those two little girls saw them as they really were—a precious creation of God's to treasure and share from loving hearts to brighten the day of a lonely old "Grandma."

~Bonnie Hanson
Chicken Soup for the Grandma's Soul

57

In the Eye of the Storm

Golden leaves fell across the country in mid-November, but the autumn beauty would soon not matter to Helen Weathers. For on the night of her fifty-ninth birthday, her life was swept completely out from under her. She had just finished celebrating at a restaurant with some of her closest friends and was getting ready for bed when she felt like a jagged piece of glass pierced her head. Then, the lights went out for Helen. For a long time. Most signs of life disappeared instantaneously when an aneurysm struck down this vivacious woman.

Five days later, her dearest friends, her husband, Robert, and the rest of her family waited patiently through a six-hour brain operation to see if Helen would survive. Her unopened birthday gifts sat at home on her table just the way she left them. The gifts would remain untouched for months, for after the surgery, she suffered a stroke.

Helen had always dressed with flair and elegance. This now bald woman lay helpless in a hospital bed day after day. She probably would have been embarrassed had she been herself and able to see the friends pouring in and out of her room. Later, she would be grateful. The endless stream of visits, flowers and food for her family gave her relatives the buoy they needed to survive the icy waters.

Helen believes the love and support also kept her alive in the midst of the storm. Within a few weeks, many friends had a prayer chain going for her, hoping to bring her back from the brink of death. Their hopes and prayers were answered. But Helen could barely recognize herself. "I couldn't remember what I looked like before," she says. "I don't remember when I discovered I had no hair. My cousin Elsa said that when I looked in the mirror and saw I had no hair, I turned to Robert and her and said: 'I have no teeth.'"

Helen's friends continued to send flowers, food and cards. One of her closest friends brought her pictures of all her dogs: Doodles, Ms. Liberty and Taffy.

Robert and their daughter, Sandra, brought her new make-up.

Everyone wanted her back even though it became clear that Helen might never be the same woman again. At times, she was like a stranger. To others — and to herself.

When she started recovering, she had much to learn. How to write her name again. How to walk. How to speak clearly. How to dress herself. Sometimes, she felt like a baby. But her brain surgeon said it was a miracle she was alive.

Helen was almost like a child. Her sentences were gibberish. She giggled uncontrollably. Then she'd cry. She was hospitalized for nearly half a year undergoing rehabilitation and trying to return to her former self.

She was placed in intensive therapy and was given classes in arithmetic, which confounded her and left her trying to count things out on her fingers. Finally, she gave up and started using a calculator. "One of my favorite bon mots is: 'In real life, there is no algebra!'"

In therapy, one of the happiest incidents she recalls was being allowed to go out to a Wal-Mart to Christmas shop so her doctors could see if she could make it in the "real world." Helen was delighted, though confused a bit, and finished all her shopping in the first two aisles.

After seven months, she made it home to husband, Robert, and dogs, Doodles, Ms. Liberty and Taffy. Today Helen is restored to her former self and has gained back her abilities to paint, walk and speak.

"I am convinced that the only reason I was spared is to inspire others," Helen says from her home where she receives dozens of calls a day from people seeking help with similar disabilities. "I have been in the trenches with people who have suffered like this. I know lots of people were pulling for me. Now, it's my turn to encourage people to go to rehabilitation and hang in there."

Helen is often asked: "How long did it take you to learn to write again?"

"Seven months," she replies and then adds, "and almost that long to keep from putting lipstick under my nose."

When Helen receives phone calls for help, she never turns anyone away. Because she knows deep in her heart that it was love and caring that guided her out of the storm and helped her wade safely back to shore.

~Helen Weathers as told to Diana L. Chapman
Chicken Soup to Inspire the Body & Soul

58

The Fishermen

Peppy was an old dog put together with a few genes of this and that. His body was a mass of gray curls that still had traces of the black that once covered him from head to toe. A lot like my own hair. But it was his eyes that could melt your soul. Dark-brown disks were clouded milky white. Pep was blind and a stroke had rendered his legs useless. The poor dog had to be carried everywhere. He was 15, 105 in human years, and I was nearing 80. We could commiserate.

We met for the first time in an elevator that took us down from the thirty-second floor. Peppy's master, Nick, held the old dog in his arms. They were my new neighbors and had come to Florida from the north. I said a few words to break the awkward silence, and Peppy immediately lifted his drooping head at the sound of my voice. His nose sniffed in every direction searching for this new stranger in his midst. Reaching out his snow-white muzzle and shaggy white head, he licked my fingertips with a warm tongue. I stroked his head. His tail wagged a little faster, and his backside moved to the same tempo. By the time we reached the lobby, I knew I had a friend.

With Nick's enthusiastic approval, I started taking care of Peppy while Nick was off at work. I'd spend hours telling him about my life. He would close his sightless eyes and listen to everything I had to say. His curly tail would wave slowly, and his nose would punch the air catching the different tones of my voice.

After a while, Nick rigged up a baby carriage with a platform built on its frame. How wonderful — Pep now had a set of wheels. I even began taking Peppy to my favorite fishing spot. Peppy loved being wheeled along on the quay. The wind pushed back his floppy ears, and he lifted his nose to drink in the many fascinating, fishy smells.

It wasn't long before another old critter joined our party. It was a pelican that usually sat nearby and waited for a meal every time I threw over the line. I knew what an effort it was for him to fly. He was too old and worn out to join his wingmen, diving from high altitudes and skimming fish from the edge of the sea. The other pelicans flew off in perfect formation, but the old one just sat there and watched. He survived by gliding a few feet off the dock and snaring baitfish in his huge mouth. Between that and my handouts, he just barely survived.

Peppy and the pelican hit it off from the first time they met. They sat close to each other and developed a special kind of rapport. What a picture we must have made, Pep on his platform carriage, the tattered bird dozing and me, still casting in the twilight of my own ancient life.

One day I dropped a baited hook in the water and waited as the line swayed gently in search of a fish. Suddenly Peppy whimpered, not loud, more like a purr. He could see nothing, but his head stretched over the platform till he was facing directly into the sea. His tail beat faster, and his ears stood erect. Somehow the old dog was trying to help me catch a fish. His motions and whimpering alerted the pelican. The old bird stood up and also peered into the water. His yellow eyes bulged, and he stared at my line.

The two clairvoyants were telling me something was about to happen. Sure enough, it did! The line became taut! Wham! We had a hit! The pole bent in half, and I strained with all I had to bring something up to the planks. Peppy was half-crazy with excitement; he even pulled himself up on his haunches to get closer to the struggle. And the pelican waddled over to keep an eye on the end of my pole.

With a lot of grunting, I finally brought up a big, beautiful yellowtail snapper and laid it at Peppy's feet. Peppy sniffed at the fish madly, then rested on his blanket and seemed to enjoy the sound of the pelican eating his freshly caught lunch.

These days I'm spending more time at the quay than ever and catching loads of fish. My two pals never disappoint me. Alerted by a wagging tail, a whimper and a flutter of wings, I'm always ready when the magic begins. Everyone knows about bird dogs, but who's ever heard of a fish dog? Or a fish bird? Who'd ever believe I have pets like this?

These are wonderful days for old Peppy. Instead of moping indoors, alone all day, he's out in the sunshine with a whole new mission in life. Just last week, Peppy celebrated his sixteenth birthday with some of the most exciting catches of his new career.

And the pelican? All this activity's had an effect on him, too. As dusk came to the quay not long ago, I watched as he unfurled his trailing feathers and actually lifted himself off the ground. He pumped his long, weathered wings, and slowly made it to a roost to sleep for the night.

We're a threesome of old fishermen. A sightless dog, a flightless bird and an old man who's having the time of his life.

~Mike Lipstock
Chicken Soup for the Fisherman's Soul

Older & Wiser

Chapter 7

Laugh Wrinkles

With mirth and laughter let old wrinkles come.
~William Shakespeare

59

The Right Approach

Put a grain of boldness into everything you do.
~Baltasar Gracian

Back in 1959 Bud and I, new army second lieutenants, received orders for the same unit at Fort Sill, Oklahoma. We graduated together from OCS but did not know each other well as we had been in different sections. Our new assignments brought us in daily contact and soon we became good friends. An outgoing Irishman, Bud enjoyed telling tales of growing up in the Bronx and recounting humorous situations involving parents and siblings. The family picture displayed in his room included an attractive younger sister. From the way he spoke about her she was obviously popular and not lacking "gentlemen callers." The attraction was there—this was someone I wanted to meet. But she was in New York and I was in Oklahoma—a long way to be dating.

Eventually I got up my nerve and asked Bud if he would mind if I wrote his sister a letter. He looked a bit quizzical, but gave me the address and wished me luck. I pondered what approach would have the best chance of hooking her interest and receiving a reply. The standard "Let's be pen pals" did not seem the way to go. After some thought, I sent the following letter:

Dear Rita:

I'm a friend of your brother. I'll come right to the point. I owe him some money. He said he would cancel the debt if I would marry his sister. As he related, the family has been trying to marry you off for some time — with little success! As fate would have it, I am looking for a woman of childbearing age who is in good health, capable of hard work, reasonably intelligent and comes from good stock! As you appear to meet these criteria, I have accepted your brother's offer, and so for better or worse, we will be married. Thus, consider yourself engaged!

Enclosed you will find a temporary engagement ring (cigar band). Wear it with pride! If you have any questions about the details of the marriage, our future life together or other minor points just let me know. I will complete my active duty obligation in the near future. You may select an appropriate date for our wedding any time following my discharge.

Your husband-to-be,
Ed

I had no idea if she would reply, or if she would toss the letter out, thinking, "What nut did my brother meet and why did he give him my address?" On the other hand, if she did reply this could be fun. About a week later a perfume-laden letter arrived.

She had taken the bait! It read:

Dear Ed:

Your letter certainly came as a surprise! I am grateful that my brother has arranged for someone to take me "off the shelf." I planned to wear my "temporary engagement ring" until I found out that it comes from a very "cheap" cigar! I don't mind the marriage commitment, but I want to do it in style and comfort. This brings me to certain "conditions" of our intended betrothal. Naturally you plan to keep me in the manner to which I hope to become accustomed. To be specific, we will need a maid/cook as well as someone who takes care of the house and grounds. I hesitate to set a date for our entry into marital bliss until you can assure me that such will be the case.

Awaiting your reply with a fluttering heart!
Rita

Ah, the challenge! This was getting good. I replied:

My dear bride-to-be:

It was gratifying to hear that you have accepted my proposal. Now we can plan our life together. Further, I can understand your reluctance to wear that cigar band, as it was from an inexpensive brand. You are absolutely right! I should have known that you were a girl with "class." Thus, enclosed is a band from a Dutch Master, a much better brand. You can wear this one with pride!

I am happy to report that the conditions you specified (housekeeper/cook and groundskeeper) can be met. You see, we will be living with my parents and, as you will soon find out, Mom keeps a clean house and is a good cook while Dad keeps the lawn cut and the house in good repair. If you would want Mom to wear a special apron or something, I'm sure I can talk her into it. We can even get a bit of a uniform for Dad. I'm sure that this arrangement will satisfy your demands.

I did have one other question. You signed your letter "with a fluttering heart." Were you implying that you have a heart murmur or some other type of cardiac condition? Your brother assured me that you were "as healthy as a horse" when I agreed to marry you. I'm just checking, as one can't be too careful these days! Also, I have no picture of you. Please send one at your earliest convenience.

Your husband-to-be,
Ed

Her reply came in about two weeks.

Dearest Ed:

Your plan for us to live with your parents is certainly an interesting arrangement. I can't wait to hear about other plans you have for our life together, as you seem so sensitive, romantic and intuitive. How lucky can a girl get! By the way, how much money did you owe my brother?

In response to your inquiry about a possible "heart condition," the answer is "neigh." You see, I am as healthy as a horse. However, the thought occurs to me that if

I continue to respond to your letters perhaps I should have my head examined.

Sorry, I have no picture of me alone to send you. I have some with boyfriends, but somehow it would seem "tacky" to send one of those. Thus, I've decided not to send a picture and I'm sure you'll understand. You'll have to admire me without the benefit of external props. Just think of me as perfection!

With bated breath I await your response!
Rita

Hum, how to respond? This one took some thought and a bit of research. The final product was as follows:

My dear Rita:

In your last letter you wondered what our life would be like together. A great question! I see you as the perfect wife. The life of such a woman is described clearly in the Bible, specifically in the book of Proverbs, chapter 31. I quote some of the verses:

> *"She does her work with eager hands.*
> *She gets up while it is still dark*
> *Giving her household their food.*
> *She puts her back into her work*
> *And shows how strong her arms can be.*
> *She weaves linen sheets and sells them,*
> *She supplies the merchant with sashes. Etc.*
> *Also: Her husband is respected at the city gates,*
> *And praises her good works to the elders."*

Obviously, the message needs to be updated to reflect our current culture, but the meaning is clear—you'll work your fingers to the bone and love it! Now be honest, isn't that the type of wife you always imagined yourself to be?

This brings up another point, namely, the picture. Perhaps I wasn't clear regarding this. My words, or at least my intent, was not to give you an option regarding sending a picture. So let me be clear—send a picture. Again, it is important that we establish the proper line of authority for our life together. Remember St. Paul's statement, "Wives be subject to your husbands." The fact that we are not yet married is a minor technicality. So, I expect a picture!

Regarding the money I owed your brother—it was $3. He said you were worth every penny.

One last point. You signed the last letter—"with bated breath." I just want to make sure that you weren't implying that you have a lung problem or persistent halitosis. I await your picture!

Your sensitive husband-to-be,
Ed

In a few weeks a small package arrived that obviously was a picture frame.

Enclosed was a picture of a girl of about seven or eight seated on a piano stool. She displayed a broad smile that reflected the absence of her two front teeth. A large bow in her hair complemented a fluffy dress. Score one for her! How do I respond? It took a while to develop the following:

My dear Rita:

Just a short note to let you know that your picture arrived safe and sound. I know our life together will be conflict free, given your willingness to follow the dictates of your husband-to-be. However, I would be less than candid if I did not confess that the picture took me by surprise. You see, in the picture you seem more mature than your letters have indicated to date! But, I guess some surprises are to be expected in any relationship.

One item we have failed to discuss—the dowry. Please let me know the assets you will bring into our marriage.

Your husband-to-be,
Ed

Several weeks went by without a reply. Had I pushed it too far? On the surface it was just good fun, yet I felt we were developing a relationship. I wanted to meet her and thought she had similar feelings. Well, I thought, guess again.

Shortly thereafter Bud advised me that he received a letter from Rita telling him that she was entering a convent, something she had always considered. She asked him to say goodbye to me and to let me know that she had enjoyed the letter writing and was sorry that we didn't have a chance to meet. Were my letters the last straw, driving her into the convent? I muttered to myself, I guess it was the wrong approach!

Soon my required active duty time was up and I returned home. Bud's commitment kept him in the army a bit longer. About six months later I received a letter from Bud inviting me for a weekend in the Bronx to celebrate his discharge. He noted, "As an added incentive I am featuring one ex-nun." How could I resist? I flew to New York and we met.

Our fortieth wedding anniversary is not too far away. It was the "right approach."

~Edmund Phillips
Chicken Soup for the Romantic Soul

60

In Over Their Heads

By ninety-six years of age, Marie had outlived two husbands and both her children. But she still lived in her rural home, thanks to her support crew—thanks to her friends.

Marie relied on them all. Each helper had an assignment. One brought the mail every day; another picked up her groceries. This one did her laundry; that one chauffeured her to the beauty shop. Someone else drove her to church and the rare doctor appointment.

But she had an especially close relationship with Jean. Almost half her age—and nearly half her size—petite Jean was a bubbling bundle of energy.

Jean brought over racy romance novels; Marie recited improper limericks. The two shared a feisty history of heart-to-heart confidences and irreverent jokes, touching stories and outlandish lies—and Christmas.

And it was Jean who was "sitting" with Marie that night after medication for an infection left her aged friend shaky, disoriented and confused.

"I believe I'd like to soak in a bath," Marie suggested.

"Are you sure you feel up to it?" Jean worried that Marie was weaker than she thought.

But Marie insisted. So after helping her elderly friend

from bed to bathroom, Jean sat outside the door to keep her company and to give her privacy. After a time, she heard the water draining.

"Do you need some help, Marie?"

"No, I'll pop right out. You just wait."

She waited—and waited. "Marie?"

"I can't do it. I can't get out. My knees won't work."

Jean stood in the doorway to assess the situation. There sat Marie, folded in the bottom of the deep, claw-foot tub. Ancient, wrinkled and naked as a jaybird. Her once-buxom friend's solid frame had dwindled in recent years until she was nothing more than bones and lots of sagging skin. But she was still considerably larger than Jean.

"Uh, Marie, I think I'd better call the fire department. They've rescued other people in similar situations."

"No, you won't call the fire department." Marie was horrified. "I know those people. They're... men! Why, I'd be the talk of the entire community." She looked down at her accordioned body. "Besides, I need a good ironing."

They both began to laugh. Still grinning, Jean climbed into the high-sided tub, shoes and all.

She edged behind Marie, put her arms around the water-slick woman and lifted. Up came a lot of loose, corrugated flesh—but Marie stayed put. Jean tried again. The same thing happened. Tears of hilarity weakened them both as she strained even harder. But only Marie's skin cooperated.

Exasperated, Marie finally ordered, "Jeannie, just throw my tits over the side and maybe the rest will follow!"

Marie leaned forward, Jean's adrenaline kicked in for one final heave, and they were soon on dry ground. Giggling like girls, the two of them dried off, dressed for bed and added a new story to their repertoire — a "steamy" one.

~Carol McAdoo Rehme
Chicken Soup for the Caregiver's Soul

61

Caution:
Follow Directions

I don't know about you, but I have a hard time reading directions. I'm embarrassed to talk about how many cars I have driven out of oil, or the sewing machine that locked up because I never oiled it, or the appliances I've burned up, or the clothing I've shrunk—simply because I failed to read the instructions. I seem to slip into a kind of mental sleepwalking when I try to read the directions for the VCR, CD player, cellular phone, pager or fax machine. God's good humor is solely responsible for me even turning on a computer.

One Christmas our son gave us a "New Age" clock radio. I describe "New Age" as anything that is new to me at my age! This radio has an extra feature. It's a menu from which you can select an assortment of relaxing sounds that are meant to serenade you into a deep, tranquil slumber. You can choose the sound of ocean waves, gently falling rain, a heartbeat, whales communicating, a gentle running stream, or a bird quietly singing. It was all I could do to keep from bursting into laughter as my son explained how to use the remote control to select these sounds and, better yet, combine them. I envisioned myself walking to the bathroom all night while listening to water running to the beat of a heart.

But the thing that made me giggle the most was that my son actually believed we could ever figure out how to actually use the remote control, or find it in the middle of a dark night!

Yes, following instructions is something I struggle with. I will do just about anything to get out of it. In fact, I'm reminded of the time my husband, Orvey (yes, that is his real name), and I decided to paint our house instead of hiring a painter. We couldn't wait to spend all the hundreds of dollars we were going to save by doing it ourselves. After all, we were young, industrious and energetic. Why hire a professional?

Orvey commuted every day into Los Angeles, which left him no time to pick out or pick up paint. That job was left to me. On the morning I was going to pick up the paint, Orvey had an idea. "Judy, why don't you rent a compressor? It will save us a lot of time and energy," he chirped.

Being the godly submissive woman I am (I just heard thunder), I dutifully trudged down to the paint store and picked out the paint. I also reserved a compressor to be picked up the following weekend. The owner of the store then introduced me to a man who would share his expertise on operating the paint compressor. But there was a slight problem. The man was drunk. I felt myself nodding off as he slurred his words and tried to flirt with me at the same time. I thought, Get me out of here. We'll figure it out ourselves, for heaven's sake. If this guy can paint while he's drunk, surely my sober husband can manage this dumb thing.

The next weekend, my husband completed his preparations for painting our house, while I picked up the compressor. He power-washed the siding, taped all the windows and covered the bushes with tarps.

I gave him a few directions on how to operate the compressor, and Orvey declared "Let the painting begin! I'll be done in no time." Little did he know!

Soon he was filling the large bucket with paint, ready to engage the compressor.

"Here she goes!" he bellowed.

He pulled the trigger on the nozzle, and the force from the compressor nearly knocked him off his precious little feet. Paint flew everywhere! It blew the plastic off the windows, the tarps off the shrubs and the newspapers off the cement. Within minutes, our home, yard and birds flying by were sprayed white!

Orvey hunkered down, tightened his grip on the nozzle and went forth like a soldier in battle. Paint blasted out a mile a minute. Everything in sight was turning white, and it looked like a blizzard had hit California. Our terrazzo front porch was covered in paint, as were the sidewalks, trees, shrubs and mailbox.

By now, both our moods had deteriorated to an ugly state. Our children quietly packed their belongings and moved in with the neighbors. I know I should have kept my mouth shut, but that's another lifetime.

"Honey, you are ruining our home!" I shrieked.

Orvey turned to me with a look that would have scared Hitler, pointed the nozzle at me (but didn't pull the trigger), and I ran into the house.

By evening, the neighbors had bolted their doors, contacted realtors and the street was silent. My husband was finished. He looked like someone from a science fiction movie. Only the circles around his eyes, where his glasses had been, remained untouched by white paint.

When he returned the compressor, he told the store about his experience, and commented "I think this compressor must be broken. The paint shot out like a nuclear missile."

"Mister, why didn't you turn the pressure down with this knob here on the right?"

The blood drained from my husband's face. He didn't know about the knob. I never told him, because I hadn't listened to the man's directions.

We've had many laughs over that paint day through the years. It was harmless enough. All it cost us was a few gallons of paint and some marriage counseling.

I wish it were just as harmless and laughable to ignore the counsel of God's word and how important it is for my life. Oftentimes, when I read the Bible, I slip into my spiritual sleep mode and ignore God's directions. The consequences are not as harmless as a broken VCR.

Out of His marvelous grace and mercy, God forgives me when I stray. It has taken me years to understand how life changing His love and wisdom are.

And it sure beats listening to whales talk in the middle of the night.

~Judy Hampton
Chicken Soup for the Christian Woman's Soul

62

Computer Granny

Back up my hard drive? How do I put it in reverse?
~Author Unknown

My eyes filled with tears as I kissed my family good-bye at the Sydney airport. Because the trip from America is so expensive, I knew I wouldn't be returning to be with my son, my Australian daughter-in-law or my precious grandchildren for at least two more years.

Tracy, nine years old, and Phillip, eleven, were born there. I'd seen them only five times in their short lives—one month every two years. I so wanted to be a good grandma to them, like my grandma was to me. I wanted to bake them homemade cookies, visit their schools, watch Tracy's dance recitals and Phillip's bowling tournaments. I wanted them to be able to come to me when they were hurting and let me wipe their tears and give them hugs. I wanted to be able to talk with them every day—to listen to their laughter, to know their dreams, to say "I love you."

Each time we parted, my heart ached a little more. But on this visit, Tracy and Phillip had given me exciting hope for the future. They had talked incessantly about their new computer and how, if I bought one, we would be able to communicate daily!

"Remember, Granny," Tracy squealed as I waved good-bye, "get a computer! And write to us!"

"Every day!" Phillip shouted. "We'll write to you, too."

And so it was that I abandoned my outdated typewriter and made a frightening leap into this fast-paced, high-tech era of e-mail. Everything about my new computer scared me. I was afraid to touch the keyboard for fear I'd delete something important or do some sort of damage. I even had trouble getting started with the one-page, loose insert of quick tips:

Click on the Windows Icon.

(Wait! I wanted to scream. How do I turn on the computer?)

Click on the Start button, located on the Taskbar.

(What's a taskbar?)

Point to Programs with the mouse cursor.

(What part of this silly-looking mouse thing is a cursor?)

Gramps started questioning my sanity when he heard me talking to my machine, aloud, on a regular basis:

WARNING! Invalid MAPI.DLL present. Cannot provide MAPI.DLL service.

(Did I ask to be serviced?)

WARNING! This program has performed an illegal operation and will be shut down.

(So shut down already. I don't want to work with something illegal anyway.)

WARNING! A printer time-out has occurred.

(What?! My printer is taking a break? Who's in charge here?)

My first few weeks of learning were not fun. I spent full days and nights reading tutorials. I bought *Windows for Dummies*. I waited on hold for hours, the phone glued to my ear, trying to connect to a live helper on the "helpline." I harassed my friends with annoying calls—at 7:00 A.M., at meal time, at bedtime—pleading for a simple escape from some program jam that had me trapped in limbo.

The machine became my nemesis, and at the same time, the hero that could link me to my family. It was definitely a love/hate relationship. But no obstacle, technological or otherwise, could deter me from the possibility of hearing from my grandchildren every day!

I've missed out on so much of their lives. But with electronic mail, everything has changed. Now, one month and dozens of messages later, I'm up-to-the-minute with news from Tracy and Phillip!

By e-mail, Phillip tells Gramps and me about his role in the school play. He regales us with his account of getting caught in the rain on his bike. And he makes us proud as he announces his test scores in math.

On my last visit I taught him a goofy language called "Op." He recently sent a complete e-mail message using our "secret code"—no easy task. The best part was "OpI lopove yopou sopoopoopoopo mopuch!" Translation: "I love you soooo much!"

Tracy turned ten last week. We were in on the birthday plans from day one—the porcelain doll she was hoping for, the anticipation of a slumber party with three of her friends and a Lion King cake.

On the night of her sleepover, we smiled at the computer message from her dad complaining about the unbearable noise level. We quickly responded to Tracy by saying, "We had to close our windows because we could hear you and your friends all the way across the ocean!"

Her mom immediately replied, "I just went in and read your message to the girls. They started to apologize, then realized it was a joke. The look on their faces was priceless!"

Before long we received a short note from Tracy. It was almost as though we were right there enjoying her party in person.

The kids write to me when they're happy. And they write when they are hurting. They share some secrets they don't even tell Mom and Dad, and they ask me questions that only a grandma could answer.

I can't wipe their tears or put my arms around them and hold them close. But I can "listen" and show how much I care with my empathy and advice. I can send them funny jokes and precious poems. I can tell them how much I love them—every day.

I still make lots of mistakes on my computer, and my heart still jumps when I get one of those obnoxious, threatening, WARNING! alerts. The most recent one said I had committed a "fatal error." Fatal! I nearly threw in the mouse pad! But on the same day we received a message from Tracy saying, "I love you guise bigger than the entire world!"

For that I'll take any abuse this whiz-bang wonder of chips and a motherboard dishes out.

Just call me Computer Granny!

~Kay Conner Pliszka
Chicken Soup for the Grandparent's Soul

63

Garden Crime

Never say, "oops." Always say, "Ah, interesting."
~Author Unknown

Now that we've retired and live in the country, I have finally started gardening, as I've wanted to all my life. I love it, and I'm learning a lot. My husband likes to help out. He often comes home with plants he's found along the side of the road.

Two years ago he came home with a plant about fifteen inches tall. He told me he had found a whole field of them. As always, I faithfully planted it in front of our house in a nice, sunny spot. It grew quickly, and I had a lot of admirers — people even took pictures. But I was disappointed because it produced no flowers. That was unfortunate. I wanted a flowering bush in that spot.

As I was digging it up to transplant it, a very nice police officer stopped and asked me where I had found that plant.

"You can have it if you want it," I told him. "It doesn't produce any flowers and I have no use for it. My husband says there's an entire field of them, so if you want more, he can tell you where to find them."

"Thank you, ma'am," he replied. "I think I would like to talk with your husband." He waited in his car in front of our house while I kept puttering in the garden, feeling rather strange.

Finally, my husband arrived home. When asked by the police officer where more of these "beautiful" plants could be found, my husband said, "I don't remember!"

Well, you can imagine my horror when the policeman informed us we were growing marijuana, which of course is against the law. But, since we are in our seventies, to my relief, he believed my husband's loss of memory and we weren't arrested! And, to my delight, the police officer dug up the plant himself and took it away, saving me the work!

The next time my husband goes on plant foraging expeditions, I'm sending along a plant identification book. Who knows what he could bring home?

~Ursel Rabeneck
Chicken Soup for the Gardener's Soul

64

Encounter on a Train

It's a strange world of language in which
skating on thin ice can get you into hot water.
~Franklin P. Jones

When I first saw her in the station at St. Margrethen, she was boarding the railroad car in which I sat, shoving an enormous brown leather suitcase up the high step with her knee.

She was wearing earth colors: pants of brown corduroy, knitted vest patterned in orange and brown, Kelly green shirt with up-rolled sleeves. Dark eyes, dark hair, dark complexion, young, mysterious. After heaving her burden onto the overhead rack, she collapsed into a seat across the aisle from me, perspiring sedately. Then the silver, air-conditioned train quietly sealed itself to continue its five-hour run westward across Switzerland.

Alpine streams bubbled with icy meltwater, and the fields were ablaze with poppies, for the month was May. I attempted first to doze, then to strike up a conversation with the person next to me. No success there. I tried to doze a second time and couldn't, and then I noticed her again. She had produced a posy of wilted wildflowers from somewhere and was now holding it on her lap, her thoughts apparently upon whoever had given it to her. She

Encounter on a Train: Laugh Wrinkles   249

had a strong but tranquil face. She was looking at the flowers and lightly smiling. I moved across the aisle and sat down facing her.

"Wie heissen die Blumen?" I asked. I knew that the salad bowl of German words at my disposal would not get me far. Perhaps speaking to her at all was a mistake. At any rate, her only answer to my question about the flowers was a smile. Ah, I thought, not German. Italian, of course. She's dark.

I leaned forward to craft a more careful question about "i fiori," knowing that if the conversational terrain should dip in that direction I'd have to beat an even quicker retreat. She still didn't answer me. The thought that she was mute crossed my mind, but I dismissed it. Since this was Switzerland, I had a final choice: French. The reply, however, was as before: a Mona Lisa smile. I began to wonder. I'd seen a stationful of Yugoslavs in Buchs that morning, back toward the Austrian border. Could she be one of them? The prospect of hearing her speak at last in Serbo-Croatian was discouraging. Better to go slowly now.

I leaned back, relaxed, and returned the smile as enigmatically as I could. I tried to look mysterious—a foredoomed task, considering my garb of crushable fisherman's hat, red long-john shirt, pin-striped mustard slacks, and leather running shoes. It didn't work. Just as I was about to pack it in, Mona Lisa spoke. "Habla español?" she asked. Why hadn't I thought of it? She's Spanish! A tourist, maybe, but more likely a "Gastarbeiter." There were loads of Spaniards working in Switzerland.

With all circuits snapping to life, I strove to call up my meager store of Spanish while rummaging frantically through my bag for the right *Grosset's* phrase book. I commenced to address this person, whose national origins were beginning to take form. She turned out indeed to be a Spaniard, on her way home to see her family. She was single, employed in a home for the aged in Altstätten, and incredibly, her suitcase was stuffed with Swiss chocolate.

Our conversation, unfortunately, was hampered by more than language difficulties, since I had been ill for twenty-four hours and was still required to take periodic and sudden absences. She proved to be understanding. She turned out, however, to be a poor judge of national costume or accents, taking me first for an Englishman and later for a German. I was apparently the first specimen she'd encountered from the Land of the Free and the Home of the Brave.

What we spoke of, exactly, I can't remember, but the day flew past, and I do recall we were in marvelous accord on a number of important issues. I dreaded our arrival in Geneva, where we would part, but by day's end we were there. We strolled for a while through the city's pretty streets, dallied over cappuccino in a sidewalk cafe, inspected shop windows in the day's failing light, laughed together, and filled conversational voids with banalities until my train came. Hers was due later, at midnight. I said goodbye with great reluctance. She appeared to share my feeling, but her people were beckoning from across the Pyrenees, and my schedule called me to Italy before returning home. We exchanged addresses. I then boarded the train and left.

Today my life doesn't have the broad margin it had then. Like many other people, I raise children, commute, remodel and mow the lawn. But I sometimes think of those days when life could become so quickly and intensely bittersweet, when great possibilities could yawn in an instant.

In fact, one way I'm able to retain perspective on the

here and now is by recalling the details of that particular spring day, with its chance meeting and sad goodbye. Occasionally I've recounted the event to others, too, but there I enjoy taking some liberties with the facts, making the girl somewhat more desperate and myself a bit more dashing or distant. In one of my versions the girl unabashedly pursues me. My wife especially enjoys hearing me carry on in this vein.

Even though she likes the story, my wife does find its variations astonishing. She insists that on the train she was not desperate, that I was not distant or dashing, and that she left Switzerland the following year to marry me despite the way I was dressed that day.

~Kevin H. Siepel
Chicken Soup for the Romantic Soul

Lunch with Grandma

Next to a good soul-stirring prayer is a good laugh.
~Samuel Mutchmore

Although uncertain, unprepared and unaware of the challenges of Alzheimer's disease, I headed to Charlotte to help Mom care for Grandma.

With my usual upbeat, positive attitude, I rose the first morning full of enthusiasm and knowing exactly what to do, or so I thought. Before my first cup of coffee, I entered the bathroom to find Grandmother attempting to brush her teeth with a razor! Shocked and near hysterics, I yelled for mother while trying to retrieve the razor without hurting Grandmother or myself. Mom quietly walked into the room, took the razor and control with a smile and what looked like an invisible tear. Tears were many as the day went on. The "tuff one," as I had been called, had met her match.

A few days passed and I became more confident as Mom and I realized that Grandmother did things born of habit. So we began playing on her habits—messing up the living room so she could straighten up again and again—assigning her the chore of sweeping the porch—washing unbreakable plates and cups as I dried them and put them away.

Convinced I could handle any situation with ease, not

to mention that mother was impressed with my ability to keep Grandma busy, my confidence grew. So I decided to take Grandma to lunch, just the two of us. Against mother's better judgment, plans were made to take her to a steakhouse with a salad bar, so Grandma could pick out what SHE wanted to eat.

Riding to the restaurant was no problem; she just loved these new-fangled vehicles. Happily, we entered the steakhouse, got our plates, and ventured to the salad bar. But Grandmother didn't know what anything was, not even a roll. She refused to eat anything accept the pretty "red stuff" that wiggled. Finally, with only gelatin on her plate, we sat down and had a wonderful lunch. She swirled the good "red stuff" around in her mouth, thoroughly enjoying herself.

All of a sudden, out of nowhere, she grabbed my arm and yanked me to the floor, pulling me under the table. I was too shocked to scream or I would have. I took her arm and gently coaxed her to stand, but she clutched my arms with a strength I couldn't imagine and jerked me back to the floor "Indians!" she cried out in a hushed tone. "We must escape!"

Trying desperately to understand, I said, "Where are the Indians?"

Frightened, she pointed to a group of people that had just entered the restaurant. Then she started crawling on the floor, dragging her purse behind and motioning me to follow her. I knelt still.

"Come on!" she commanded, her irritation and my embarrassment mounting.

What the heck, I thought, swallowing any pride I had left. I crept behind her between and under empty tables, making our way through the great Wild West toward the salad bar. Once we arrived safely to our "cover," she pulled me toward her and said, "That way, to the door! We can make it," she said, "be brave!"

Off we went in a fast crawl, her in her dress, me in cut off blue jeans, both of us dragging a purse and turning our heads from side to side. She was looking for danger and I was looking to see who was staring. Just when we were getting close to the door, the manager came from behind the counter. Terrified, Grandma flung herself over my body to protect me.

The manager gazed down at the two of us piled in a heap on the floor and asked, "Can I help you ladies?"

I burst out laughing. Grandma pulled herself up and bent over to help me since I was laughing so hard I couldn't stand. She brushed me off and asked me, "Are you okay, honey?"

The confused manager asked the obvious question. "Is anything wrong?"

"Of course, everything is quite all right," Grandmother said, "now that you are here, Marshall Dillon."

With tears of hysterical laughter streaming down my face, grandmother pulled me along to the door. Once she got there, she turned back to the manager and said, "I'm sorry sir, we forgot to pay." She took a dime out of her purse and placed it on the counter.

"Thank you, ma'am," he said and gave her a big smile.

By now I was laughing so hard I could hardly breathe. My grandmother gripped my arm and jerked me toward the door. "We have to get out of here, Teri," she said. "You're embarrassing me."

~Teri Batts
Chicken Soup for the Caregiver's Soul

66

At Ease

Now in their late sixties, the widow and widower, long-time friends before their spouses passed away, chose to marry. The groom—a proud and valiant ex-Marine—arranged the wedding at the unobtrusive Marine Corps Chapel tucked over the gymnasium at Headquarters Battalion USMC, Henderson Hall, in Arlington, Virginia.

At the close of the simple ceremony, my cousin Larry—officiating chaplain—presented the couple to the audience and introduced them as "Mr. and Mrs." Then he suggested it was time for the groom to acknowledge his bride.

Larry waited expectantly. The bride looked up adoringly. And the small audience held its collective breath, eager to witness the traditional first kiss as husband and wife.

But guests collapsed into gasps and gales of laughter when the feisty groom snapped to attention and, in true military style, "acknowledged" his bride with a proper Marine... salute.

~Carol McAdoo Rehme
Chicken Soup for the Bride's Soul

Older & Wiser

Chapter 8

Final Gifts

*Memory is a way of holding onto the things you love,
the things you are, the things you never want to lose.
~From the television show*
The Wonder Years

67

Gone Fishing

Sometimes our light goes out but is blown into flame
by another human being. Each of us owes deepest thanks
to those who have rekindled this light.
~Albert Schweitzer

When I entered her room, Mrs. Johnson was sitting in a chair by the window reading the Bible. Her thin frame bathed in the morning sunlight as she quietly thumbed through the worn pages. I stopped in the doorway and studied the elderly woman. The room was quiet and very peaceful.

I had only recently started my third year of medical school, and it was my first day on the urology service. Mrs. Johnson had end-stage ovarian cancer that had spread throughout her abdomen, obstructing her ureters and causing her kidney function to decline. I had spent two hours reviewing her chart, X-rays and old records. I also read all that I could find about ovarian carcinoma. For a moment, I felt very uncomfortable. Although I had a considerable amount of knowledge about her condition, I knew absolutely nothing about her as a person. She was dying, and I had been worrying about trying to impress my chief resident with my fund of knowledge. After taking a deep breath, I stepped into her room.

"Hello, Mrs. Johnson," I said while reaching for her bedside chart. "How are you doing this morning?" I asked.

"Sweetie, I'm doing just fine on this glorious day," she said, turning towards me with a warm smile on her face. "You look a little young to be wearing one of those white coats," she said, examining me over the bifocals perched on the end of her nose.

"Well, it's the only thing I could find to match these pants," I teased.

She chuckled softly as she closed the Bible on her lap. She turned her attention back toward the window and took a long, slow breath. "Sure is a glorious day," she said as she shook her head.

An unexpected calm came over me as I stood beside her. She seemed completely at ease as she basked in the morning sunshine that poured in through the window. I sat on the bed next to her chair and asked if she could spare a few minutes to discuss her medical condition.

For the next fifteen minutes, I talked with her about all aspects of her disease and how it related to her kidney failure. "Without functioning kidneys, toxins will build up in your bloodstream and will lead to your death. We can place stents in through your bladder, which will relieve the obstruction and save your kidneys from shutting down. It is a quick and painless procedure."

"My, my, my... just look at this glorious day," she said.

"Mrs. Johnson, do you understand everything that we have talked about?" I asked, with a confused look on my face.

"Honey, I'm dying," she said, with no change in her expression.

"You don't have to die from renal failure," I interrupted.

She sat quietly looking at me. I felt uncomfortable in the silence. She turned back to the window and asked, "So dying from kidney failure would be worse than dying from cancer?" She already knew the answer. Suddenly, the notion of getting consent for the procedure seemed absolutely ridiculous. Who was I treating, the patient or myself? I was saving her from a more humane death, only to have her meet with a long and painful demise.

"Sweetie, the Lord takes care of all his children. He doesn't want me to suffer and neither do you," she said. She obviously sensed my sadness as I stared intently at the floor. "Look at me," she said. "It is okay to die. It is as much a part of life as being born. I have been on God's green earth for seventy-eight years and have loved every minute of it. Life is a gift. You take the good with the bad."

I didn't even try to hide my tears as she continued talking.

"I know this is difficult for you to understand, but I'm tired, very tired. God has a plan, and it is my time to go," she said. "You are a good doctor. Just listen to your patients, listen to your heart and do what is right."

I was numb. Why was this dying woman comforting me? She eased back in her chair and said, "Sure is a glorious day."

"Mrs. Johnson, what can I do for you?"

"Honey, why don't you go sign my release papers?"

"What are you going to do, Mrs. Johnson?"

She smiled and said, "I'm going fishing. I am going to pick up my grandchildren, and we are going to go down to the lake and catch some big ones."

I left and completed all of the necessary paperwork then returned to her room. We talked for a long time about her life and her experiences. I enjoyed getting to know her as a person. She was wonderful. She hugged me, and before I left she said, "Never forget what's important. No matter how busy you are, take the time to look around. In the end, the only things that really matter are the relationships you have with God and your loved ones."

I paused in the doorway as I left. She was staring out the window with a peaceful smile on her face.

"Sure is a glorious day," I said.

~Adam Gold, M.D.
Chicken Soup for the Caregiver's Soul

Daddy's Dance

The heart that loves is always young.
~Greek Proverb

I loaded the last of my retreat supplies in the back of my minivan, then kissed my husband and son goodbye. Not only was I excited about the ladies' overnight retreat where I would be speaking, but I had mapped out a driving route that took me right through the town in which my parents lived. I planned to stop and spend a few hours with them, welcoming any opportunity to visit my mother and father, now eighty-three and eight-six years old. But often the visits were difficult.

Daddy was in the throes of Alzheimer's disease, and his comprehension and communication were severely impaired. The progression of the illness was devastating, especially to my mother, his mate of sixty-six years. She was now more a caregiver than a wife, and often Daddy was unable to even recognize her face. I grieved for both of them as well as myself. I wasn't ready to let go of the father I had known forever. He had been so full of life—singing, dancing, joking, laughing. Where had he gone? How did those Alzheimer's tangles in his brain rob him of words, faces and places?

Many times, Mama wanted to tell me of personal incidents, thinking I would understand, being the mother and caregiver of an adult son with special needs. But I didn't want to hear humiliating details of Daddy's debilitating disease. This was still my father, the man who held me on his lap and rocked me as a child, put me on my first horse to ride and taught me to drive in an old 1948 Ford pickup truck. This was the daddy who used to show up at my college dormitory to bring me home on weekends when he thought I had stayed away too long. There was no way to divorce myself from those memories, nor did I want to. I held them close to my heart.

Even with the progression of the disease, there were still small windows when Daddy was coherent, like the Christmas he hugged me and looked into my eyes and said, "You don't come home enough." I blinked back tears and said, "No, Daddy, I don't." He didn't remember the responsibilities I had at my own home.

And just a few months earlier, when I called to tell him "Happy Birthday," he gave me a delightful recap of his day before regressing into unintelligible words and phrases. Once when I presented him with a framed picture of myself as a gift, Mama asked, "Do you know who's in that picture?"

He smiled and pointed directly at my face and said, "That's my baby."

Indeed, I would always be his baby girl.

But today, after arriving at my parents' home, Daddy gave me a quick hug, then went to the bedroom to take a nap while I sat at the kitchen table with Mama. She spilled out her fears, resentment and pain. She had no idea how to cope with Daddy's anger when she didn't fulfill his requests. But how could she possibly know what he wanted when she couldn't understand his words or gestures?

Because of my own son's lack of communication, I could

identify with her frustration, but it seemed harder for my mother. This was her husband, and it wasn't supposed to be this way. This was the time she had dreamed of traveling and relaxing after many years of hard work. Daddy got up from his nap several times to make trips to the bathroom, always requiring Mama's help with snaps and zippers on his clothing. Neither of them liked this situation, and both were argumentative and irritated with each other.

Finally, I left for the retreat, but my heart was heavy. As I drove, I thought of the anger, fatigue and emotional pain that my parents were experiencing and wondered if they ever had a happy moment. I loved them and wanted to help, but had no idea what to do. As I guided the car along the highway, I prayed for peace, harmony, love, health and even joy in their lives.

The retreat provided a refreshing respite for my body and soul, and I was in great spirits as I headed back home. Again, I stopped for a visit with my parents, hoping things had improved.

I pulled into the driveway just ahead of my brother, and we congregated in the living room with his guitar. Monte played and sang several songs; then Mama and Daddy joined in. By the time they hit the old hymn, "I Saw the Light," Daddy was singing every word from memory and smiling from ear to ear. I sat in awe as I watched his whole countenance change.

Suddenly, Daddy, who normally shuffled and slumped when he walked, jumped up from the couch and began to dance a jig to the music, his face alive with pure joy and fun. Then he put his hands out toward Mother. She stood up beside him, and together they two-stepped across the living room floor, both of them laughing and gliding as I remembered them doing when I was a child.

I sat in a chair, clapping my hands in time to the music and wiping away tears. I had forgotten how much music had been a part of our family while growing up. I couldn't count how many times Mama and Daddy had stood beside our old upright piano and sang while I barely plunked out a melody. Daddy also led the singing at our little country church and even sang while he worked in the fields, often letting me ride on the horse's broad back while he guided the plow behind. My mind flooded with wonderful memories. Good times and hard times, but happy times. Soon Daddy plopped down on the couch, a smile still lighting up his face.

I left for home with a new peace and joy in my heart and again prayed for my parents while I drove, this time thanking God for the love and happy times they still enjoyed.

I know there will still be hard times in the future, but I'm thankful for this beautiful memory and reminder to celebrate every moment in life—perhaps, even dance in it!

~Louise Tucker Jones
Chicken Soup for the Father & Daughter Soul

Roses for Rose

The sweetest flower that blows, I give you as we part.
For you it is a rose, for me it is my heart.
~Frederick Peterson

Red roses were her favorites—
    her name was also Rose—
And every year her husband sent them,
    tied with pretty bows.
The year he died, the roses were delivered to her door.
The card said, "Be my Valentine,"
    like all the years before.

Each year he sent her roses,
    and the note would always say,
"I love you even more this year
    than last year on this day.
My love for you will always grow
    with every passing year."
She knew this was the last time
    that the roses would appear.

She thought, "He ordered roses in advance
    before this day."

Her loving husband did not know
    that he would pass away.
He always liked to do things early,
    way before the time.
Then, if he got too busy,
    everything would work out fine.

She trimmed the stems
    and placed them in a very special vase,
Then sat the vase beside the portrait
    of his smiling face.
She would sit for hours,
    in her husband's favorite chair,
While staring at his picture
    and the roses sitting there.

A year went by
    and it was hard to live without her mate,
With loneliness and solitude
    that had become her fate.
Then, the very hour, as on Valentines before,
The doorbell rang,
    and there were roses sitting by her door.

She brought the roses in,
    and then just looked at them in shock,
Then went to get the telephone,
    to call the florist shop.
The owner answered and she asked him
    if he would explain,
Why would someone do this to her,
    causing her such pain?

"I know your husband passed away
    more than a year ago,"
The owner said. "I knew you'd call,
    and you would want to know,
The flowers you received today
    were paid for in advance.
Your husband always planned ahead,
    he left nothing to chance.

"There is a standing order that I have on file
    down here,
And he has paid well in advance;
    you'll get them every year.
There also is another thing that I think you
    should know:
He wrote a special little card...
    he did this years ago.

"Then, should ever I find out
    that he's no longer here,
That's the card that should be sent to you
    the following year."
She thanked him and hung up the phone,
    her tears now flowing hard,
Her fingers shaking,
    as she slowly reached to get the card.

Inside the card she saw that he had
    written her a note.
Then, as she stared in total silence,
    this is what he wrote....
"Hello, my love, I know it's been a year
    since I've been gone,

I hope it hasn't been too hard for you
    to overcome.

"I know it must be lonely,
    and the pain is very real,
For if it were the other way,
    I know how I would feel.
The love we shared made everything
    so beautiful in life.
I loved you more than words can say.
    You were the perfect wife.

"You were my friend and lover,
    you fulfilled my every need.
I know it's only been a year,
    but please try not to grieve.
I want you to be happy,
    even when you shed your tears.
That is why the roses will be sent to you for years.

"When you get these roses,
    think of all the happiness
That we had together,
    and how both of us were blessed.
I have always loved you, and I know I always will.
But, my love, you must go on,
    you have some living still.

"Please try to find happiness,
    while living out your days.
I know it is not easy,
    but I hope you find some ways.

The roses will come every year,
    and they will only stop
When your door's not answered
    when the florist stops to knock.

"He will come five times that day,
    in case you have gone out.
But after his last visit,
    he will know without a doubt
To take the roses to the place where I've
    instructed him,
And place the roses where we are,
    together once again."

~James A. Kisner
Chicken Soup for the Gardener's Soul

Delayed Delivery

Happiness is a warm puppy.
~Charles M. Schulz

Stella had been prepared for her husband's death. Since the doctor's pronouncement of terminal cancer, they had both faced the inevitable, striving to make the most of their remaining time together. Dave's financial affairs had always been in order. There were no new burdens in her widowed state. It was just the awful aloneness... the lack of purpose to her days.

They had been a childless couple by choice. Their lives had been so full and rich. They had been content with busy careers and with each other. They had many friends. Had. That was the operative word these days. It was bad enough losing the one person you loved with all your heart. But over the past few years, she and Dave repeatedly coped with the deaths of their friends and relations. They were all of an age — an age when human bodies began giving up. Dying. Face it — they were old!

And now, approaching the first Christmas without Dave, Stella was all too aware she was on her own.

With shaky fingers, she lowered the volume of her radio so that the Christmas music faded to a muted background. To her surprise, she saw that the mail had arrived. With the inevitable wince of pain from her arthritis, she bent to retrieve the white envelopes from the floor. She opened them while sitting on the piano bench. They were mostly Christmas cards, and her sad eyes smiled at the familiarity of the traditional scenes and at the loving messages inside. She arranged them among the others on the piano top. In her entire house, they were the only seasonal decoration. The holiday was less than a week away, but she just did not have the heart to put up a silly tree, or even set up the stable that Dave had built with his own hands.

Suddenly engulfed by the loneliness of it all, Stella buried her face in her hands and let the tears come. How would she possibly get through Christmas and the winter beyond it!

The ring of the doorbell was so unexpected that Stella had to stifle a small scream of surprise. Now who could possibly be calling on her? She opened the wooden door and stared through the window of the storm door with consternation. On her front porch stood a strange young man, whose head was barely visible above the large carton in his arms. She peered beyond him to the driveway, but there was nothing about the small car to give a clue as to his identity. Summoning courage, the elderly lady opened the door slightly, and he stepped sideways to speak into the space.

"Mrs. Thornhope?"

She nodded. He continued, "I have a package for you."

Curiosity drove caution from her mind. She pushed the door open, and he entered. Smiling, he placed his burden carefully on the floor and stood to retrieve an envelope that protruded from his pocket. As he handed it to her, a sound came from the box. Stella jumped. The man laughed in apology and bent to straighten up the cardboard flaps, holding them open in an invitation for her to peek inside.

It was a dog! To be more exact, a Golden Labrador Retriever puppy. As the young gentleman lifted its squirming body up into his arms, he explained, "This is for you, ma'am." The young pup wiggled in happiness at being released from captivity and thrust ecstatic, wet kisses in the direction of the young man's face. "We were supposed to deliver him on Christmas Eve," he continued with some difficulty, as he strove to rescue his chin from the wet little tongue, "but the staff at the kennels start their holidays tomorrow. Hope you don't mind an early present."

Shock had stolen Stella's ability to think clearly. Unable to form coherent sentences, she stammered, "But... I don't... I mean... who...?"

The young fellow set the animal down on the doormat between them and then reached out a finger to tap the envelope she was still holding.

"There's a letter in there that explains everything, pretty much. The dog was bought while his mother was still pregnant. It was meant to be a Christmas gift."

The stranger turned to go. Desperation forced the words from her lips. "But who... who bought it?"

Pausing in the open doorway, he replied, "Your husband, ma'am." And then he was gone.

It was all in the letter. Forgetting the puppy entirely at the sight of the familiar handwriting, Stella walked like a sleepwalker to her chair by the window. She forced her tear-filled eyes to read her husband's words. He had written the letter three weeks before his death and had left it with the kennel owners, to be delivered along with the puppy as his last Christmas gift to her. It was full of love and encouragement and admonishments to be strong. He vowed that he was waiting for the day when she would join him. And he had sent her this young animal to keep her company until then.

Remembering the little creature for the first time, she was surprised to find him quietly looking up at her, his small panting mouth resembling a comic smile. Stella put the pages aside and reached for the bundle of golden fur. She thought that he would be heavier, but he was only the size and weight of a sofa pillow. And so soft and warm. She cradled him in her arms and he licked her jawbone, then cuddled into the hollow of her neck. The tears began anew at this exchange of affection and the dog endured her crying without moving.

Finally, Stella lowered him to her lap, where she regarded him solemnly. She wiped vaguely at her wet cheeks, then somehow mustered a smile.

"Well, little guy, I guess it's you and me." His pink tongue panted in agreement. Stella's smile strengthened, and her gaze shifted sideways to the window. Dusk had fallen. Through fluffy flakes that were now drifting down, she saw the cheery Christmas lights edging the roof lines of her neighbors' homes. The strains of "Joy to the World" floated in from the kitchen.

Suddenly Stella felt the most amazing sensation of peace and benediction wash over her. It was like being enfolded in a loving embrace. Her heart beat painfully, but it was with joy and wonder, not grief or loneliness. She need never feel alone again.

Returning her attention to the dog, she spoke to him. "You know, fella, I have a box in the basement that I think you'd like. There's a tree in it and some decorations and lights that will impress you like crazy! And I think I can find that old stable down there, too. What d'ya say we go hunt it up?"

The puppy barked happily in agreement, as if he understood every word. Stella got up, placed the puppy on the floor and together they went down to the basement, ready to make a Christmas together.

~Cathy Miller
Chicken Soup for the Pet Lover's Soul

Grieving Time,
a Time for Love

If a loved one has departed,
And left an empty space,
Seek the inner stillness,
Set a slower pace.
Take time to remember,
Allow yourself to cry,
Acknowledge your emotions,
Let sadness pass on by.
Then center in the oneness,
Remember... God is here,
Death is but a change in form,
Your loved one is still near.
Treat yourself with kindness,
Allow yourself to feel,
God will do the mending,
And time will help you heal.

~Barbara Bergen
Chicken Soup for the Grieving Soul

Angel on the Beach

"Thank you."

"I appreciate all you have done."

"It was kind of you to come."

The same words over and over again. None of them would bring Tom back, nor would any of the flowers, charitable gestures, cards or notes. He was dead—dead! My best friend, lover, husband would no longer come through the door, cook his specialties, leave his socks on the floor or hold me with a warmth I had never known before.

Tom suffered a terrible end. No dignity, just pain—endless pain. The cancer had ravaged his body so he was no longer the person I knew physically. However, his aura, his being never changed and his bravery amazed me every day. We had the life together people hear about but never really believe exists outside the movies or books. "Twenty-six years and holding—and not letting go!" Tom would say and then hug me. "Not sure I'm going to keep her, I may want a younger version soon."

My reply was an automatic, "And what would you do with a younger version, my dear?" Our routine amused our friends and family but it also confirmed our commitment to each other. A commitment based on love, trust and true friendship.

Tom and I were confirmed "singles" prior to our meeting. He was forty and I was thirty-two when we met—neither one interested in a relationship. "Too old for that nonsense," we said. Friends decided we would be the perfect match for companionship since our interests were similar and included fine dining, classical music and the theater. We both had successful careers and no interest in a relationship. Absolutely no interest in a relationship.

Our first meeting was not at all what we expected or wanted. It was not love-at-first-sight but it was certainly something-at-first-sight. We were very attracted to each other, but since we were sophisticated New Yorkers, we tried to be "cool" about the attraction. It did not work. We talked only to each other and totally ignored everyone at the party. We left at the first possible moment and were married three months to the day we met.

Friends and family were sure we had both lost our minds and that the marriage would not last as long as the courtship. We knew better. Tom and I had found our missing parts. We complemented each other in every possible way. We enjoyed the same things, but each one brought something new to the relationship. We reveled in our sameness but respected our differences. We loved to be together but loved being alone. We were friends.

Our careers were demanding but fulfilling for both of us. However, our careers never took control of our lives and we always had time for each other. We traveled, kept an active social life, and surrounded ourselves with family and friends. We had not been blessed with children, but we accepted that fact easily, for our lives were full and happy.

The change came when we were preparing for one of our trips. "Tom, please pack your suitcases today or at least lay out your clothes and I'll pack for you," I shouted up the stairs. "Tom, Tom, do you hear me?" He quietly replied, "Hon, I don't feel well, please come up here." That was the beginning.

A feeling of great fatigue came over Tom, very unusual for a man who was never tired. We went to the doctor (doctors, really), had countless tests, and then the diagnosis. "They are wrong. Doctors make mistakes. We'll go to other medical centers, other doctors, anywhere, this is not correct!" But it was.

We were soon totally consumed by the disease. Every waking moment was turned over to doctor visits, hospitals, chemo, radiation and medication. It was all we talked about and all we read about. New and innovative treatments. Holistic approaches. Traditional medicine. Surgery. Everything was tried and nothing helped. Tom was leaving me. Every day he got weaker, unable to hold on, and then he was hospitalized for the last time.

As we entered the hospital room, a volunteer followed with magazines, books, toiletries and a gift. "The gift of hope," she said, "for no matter what happens, you must have hope." She placed a tiny angel pin on Tom's hospital gown and it stayed with him the entire five days he was in the hospital. On the fifth day, the doctors asked if he would like to go home "to rest more comfortably," but we both knew the end was near. We decided to go to our beach house since it was a place we both loved dearly.

We entered the beach house together and spent the next two weeks holding on to whatever we could. Friends and family visited for short periods to not tire him. I did not leave his side and, with the help of an aide, was able to care for his needs. I read to him, I talked to him, I loved him for as much time as we had left together. And then he was gone — one year from the diagnosis.

I took early retirement from my job and stayed at the beach house. It was where we loved to be and where he had spent his last days. I needed to keep his memory alive. I wanted nothing to do with anyone because they took my thoughts away from Tom, and I could not have that!

I kept his clothes near me because they smelled like him. I wore his favorite sweater because it felt like him. I read our favorite books and listened to our favorite music over and over. It was the only way to hold him close. Our favorite time to walk the beach was at dusk—just before the sunset. That became my ritual.

Time went on and the first anniversary of his death arrived. I truly believed I had no life without Tom. Absolutely no reason to go on without him. Friends intervened, family called, visited, nothing helped. I needed Tom to tell me what to do. I needed him to answer me when I spoke to him. I needed a sign.

With the help of friends, I agreed to clear out Tom's closet, bureau, desk and bookcases. However, after hours of sorting, I could not find the angel pin that Tom had close to him at the end. Where was it? Was it still in the house, or had it been thrown out in the confusion of his last hours? I wanted the angel pin because it had been a part of Tom's last hours, and it represented hope to me. Hope for the future, if I really had one.

With the cleaning out of Tom's belongings, I decided to return to our apartment in town and close the beach house until the summer. It was close to dusk and I decided to take a walk on the beach. My walk was brisk and invigorating, and I felt refreshed. As the sun set, it sent a glow over the ocean and a bright reflection on the sand. I bent over, picked up a shiny object and, in disbelief, cradled it in my hand. It was the angel pin that had been lost since Tom had died.

An omen? A message from beyond? The sign I had been asking for? I did not know. All I did know was that I felt a calm I had not felt for years and, suddenly, I knew everything would be all right.

~Helen Xenakis
Chicken Soup for the Romantic Soul

73

A Timeless Gift

Sorrow makes us all children again—
destroys all differences of intellect. The wisest know nothing.
~Ralph Waldo Emerson

Emerging from shock after my husband, Ken, died, I discovered strange things happening around me. Each morning I found doors unlocked, the television blaring and sprinklers spraying. Something shattered my life, and I felt utterly unprotected and vulnerable.

Once I had been a mentally strong, independent woman—handy qualities for a young Navy wife living in strange places and rearing four children alone. My husband's ship cruised half a world away, often through hostile waters toward secret destinations. The possibility that he might not make it back was never far from my mind. After all that experience living apart in the early years of our marriage, I now wondered if I had what it took to live alone.

A friend's words helped me understand what I was feeling. "You lost someone you love, and nothing has prepared you for what happens next. You're reacting to intense pain by closing down and buying time to heal. You still function," she said, "but now you are operating on automatic. And don't forget, nobody is doing your husband's chores."

Ken had efficiently taken care of making my world safe

by quietly fixing, renewing or replacing what needed to be done. In my current state of mind, if I remembered to turn anything on, I usually forgot to disconnect it, taking for granted that what needed to run, sprinkle or turn off would do so on its own.

As friends and relatives gradually drifted back into their own routines, I stayed home, stared off into space and withdrew from life. It was obvious I needed help, but it was easier to do nothing, live in the past and feel sorry for myself.

Moving forward was hard, and I looked for excuses not to try. Day after day I prayed for guidance. Finally, one Sunday about two months after Ken died, the church bulletin included an announcement for the beginning of a new grief-recovery workshop. One statement caught my attention: "Grief is real, powerful and has a devastating impact on our ability to function." The class started in two days. This must be an answer to prayer, I thought, so I followed God's direction and signed up. It felt right to be in his hands.

My confidence wavered as I walked to the first session. It was more difficult than I ever imagined. I felt as though I wore a sign saying, "No spouse! All alone! Abandoned!"

Beginning with that first night, the seven members in my group empathized with each other's tragic loss as our bonding included advice from the heart, the hand of friendship and a sympathetic ear. Joining this group was the first step I had taken to help myself and one that would eventually make me feel better, stronger and less vulnerable.

Our homework assignment? Do something pleasurable for ourselves. I splurged on new plum-colored sheets, transforming "our" bedroom into "my" room with a cheerful, feminine décor. Then, because I never owned one before, I bought a navy blue designer baseball cap. Checking out the hat, I glanced in the mirror and smiled. Being good to myself could easily become a habit.

Facilitators cautioned us about letting painful reminders of the dead person stay in our lives. Guilt can lure us into making our homes a shrine to their memory. I called mine "the recliner shrine." Grandchildren's crayon drawings, an old newspaper and a mug inscribed "Dad's Cup" remained where he left them on a small table beside the recliner.

The chair's emptiness served as a constant reminder that he was gone. My children looked for Dad in his favorite place each time they entered the room. It was just too painful, so they took action. They reorganized the house. Immobilized by his death and still too stunned to move, I sat in the rocker and watched them work. Couches and chairs, followed by end tables, lamps and pictures, all ended up in a new spot or a different room. I loved the way it looked. The recliner, hidden under a floral cover, was relocated to an inconspicuous corner of the house, still with us, but no longer a blatant reminder.

Grief facilitators taught me how to face the finality of my partner's death. I realized that grieving is not a place for me to stay, nor can I go back, for my old life is no longer there. Accepting that it's all right for me to survive is a big part of healing.

In addition, facilitators admonished each week, "Take care of yourself." Since my husband was no longer here to make my world safe, I would do it myself. Using a twelve-point system, I secured the house, counting each job: (1) lock the door; (2) close the windows; (3) turn off the TV, etc. If I reached my bed with less than twelve, I knew I had missed a room and had to start over. Counting brought me security and peace of mind.

I resolved to simplify and reorganize my life. Feeling easily distracted and maddeningly forgetful, I bought a monthly planner that I kept in full view on the kitchen counter. I made a do, buy or be list: Do call plumber, wash car, buy milk and bread, be at vet 4 P.M. (don't forget the dog). This visual reminder lessened the stress of trying to remember everything.

On the first-year anniversary of my husband's death, I filled a basket with strawberries, pears, grapes, plums and other colorful fruits. Then I attached a note of appreciation and delivered it to the hospital intensive-care staff. I had been too devastated before to thank them for such compassionate care of both patient and family.

My daughter asked, "You're not doing a shrine thing again, are you?"

"No," I promised, "these gifts are to nourish the living, so they can continue helping others in need."

Later that day while emptying my husband's desk, I found a torn piece of paper from an artist's sketchbook. The unexpected note was not dated, but I recognized Ken's handwriting immediately. "Dearest wife and children, Forgot to tell you how much I love you—I do." My eyes filled with grateful tears.

Ken always said things happened for a reason. This gift that arrived without a date on the anniversary of his death was very special. It reminded me that I was loved deeply, I loved him in return, and our love became part of us forever—even when one left and the other moved toward a new life alone. Eventually, the pain of parting diminishes, but the love remains forever—like a timeless gift.

~Gloria Givens
Chicken Soup for the Grieving Soul

74

Saturday Mornings

First we are children to our parents,
then parents to our children,
then parents to our parents,
then children to our children.
~Milton Greenblatt

I hate it when that happens... you know, it's Saturday morning, and the only plans you have made are to sleep in; but you are suddenly brought into the day by the sound of a too-early phone call. There's no recapturing that wonderful feeling of being suspended between the past worries of yesterday and the eagerness of tomorrow. You're awake, and you might as well put your feet on the floor and begin the journey for today.

When we were first married, our Saturdays were spent mowing lawns or heading for the river to fish and picnic. Our family grew. Our treasured weekend time began with early morning feedings, giving baths in the bathroom or kitchen sinks and some great one-on-one time in coos, song or patty-cake.

As the boys grew, Saturdays were days you were awakened by cold, little noses pressing to your cheek. With their warm breath and in a faint whisper, they would cup your ear in their hands and say loving things like, "Mom, I can't reach the Count Chocula." Lesson well taken, you would rearrange the shelves so that the cereal was within their limited reach.

Assuming more responsible roles, the boys would get up, fix their cereal to hold them over until something warm, like pancakes, could be prepared. They would find solace in the only babysitter available at 7:00 on Saturday mornings and watch their favorite cartoons. They would keep the volume down, but their giggles and laughs would float down the hall to remind you that sleeping late was a definite thing of the past.

Saturdays were often filled with scouting events or school-related commitments. I remember the time we hiked four miles on a park trail and finally sat down at its end on the base of a monument bearing the inscription, "May they rest in peace." Or the Saturday soapbox race where one of the boys ran off the ramp at the start, dropping about three or four feet to the pavement. I prayed that wouldn't be an indication of his driving abilities later in life. There were river-raft races, ballgames, camping trips and our very favorite—high school band competitions. October was band month. Every weekend was a trip to some competition, and it always began early, early on Saturday morning.

When schedules did allow us to be at home on Saturday morning, it often turned into washing the dog, changing oil in the cars or their very favorite—cleaning their rooms. As any parent knows, cleaning the room of a teenager usually takes more than the morning hours. No matter how early they start, it seems they manage to draw it out through the entire day. This frequently results in a bit of banter about why this is necessary, as it will all have to be done over again next Saturday.

The boys are grown now. One's room has been

completely redecorated to accommodate guests, as he has moved with his sweet wife to another town. The other boy's room, while he's away at college, still bears evidence of his "youth" by posters, movie memorabilia and a massive Star Wars collection. The lights may go for days without even being turned on in their rooms. The carpet is visible, no clothes scattered here and there. The things on the shelves remain on the shelves in their respective places. The beds stay made for weeks.

So I guess I've come full circle. Saturday mornings are mine again. Sleep late, get up and sit on the screened-in porch with a cup of coffee and listening to music (my choice) on the local radio station. In all the quietness of the morning, I can read or write without interruption. If I choose to watch television, I can flip over the cartoons and go straight to the Discovery Channel. I don't have to watch for toys on the stairs or shoes in the hallway. The towels in the bathroom hang where I last put them, and the tub has no ring. The refrigerator is always full. Our kitchen cabinets aren't cluttered with cereals that are pink or multicolored. When I get in the car, the gas tank is full. The house is free of brotherly squabbles, no frantic schedules to meet, no emptying my wallet for gas money or spending money to take on trips. But you know what—I hate it when that happens.

~Andy Skidmore
Chicken Soup for the Mother and Son Soul

75

Cracking Up

After fifty years of marriage, her husband died. The widow painfully selected the granite marker to place over the gravesites reserved for them both. She gave instructions to put her name and birth date on the marker and also requested that wedding bands be placed between their names along with the year of their marriage.

The widow wanted the marker finished in time for their fifty-first wedding anniversary only a few weeks away. The marker would be the last gift she would give her husband. As workers at the cemetery monument company, we immediately ordered the special color granite she had chosen in hopes we could finish the marker in time.

The marker was finished ahead of schedule. When we called the widow to let her know, she told us she would like to come in to see it before we took it to the cemetery. The guys in the shop loaded the marker on the straps of the crane to place it where she could see it best. With no warning, the unthinkable happened. The marker slipped off the straps and fell to the ground, cracking in half!

Frantically, we were trying to figure out how we could finish another marker when the widow walked in. There she stood in front of us, fully expecting to see the beautiful marker she had so carefully chosen. Wild thoughts raced through our minds. Even though we knew we shouldn't lie, we wanted desperately to spare the feelings of a woman who had already suffered far too much grief. We stumbled for words and finally simply told her the truth.

We expected anger. We expected tears. We never expected laughter. But as soon as she saw the marker cracked perfectly in half, her solemn expression turned into one of amusement and then heartfelt laughter! Seeing our astonishment, she composed herself and explained, "At our wedding reception fifty-one years ago, my husband and I solemnly held the knife in our hands and cut into the wedding cake. The cake instantly cracked down the middle and broke in half.

"How fitting it is," she added, "that this happened to the marker. I really wanted my last gift to my husband to be something special, and it is. I have a feeling he's laughing right along with me, just like we did for those fifty-one years."

~Maureen S. Pusch
Chicken Soup for the Golden Soul

76

Pomp and Ceremony

And I'm proud to be an American,
where at least I know I'm free.
And I won't forget the men who died,
who gave that right to me.
~Lee Greenwood

My husband is enlisted in the Navy. We live in Hawai'i, on a tall, red-dirt hill that overlooks the electric blue waters of Pearl Harbor. In the evenings when the weather is fine, we watch the enormous sun set low over the bright white structure of the USS Arizona Memorial, its edges trimmed brilliant gold with the sunset's smokeless fire, and it brings to mind a story of my husband's.

As an act of respect and acknowledgment, when commissioned naval ships pass each other on the water, sailors stop what they are doing, stand at attention and salute the oncoming ship.

The sight is striking: Sailors line the upper deck while standing at attention and whistles blow to prompt the changing positions. It is quite an emotional moment, especially if one is a returning ship which has been away from an American port for a long time. The crisp white uniforms appear like pillars against a clear ocean sky as these enormous gray floating cities pass each other with magnificent dignity.

Once a young seaman recruit was out at sea for the first time. His ship had been in foreign waters for several months, and the crew was eager to touch American soil again. But none was more eager than the young seaman recruit. He disliked the daily grind of ship life, working every day and never seeing anything but the endless, flat blue ocean. He especially detested the ceremony and ritual of Navy life and the restrictive uniform. He simply couldn't see the point to all that pomp and ceremony.

Finally they were on their way home to the United States. He was looking forward to his freedom and time away from the monotony of ship life.

Their first stop was Hawai'i. The weather was perfect, and the ship's path was clear and open. The Pacific Ocean was calm, and there were no other naval ships around as far as the eye could see. All hands lined the deck, to "man the rails," as was the custom when heading into port.

But this time was different. A whistle blew over the loudspeaker, calling the sailors to attention. The seaman recruit was irritated at yet another pointless ritual. He couldn't understand why they had to do this when theirs was the only ship in sight. So he complained to the chief petty officer standing beside him.

"Why are we at attention when there's no other ship around?" he asked.

"But there is a commissioned ship around," the senior man replied. "And we are honoring this ship as we would any other."

All the seaman recruit could see was the bright white arching structure of the USS Arizona Memorial.

"But, it's just a museum," he countered. "That ship sank fifty years ago!"

The chief petty officer continued to stare straight ahead, his hand now saluting. "The USS Arizona is still a commissioned ship, seaman recruit, and there are more than 1,100 men still entombed in it. They are all U.S. sailors, and you will treat them as such."

The chief petty officer did not move his head, but the seaman recruit could see the emotion in his eyes. "My grandfather is one of them," he added, his voice hoarse but steady.

The gray carrier dotted with bright images of several thousand sailors standing at attention gently eased into Pearl Harbor. The seaman recruit stared at the ocean surface. Then, as he stood straight and tall, eyes now cast ahead, his hand set in a firm salute, he wondered if there had ever been a more beautiful sight.

~Nicole Hayes
Chicken Soup from the Soul of Hawai'i

Love, Leo

I t wasn't fair! Leo, my devoted husband who was seldom sick, was diagnosed with acute leukemia in 1991, at the age of fifty-nine. Twenty-three days later, just before our thirty-fifth anniversary, he died. We were counting on so many more years together! We didn't have enough warning!

The daughter of a pastor, I couldn't remember a time when I didn't feel close to God. But I never felt further from him than now. I wanted to cling to him, but I was so bitter that he would allow somebody as strong as Leo to die, and leave someone as emotionally fragile as I. Well-meaning friends gave me a print of Jesus welcoming a man into heaven with open arms. Sometimes I put it out of sight and ranted at God, "You've had Leo long enough! I need him more than you do!"

Leo and I had truly been one—I felt ripped apart. Another widow told me it would be three years before I began to feel whole. "Lord, will the pain always be this intense?" I anguished. "I need to feel your love! I need to feel Leo's!"

I lived on automatic pilot, going to my nursing job, coming home to my Leoless house. Every problem seemed overwhelming. One morning I saw ants in the kitchen; Leo used to get rid of any ants. I grabbed a broom and jabbed at them futilely, growing angrier and angrier, screaming, "Leo, where are you? You belong here!" I flung open the back door and wailed into my suburban backyard. A neighbor rushed over, asking, "Is anything wrong?"

"No, I just have to scream," I answered, crumpling at the enormity of my loss.

Leo and I had grown to love each other deeply, but we weren't really in love on our wedding day in 1956; we hardly even knew each other! Poor, dear Leo. We married unaware that we were opposites. He was immaculate—almost perfect!—and assumed his nurse wife was also; cobwebs didn't faze me. He loved classical music; I fell asleep at the first concert he took me to. He was a gourmet cook; I rotated the ten recipes I used as a bride. He was reserved; I hugged spontaneously.

Our first years of marriage, Leo was not demonstrative. I desperately needed to hear him say "I love you," but he couldn't bring himself to say it. He'd say, "I like you—isn't that enough?"

After we'd been married about twenty years, we attended a marriage renewal retreat. The leaders encouraged us to write each other a love letter, mail the two letters in about a month, read them, and hide them to rediscover later. Leo wrote a beautiful letter full of words he found difficult to say in person. From that time on, he had no trouble telling me he loved me.

But now he was gone.

I couldn't bear to part with Leo's belongings. Any scrap with his handwriting—even doodling—was precious to me. A graphic arts professor, he was a man of many interests. I spotted, on his desk, the conductor's baton our three children and I had given him because he loved to conduct the invisible orchestras of his Bach and other tapes. I cried at that and mementos of his love of sailing and photography. A new wave of grief assaulted me with each reminder.

I went to our room and splashed some of Leo's cologne on me so our bed would smell like him. I glanced down wistfully at our pillows. Leo and I used to clip out cartoons and leave them on each other's pillows. One of my last ones to him was a woman kneeling by a bed praying, "Dear God, make Mr. Perfect do just one thing wrong!"

We had lots to tease each other about. Because my purse had been stolen twice, I was obsessive about keeping it nearby. Leo and the kids said they were going to have "Where's my purse?" engraved on my tombstone.

Two years went by, and I screamed less and less. One day I opened a cookbook and found a valentine from Leo I had used as a bookmark. Another day while shopping I saw a sailboat-shaped picture frame that reminded me of my beloved sailor and shutterbug. I bought the frame, put it on the TV and inserted one of Leo's spectacular sunsets. I gazed fondly, not weeping.

Another day I was going through the pockets of Leo's blazer, finally able to give it away, when I found in the breast pocket a cartoon of archaeologists unearthing a mummy with a purse and exclaiming, "It is! It is! It's the mummy's purse!" I laughed out loud, knowing Leo intended to put this on my pillow.

A realization startled me: A reminder of Leo had brought not tears, but a chuckle.

Shortly afterward, I was cleaning out a cardboard-lined dresser drawer where I keep scarves. I glimpsed a long envelope under the cardboard and felt a surge of warmth at the familiar curve of Leo's handwriting. I shivered. It took my breath away. This was the letter Leo had written after the couples retreat fourteen years before! I eagerly dug out the sheet of paper and my eyes hungrily devoured "Dearest Doris..."

Leo quoted the poet Shelley's "One word is too often profaned/For me to profane it" and went on to say, "I truly do love you in all of the true meaning of the word—even if I am negligent or hesitant to say it—I love you—We are as one and I must put forth the effort to make this a more complete oneness... We were united in Christ's name and together we will grow in Christ's Love. Amen—Let it be so.

"With Everlasting Love —
Leo (Just me)"

I was ecstatic! I needed this affirmation so badly. I clutched the letter to me and carried it from room to room, stopping every now and then to reread its words. Words I don't think I could have handled right after Leo's death, but ones that brought healing now. I folded the letter carefully and tucked it into my ever-present purse to open often. Just reading it makes me smile.

I still feel incomplete. But I feel surrounded by God's and Leo's love. When something reminds me of Leo, there's a little less grief and a little more gratitude for what we had. My eyes get watery, but I can control it better now.

And sometimes I even laugh.

~Doris Delventhal as told to B. J. Connor
Chicken Soup for the Single's Soul

Older &
Wiser

Gratitude

*The only people with whom you should try to get even are
those who have helped you.*
~John E. Southard

78

Mrs. Frieda Moves

I've seen and met angels wearing
the disguise of ordinary people living ordinary lives.
~Tracy Chapman

On my calendar in Thursday's space is written, "Mrs. Frieda moves." Avoiding this melancholy matter had almost convinced me everything would continue as always. But the day I've been dreading for so long has arrived. The phone rings. Frieda wonders if I could come over for a few minutes; she wants to say goodbye.

When my husband and I moved into the neighborhood ten years ago, Thomas was almost a year old and Barrett was four. Frieda, a sweet elderly widow who lives next door, grew fond of our children and tolerated their typically boyish behavior with an astonishing amount of good-natured grace.

When Barrett was six or seven, he decided on a whim to see if a rock, when hurled over our fence, could land on Frieda's roof. It did not. With a mighty crash, it collided with her living room window. Frieda was in a bedroom in the back of the house and almost suffered heart failure on the spot. But when I marched Barrett over to apologize, the corners of her mouth trembled with an ill-concealed smile, and she said, "I wasn't worried; it didn't break, but if it did, I knew you'd look after it."

The boys decided that Mrs. Frieda, as we christened her, has a better driveway than ours for hockey. It is shared with the people living next to her and, as a result, is wonderfully wide. The boisterous game at some point spilled over into her yard and before Mrs. Frieda knew it, her property became a giant rink filled with shouting boys, hockey sticks, pucks and nets. I wasn't aware of this development until she phoned me to say that hockey is a healthy exercise, and the boys are very good at it, but she was a little concerned for her shrubs.

On hot summer nights, Barrett would sleep out in a tent with his friends, and in the morning, I would see it set up over at Mrs. Frieda's. Thomas went through a bow-and-arrow phase and homemade arrows regularly littered her lawn and impaled her shrubbery. At Halloween she would shower my kids with goodies. Those minitreats wouldn't do for Mrs. Frieda; she filled their bags with full-size chocolate bars, bags of chips and cans of pop.

Her affection was returned enthusiastically. Without being asked, the boys would often shovel her driveway, their little arms straining to push the heavy snow. They took her garbage out to the curb faithfully every Thursday morning on their way to school. One day, I searched everywhere for Thomas only to find him in Mrs. Frieda's backyard, helping her rake leaves and stuff them into bags. I made them deliver countless dinners. "What do you have for me today?" she always asked and the boys would dutifully recite the menu. She sent them back with packets of instant oatmeal, eucalyptus throat lozenges and cans of fruit cocktail, lingering at her door to watch them peering into the bag as they hurried home.

One sleet-filled night, Thomas went over to Mrs. Frieda's with a huge piece of cherry cheesecake and fell. He came back covered in cheesecake, crying and carrying an empty plate. In the morning, we saw cherries, chunks of cake and pieces of graham cracker crust all over the sidewalk; for days, this unappetizing conglomeration remained congealed and frozen in the ice. Years later, all Thomas has to say is "Remember the cheesecake?" and we burst out laughing.

Sitting in Mrs. Frieda's kitchen for the last time, chatting about the nursing home she'll be moving into at two o'clock, my eyes fill with tears. Her hair, freshly cut, curled and colored an unusual shade of taupe, is held firmly in place by a shiny brown net. Her green cardigan is buttoned up to the neck and a mustard yellow blouse peeks out over the top. Her wedding rings are too loose on her thin fingers and her breathing is shallow and rapid, but she smiles that precious smile I love so much and asks me if I'd like a cookie. She has packed a tin of salmon, a box of pudding mix and a piece of leftover Christmas cake for me.

Her things are waiting by the door. Such a meager, lonely assortment, an inadequate sum of a richly significant life. A small blue suitcase stands upright, tarnished locks clipped shut. A worn plaid mohair coat lies over the back of a chair. An ancient alarm clock and some toiletries are set out beside her oxygen equipment.

Life is filled with these heart-wrenching chapters, yet turning their pages never seems to become any easier. Mrs. Frieda's sight is failing; she doesn't notice me wiping my eyes as she puts together her talking-book tapes and asks me to mail them back to the Canadian National Institute for the Blind if it's not too inconvenient.

I should be glad; she is moving down the street into a

new facility where she'll be well cared for, and I will visit her often, but something dear is slipping from my grasp. Mrs. Frieda is the reason my children have learned to appreciate and enjoy the elderly. She is why they think of others. She is why they believe neighbors should be kind to each other. Such priceless lessons they have learned trudging up the sidewalk with plates of food and dragging bags of garbage out to the curb. Mrs. Frieda has thanked me often for my generosity, but she has given me something far greater than I could ever give her—the opportunity to teach my children how to be beautiful human beings.

~Rachel Wallace-Oberle
Chicken Soup to Inspire the Body & Soul

79

At Every Turn

Help and support one another,
is part of the religion of sisterhood.
~Louisa May Alcott

I was an only child, hungry for siblings. I confess that I harbored envy toward my cousins. They had sisters, built-in playmates. I had none. I kept asking my parents for a sister. Even a baby brother would do. But they never listened. Okay. So I'd have to find my own sister. I could do that.

My first sister was my imaginary playmate. Punky urged me to act on my fantasies. We wandered the fields and climbed the leafy cottonwoods along the irrigation ditches. Late at night we held whispered conferences about the day. Punky encouraged me to resist parental control and share my adventuring exclusively with her. We never told about the kittens we rescued from the bottom of the outhouse. My father never understood why the sheep ran from me when I entered their pens. Who would've thought sheep could remember who chased them? And my mother asked, but neither Punky nor I ever answered her questions about the sudden decline in egg production. Watching hens flutter in fright from their nests was so entertaining. Punky and I were inseparable. But then the yellow school bus stopped for me. And Punky was left behind.

At school, I discovered hanging from the monkey bars and swinging across the rocky ground. Susie brushed me off when I fell from those bars and led me to the nurse's office for repairs. From then on, we were inseparable. We ate lunch together. We fended off marauding cowboys who rode up to us on stick horses. Clutching Dick and Jane books to our bony chests, we ached for a kitten as cute as Puff or a dog as lively as Spot. We ate our first tacos and watched crawdads lay eggs and reproduce in the class aquarium. Life was rich.

In high school, my circle of sisterhood widened. On Saturday afternoons, my sister friends and I shopped at Joplin's, stroking pastel mohair sweaters while assuring ourselves that the pleats of our woolen skirts were knife sharp. Lipstick and secret information about the heartthrob of the day were freely shared. We spent hours teasing our hair and consoling each other when pimples threatened our social life. A secret ride home in a hot rod '57 Chevy was later dissected moment by moment, with freeze-frame precision. We went to Saturday night movies together but separated in the darkness to meet unnamed boys who set our hearts afire. Relationships flowered, and we burst forth like a garden of color in our taffeta formals, wrists corsage decorated. We celebrated love and learned how to fill a senior ring with layers of white glue coated with fingernail polish so it would fit our thin fingers. And we cried together when love ended. Throughout it all, our circle of sisterhood survived, a little scratched but intact.

My collegiate sisters came from different places and offered me glimpses of other lives. We shared the thrills of fending off frostbite while wearing miniskirts and navigating icy sidewalks in stacked leather heel boots. We giggled as we threw panties at the last-ever panty raid and caught mashed potatoes in a cafeteria food fight. We sampled beer served from a pony keg out in the boonies and worried that we might not get back to our dorms before the doors were locked for the night. Professors extolled the philosophy of Kant and Aristotle. We wondered why we should care about these ancient philosophers when Bob Dylan sang his messages. Candles passed in the sorority announced the receipt of love in the form of a lavaliere, pin or, the ultimate, an engagement ring. Then it was graduation, and we moved back to our own worlds.

I have been blessed with adult sisters who have mentored and shared my travails as a wife, mother and teacher. We supported each other through childbirth, breastfeeding, divorces and career changes. While our children played in the dappled light of a spring day, we drank high-octane fruit juice and giggled. On camping trips we shared cooking duties, wiping s'more-coated children with cold mountain spring water while our husbands sipped the same cold water, only theirs was brewed in the Rocky Mountains. We baked Christmas cookies and traded them at cookie swaps. When our aging parents orphaned us, upsetting our world order, tears and hugs gave comfort like no words could. We released pent-up sighs of relief when our own children successfully moved into adulthood. And we shared advice on transforming newly embraced daughters- and sons-in-law from strangers into family without alienating them or ourselves. We listened to tales about recalcitrant bosses and professional successes.

At every turn, I have found my sisters. They have flowed through my life, renewing and enriching me with their presence. And I can't wait to meet the next one. I think she just moved in next door. Wonder if she likes to climb trees?

~Lee Schafer Atonna
Chicken Soup for the Sister's Soul

80

Gratitude

I climb up a mountain to breathe in the air,
    and leave behind, with each step,
    one more useless care.
The sun ripples like laughter across the wide sea.
I smile at a flower and it smiles back at me.
The wind lifts a scent from the meadow below,
    and reminds me of the first girl I kissed,
    long ago.
I kneel in the heather, feel my spirit expand.
A bright butterfly stops to rest on my hand.
The clouds, ever present, yet no two the same,
    give lively imaginations a game.
"Look! A sailboat! A rabbit! An angel! A swan!"

And it's the best kind of game because no one's
    ever wrong.
Everyone should have a secret place like my hill,
    just to rest and let the mind roam free
    where it will,
    far away from the traffic,
    the noise and the dust,
    in the crystal clear sunshine of a world
    they can trust.

Turn your heart to the beauty
    that's in and around you.
Walk gently, with love,
    and the same will surround you.
You will surely see further the farther you go,
    and remember,
    it's pain which helps us to grow.
For with all of its sadness, its heartache and strife,
    with all of its sorrow, it's a wonderful life.
Yes, with all of its sorrow, it's a wonderful life.

~Mark Rickerby
Chicken Soup to Inspire the Body & Soul

81

The Doorman

Gratitude is the memory of the heart.
~Jean Baptiste Massieu

The year was 1945. World War II had blessedly and finally ended in Europe. Thousands of young men were moved from the battlefields to Paris. There they waited for the day they would be sent to the Pacific to once again risk their lives.

Every one of the soldiers was scarred from the horrors he had seen and of which he had been a part. Kindness, quiet and peace were the medicines necessary to heal their wounds, at least enough to pick up their guns once again.

My husband, Gene, was one of those men. Though he was decorated several times for bravery, war was foreign to his heart. Perhaps this was why he was particularly drawn to the French, who are people of tremendous personal warmth.

The hotel he was billeted in, Hotel Napoleon, was located in the heart of Paris. The elevator was a cage with pulley ropes, and the rooms were clean but simple. The hotel's most impressive feature was its doorman, Monsieur Jean Fratoni. His job was to stand outside the hotel and to open the doors for the guests. He would greet each visitor with "Bienvenue à Paris" ("Welcome to Paris"), spoken in his rich baritone.

Monsieur Fratoni was particularly kind to the American soldiers. He treated every young serviceman as a special friend, almost like a son. He remembered their names and was not above hugging them from time to time. They had liberated his country, and he loved them for it.

Happily, the war ended in the Pacific before the soldiers in Europe had to go. Instead, they were sent home. When they left Paris and Hotel Napoleon, many shared tearful goodbyes with Monsieur Fratoni.

Forty years later, on his sixtieth birthday, Gene wanted to run the Paris Marathon, so we went to Europe. Gene hadn't been back since the war. Finally, with my emotional support, he was ready to see the towns he'd helped to set free; to travel the roads he'd walked while German soldiers on the hills on either side of the road had fired on them, picking the American soldiers off like flies; to visit cemeteries where so many of his buddies lay buried. It was a highly emotional tour, but the pinnacle was yet to come.

When we finally arrived in Paris, we went to register Gene for the upcoming marathon at an American-owned hotel. We thought we'd probably stay there as so many of the runners were doing. But then Gene had an idea: "Let's find Hotel Napoleon and stay there."

It sounded good to me. We got in the car, and after asking directions, we found it. But it was not at all what we expected. In 1945, it had been a simple hotel, definitely of the no-frills variety. Now Hotel Napoleon was one of the finest, most elegant hotels in all of Paris.

"Oh boy, it sure has changed. Must be very expensive." Gene said this softly, but there was something in his voice—I could hear how touched he was just being there.

Listening to my heart, I said, "Oh, but it's so beautiful, and to think, you stayed in this very place all those years ago. Let's at least check it out."

We pulled the car up to the curb next to the hotel and sat there, just looking. Suddenly Gene drew in a breath and whispered, "Ohhhhh."

I watched as a very old gentleman bowed and opened Gene's door. "Bienvenue à Paris," he said in a tremulous but rich baritone. Gene seemed suspended in time as he stared at the man's face. Finally, he stepped out of our car and stood facing the doorman.

I saw tears well in Gene's eyes as he placed his hands on the man's stooped shoulders. Swallowing hard, he said simply, "You were here during World War II, weren't you?"

The man nodded, holding his body very still. Gene continued, "So was I. I was one of the soldiers who lived at the Hotel Napoleon, and you were so kind to me. My name is Brody."

The old gentleman searched Gene's face and then threw up his hands and, with trembling arms, enfolded my husband, repeating over and over, "Je me rappelle, cher ami. I remember."

Finally, at Monsieur Fratoni's insistence, they gathered up the baggage and went inside. The hotel was very expensive, but they found us a tiny room with a bath that we felt we could afford. As we presented the clerk with our credit card, Monsieur Fratoni left us and went to speak briefly to an official-looking man. When we were taken to our room, it was not the "least room in the inn" but, rather, an elegant suite with antique furniture and priceless rugs.

When we said there was some mistake, Gene's friend shook his head. To Monsieur Fratoni, Gene was still the young soldier who had liberated his beloved France. The old gentleman just smiled and said, "Seulement le mieux pour vous" ("Only the best for you").

~Jean P. Brody
Chicken Soup for the Veteran's Soul

We've Got Mail

A child needs a grandparent, anybody's grandparent,
to grow a little more securely into an unfamiliar world.
~Charles and Ann Morse

A small blur flew a few scant millimeters past my nose. "I don't eat these!" Mrs. Clara Anthony wailed. This spry eighty-six-year-young resident of the Golden Years Nursing Center had quite a reputation. Glancing down at my feet, I discovered a single-serving box of cornflakes that she had just launched from her bed.

It was my first day on the job as the new activity director, fresh from college and full of ideas. I was determined to give my residents more than the traditional three Bs of nursing-home activities: Bibles, Baskets and Bingo.

Every attempt I made to pry Mrs. Anthony out of her bed and socialize with others met with failure. She would lift her glasses to her eyes and say, "I don't do those things." Shopping trips, travelogues, drama club—nothing could budge Clara.

"She's a crotchety old cuss," said Annie, a nurse's aide. "She could join in on the activities, but she prefers to sit in her dark room and wait for mail."

"Mail?" I asked.

"Ever since her only son and his family moved to Texas,

all Mrs. Anthony does is wait on mail. She misses them somethin' fierce."

Each week saw more and more residents up, dressed and ready to participate in the "goings-on," but Mrs. Anthony continued to withdraw.

"I give up," I admitted to Pam, the Adult Basic Education teacher. "I don't know what to do."

"You must be talking about Clara Anthony," said Rachel, my assistant.

"Gary, Mrs. Anthony's only interested in mail. If a day passes without a letter, watch out!" added Pam.

"What do you mean?" I asked.

Rachel replied, "If either Pam or I pass her room empty-handed, she throws the nearest thing."

"I've seen books, cups, even flowers come sailing out of her room," added Pam.

"She sounds unhappy," I speculated.

"Unhappy?" Rachel said incredulously. "After she's thrown out half her room, she breaks down in writhing sobs."

"She misses her grandchildren," Pam mused.

Several days later, I walked into the activity room amid boisterous giggles. Rachel, Pam and a dozen residents were trying on an assortment of baseball caps. "Where did these come from?" I inquired. "There must be hundreds."

"A hundred and twenty, to be exact," replied Robert, a retired airline pilot, who visited regularly to do travelogues for our residents.

"After the residents told me about the garden club and their need to wear hats in the sun, I decided to clean out my closets," said Robert. The unused caps were emblazoned with a variety of emblems.

"Hey, check me out, Gary. I'm a mailman." Stephen

grinned as he displayed his new blue cap with the words "U.S. Mail" affixed across the front. This ten-year-old son of a staff nurse would occasionally volunteer and help with arts and crafts.

As I stared at his cap, Rachel asked, "What's wrong?"

"Rachel, have you delivered today's mail to the residents yet?"

"No. Why?"

"I've got an idea. Stephen, would you like to be our new mailman?" Stephen nodded in agreement.

Pam asked, "Gary, what are you doing?"

"Mrs. Anthony loves getting mail, and she misses her grandkids. Why not let Stephen deliver her mail?"

"But she doesn't always get mail," Rachel pointed out. "Besides, I don't think Stephen really wants a pillow thrown at him."

"Why don't we see?" I concluded.

As luck would have it, Mrs. Anthony did have a letter that day. Stephen donned his mailcap, and Rachel, Pam and I trooped down the hallway to Clara's room together.

"We can't all go in," I warned, stopping in front of her door. "Knock first, Stephen, then go in."

Stephen tapped twice on Clara's door.

A delicate voice responded, "Come in."

"I've got mail for you, Mrs. Anthony," Stephen said proudly.

"Oh my, what have we here? Aren't you a dear."

"She wouldn't be saying that if he didn't have a letter," Pam whispered.

"Hush!" I hissed, leaning closer to the half-open door. Looking more like a covert CIA operative, I whispered, "I'm trying to listen."

Clara continued, "What grade are you in?"

"Fourth grade," replied Stephen.

"I taught school for forty years."

"Wow! I'd sure hate to be in school that long," Stephen quipped.

The laughter spilled into the hallway as the three of us stood spellbound by the sudden change in Mrs. Anthony.

"What's your name?" Clara inquired.

"Stephen."

"Would you read my letter to me, Stephen? My eyes aren't so good."

"Sure."

Rachel broke the silence in the hallway. "Gary, there's nothing wrong with her eyes."

"Shh... it doesn't matter," I whispered. "It's working."

"What's working?" Pam asked.

Pointing toward Clara's room I said, "Look."

Peering around the corner, we saw Stephen reading to Clara. Her smile spoke a thousand words.

"Thank you, dear," Clara said after Stephen finished.

"You're welcome. I'll come back tomorrow if you get another letter."

"You don't have to wait for me to get mail, Stephen. Come any time. In fact, I have a grandson just about your age."

"You do?"

"Yes, but he lives in Texas. I don't see him much anymore."

"That's sad. I miss my Nana, too."

"Where is your grandmother, Stephen?"

"She's gone to heaven." Stephen hesitated for a moment before asking, "Would you be my Nana?"

Clara chuckled. "Oh my. How would your mother feel about that?"

"She wouldn't mind. She works here."

"Well, honey, you come visit me any time."

No mail came for Clara over the next few days, but the staff began to notice a dramatic change taking place.

"She quit throwing things," Rachel reported.

Pam added, "And she stopped crying all the time."

While the staff and I discussed Mrs. Anthony in my office behind closed doors, we heard a gentle knock. "Come in," I said.

Stephen smiled and said timidly, "Hi."

As he opened the door we heard a familiar feminine voice. "I hope we're not disturbing you." There sat Clara in her wheelchair with Stephen at the helm, both of them wearing "U.S. Mail" caps.

"We're off to deliver the mail," Stephen proclaimed proudly. "Aren't we, Mrs. Anthony?"

She winked at us and smiled. "Yes... that is... if it's all right?"

We were speechless. In one week, Clara had gone from a sullen, sorrowful recluse to a smiling social butterfly.

After a few seconds, I managed to say, "Rachel, please give them the mail."

The mailbag perched in Mrs. Anthony's lap, Stephen announced, "Come on. We've got mail to deliver."

"Let's ride!" Mrs. Anthony shouted.

We heard the pair chanting as they disappeared down the hall. "Through rain, sleet... snow."

Pam uttered, "How about that?"

"Amazing," I added.

Stephen and Clara became a common sight. When they weren't delivering mail, Clara helped Stephen with his homework. When they weren't too busy, he showed Clara how to play Nintendo.

Stephen became our first volunteer to "Adopt a Grandparent." While he couldn't replace Clara's grandson, just as Clara couldn't replace Stephen's grandmother, they discovered the value of a little time and love between two people.

~Gary K. Farlow
Chicken Soup for the Volunteer's Soul

EDITORS' NOTE: For information on Adopt-A-Grandparent Foundation, visit the Website: www.adopt-a-grandparent. org.

Handmade Valentines from the Heart

I was the tender age of sixteen and my husband was only seventeen when we were married in 1966 in Welch, West Virginia. There weren't many jobs available in our small town. We had been married only two months when my husband found out that Trailways Bus Lines was taking applications for various positions.

My husband drove one hundred miles to Roanoke, Virginia, to apply for a job with the bus company. They contacted him the next week to come back to take a test that was one of the requirements for being hired. So once again, he drove the one hundred miles to take the test. A few weeks later, he was notified that he had been accepted to a position as an apprentice mechanic. This offer was a great opportunity for us, but I was heartbroken when I found out that the job was in Roanoke and that we would have to move. We knew no one who lived there. It was very hard for me to move so far from my family and friends at such a young age. We found a small furnished apartment, and I was lucky to find a job as a sales clerk at Woolworth's during the day, but my husband was scheduled to work

324   Gratitude: *Handmade Valentines from the Heart*

from midnight to 8 A.M. So as he came home from work each morning, I was getting ready to leave to go to work.

Naturally, we had very little money, so when Valentine's Day came around that first year, I knew we couldn't afford to buy anything for each other. I felt so bad that I wouldn't be able to buy him a present—not even a card.

After he left to go to work the night before Valentine's Day, I couldn't sleep. So I decided to stay up and make a Valentine's Day card for him. I didn't have any construction paper, so I had to use regular notebook paper. I worked so hard to compose a poem for him. I knew what I wanted to say, but I couldn't seem to put it on paper. It took me most of the night, and by the time he came home the next morning it was done!

I had made a valentine for my valentine. I felt foolish and childish as I handed him my homemade valentine, hoping that he wouldn't laugh at it. I held my breath and watched as he opened it and started reading it. On the front of the simple piece of paper, I had written the following:

We may not have a lot of money
To buy a card that's cute and funny.
But what we have can take the place
Of a paper heart with fancy lace.
We have each other, and that's the best,
Now open the card and read the rest.

On the inside, I had colored a large red heart and written "I Love You." I stood waiting and watching, afraid that he would start laughing at any moment. When he had finished reading it, he slowly raised his head and looked at me. Then the corners of his mouth started moving up! But all he did was smile tenderly.

While looking into my eyes, he reached down into his pocket. When he pulled his hand out, he was holding something. He told me that he had made it for me during his lunch hour, but he had been afraid to give it to me. He said that he thought I might think it was silly, and that I might laugh at it.

I took his hand in mine and turned it over. As I looked down, he slowly opened his fingers, and I saw a small heart made out of aluminum. While I had stayed up all night making him a valentine card, he had been cutting out a heart for me from a piece of aluminum. He said the guys he worked with had laughed at him for making the heart, and he'd been worried about giving it to me.

I still have the aluminum heart, and I keep it in my desk. Every once in a while when I open the drawer and see it lying there, all those memories come flooding back to me. Over the years, we've been able to buy each other very nice, expensive presents for Valentine's Day. But none has ever been as dear or meant as much as those hand-made gifts made from our hearts the first year that we were married.

~Evelyn Wander
Chicken Soup for the Romantic Soul

The Greatest Gift

Having a sister is like having a best friend you can't get rid of.
You know whatever you do, they'll still be there.
~Amy Li

I'm five years old, and my mother is on her hands and knees, washing the kitchen floor. I'm telling her about a new girl in school, and she suddenly looks up at me and says, "Who are your two best friends?"

I'm not sure what to say. I've been friends with Jill since I was three or so, and I really like Jaime, a friend in kindergarten.

"Jill and Jaime."

My mother stops scrubbing the floor and starts to take off her yellow rubber gloves. "Well, what about Karen and Cindy?"

My sisters? "I don't know who their best friends are," I say.

"No," she says. "I'm saying, why aren't they your best friends?"

She seems upset, like I hurt her feelings. "But they're my sisters."

"Yes, but they can still be your best friends. Friends may come and go, but your sisters will always be there for you."

At the time, the idea of my two sisters being my closest friends seemed strange to me. We fought all the time over toys, food, attention, what to watch on television—you name it, we bickered about it at some point. How could my sisters be my best friends? They weren't the same age as I. We all had our own friends in school.

But my mother never let the three of us forget it: Sisters are lifelong friends. Her wish—like most parents'—was to give us something that she never had. Growing up an only child, she longed for siblings. When she gave birth to three daughters—separated by only four years—the fufillment of her dream had only just begun. She had given us each a gift—our sisters—and she wanted to make sure we did not take that gift for granted. She would frequently tell us how lucky we were. But there were other, more subtle ways that she encouraged us to grow closer. She never showed favoritism to one daughter over the other, as not to cause jealousy or bitterness between sisters. She constantly took us places together—skating, shopping, swimming—so we developed common interests. And when we were teenagers, Mom always punished us equally, giving us yet another bonding experience.

We didn't always get along beautifully and fought just like any other siblings. But somewhere in between Mom's lectures, the family vacations and the shared memories, we realized that our mother was right. Today I share things with my sisters that I do with no one else. My sister Cindy and I ran the New York City Marathon together, side-by-side, even holding hands when we crossed the finish line. When my sister Karen got married, I was her maid of honor. Cindy and I traveled through Europe together and even shared an apartment for two years. The three of us trust each other with our greatest secrets.

It was twenty-three years ago that my mother first asked me who my two best friends were. Today she doesn't have to. She already knows.

~Christine Many
Chicken Soup for the Sister's Soul

85

Two Rockers

A sister can be seen as someone
who is both ourselves and very much not ourselves—
a special kind of double.
~Toni Morrison

My sister has two rockers.
She lives in Tennessee
And when I go to visit her
We rock and sip on tea.

The color of her rockers?
A dusty shade of blue.
They're on the porch, beside the door
Where all the folks walk through.

At times we both drink Passionfruit.
At times we sip Earl Grey,
As on the porch we rock and watch
The seasons pass away.

We've talked about our children
We've laughed and cried together
We've sat with sun upon our laps
We've rocked in rainy weather.

Dear Lord, please save two rockers
On the porch called "Glorious Day."
Make hers Eternal Passionfruit.
Make mine the King's Earl Grey.

~Charlotte A. Lanham
Chicken Soup for the Soul Celebrates Sisters

Older & Wiser

Chapter 10

Yes, I Can

Nobody can go back and start a new beginning,
but anyone can start today and make a new ending.
~Maria Robinson

86

It's Never Too Late

There is a time for everything,
and a season for every activity under heaven.
~Ecclesiastes 3:1

Character consists of what you do on the third and fourth tries.

We can all appreciate that "Behind every successful man is a good woman." But sometimes it works the other way around, as in the case of devoted husband Norman Klein. Norm is an accomplished distance runner. It wasn't always so, until one day he accepted a friend's challenge to run a ten-mile race. Norman accepted the challenge, but then he did something else: He encouraged his wife, Helen, to train with him for the race.

The rest is running history.

This story is about Helen—she takes the spotlight, which is fine with Norm. But as you read, remember the quiet hero, the strong, supportive husband (and he cooks, too!)—a dream guy, an oral surgeon whose fitness level is also the envy of many younger folks—the good man behind the amazing success story of Helen Klein.

Let's jump to present time: Helen recently broke the world marathon record in her age group—the eighty- to eighty-five-year-old class—completing the 26.2-mile run in four hours and thirty-one minutes. Maybe that's why she was labeled by one magazine as "Grambo." Or why Dr. Kenneth Cooper, who made aerobics a household word, calls her "legendary" and her accomplishments "unbelievable human feats."

Helen views herself as "an ordinary person with extraordinary desire."

Here are a few highlights of Helen Klein's remarkable achievements: At age sixty-six, Helen ran five 100-mile mountain trail races within sixteen weeks. In 1991, she ran across the state of Colorado in five days and ten hours, setting the world record for the 500K. She also holds a world age-group record in the 100-mile run, has completed more than sixty marathons and nearly 140 ultramarathons. In 1995, still getting younger, Helen ran 145 miles across the Sahara desert; in 1995 she completed the 370-mile Eco Challenge, running with Team Operation Smile, for a charity that does reconstructive surgery free of charge for indigent children.

As you read this story, Helen is now running through her eighth decade—marathons, ultramarathons, and the grueling twenty-four-hour runs, forty-eight-hour runs and six-day runs of 100 miles or more. That's when life teaches you a few things about yourself. For example, in the legendary Eco Challenge, endurance athletes from around the world strive to complete a grueling, ten-day, multisports event. Here is what Helen did in the Eco Challenge: rode thirty-six miles on horseback; hiked ninety miles through broiling desert heat; negotiated eighteen miles through freezing, water-filled canyons; mountain-biked thirty miles; rappelled down a 440-foot cliff; climbed 1,200 feet straight up; paddled ninety miles on a river raft; hiked another twenty miles; and, finally, canoed fifty miles to the finish line. "I would never have completed the Eco Challenge as an individual—only as a team member," Helen commented.

"Well, she's just a genetic anomaly," you might say. "One of those people born under a running star—luck of the DNA draw—one of the gifted ones. What does this have to do with me?"

As it turns out, a lot.

Helen was not always an athlete. On the contrary. Helen says, "Raised by a mom who abhorred sweat and believed that little girls must be ladylike and domestic at all times, I was programmed to believe I'd be an old lady who couldn't walk a mile, who played bridge for sport and went to luncheons. So I studied to become a nurse, married, and had four children, and refrained from exerting myself so as not to perspire." That is, until she turned fifty-five.

Helen was a nurse who had smoked for twenty-five years and never run a mile in her life. But the year she turned fifty-five, her husband, Norm, challenged her to train with him for a ten-mile run. She agreed to try it out, but wasn't so sure after running about a fifth of a mile. She was exhausted and panting from two laps on a track they had marked off in their backyard. "I thought I would die," she said. But the next day it was a little easier, and she ran one lap farther. One lap more each day, and in ten weeks she completed the ten-mile race. She finished last, but thought it was "cool." Spurred on by this success, Helen entered other "short" races, but soon realized she was not blessed with blazing speed. So she decided to try longer, slower marathons.

Since those days, Helen has crashed on her mountain bike, fallen asleep on her feet while running through the night, run through snow for twenty-six miles of a 100-mile race, faced pounding rain and 100-degree heat. Helen's mantra: "Relax and move. Relax and move." She adds, "When I had to drop out of my first attempt to run the Western States 100, I said that I would never do it again. But soon enough I struck the world 'never' from my vocabulary—except to remind others of one of the great lessons of my life: 'It's never too late.'"

During one six-day run, Helen covered 373 miles. There were plenty of times she could have quit, and many excuses she could have used. But she thought, "If I want to reach my goal, I'd better push past the excuses and think only about how great the results will feel." Helen has often said that if she had been told years ago that she would be where she is today, she would have laughed.

And she has laughed many times in her running career. Like the time Helen and a friend were running along a mountain trail and came across two fellow runners within the span of a few minutes. The first one exclaimed, "Helen, you have the legs of a twenty-year-old!" A short while later, the second runner said, "Helen, you have the legs of a thirty-year-old!" Helen turned to her running partner and said, "I may have to give up running—apparently, I've aged ten years in the last mile."

But it's not all laughter by any means. "I've felt fear many times," she says. "I fear riding a bike, and getting on a horse. But I will not run from fear... I will not let myself give in to the panic stage. I know for certain that anyone without physical disabilities could do what I do. They only need a little push—a challenge. I am not coordinated and have absolutely no talent for running. All I get by on is desire and determination."

In 1982, at fifty-nine, Helen was the oldest woman in

the world to complete the Ironman Triathlon, consisting of a 2.4-mile ocean swim, a 112-mile bike ride, followed immediately by a 26.2-mile run. "I had played around in the water before — I snorkeled and scuba dived and collected shells — but had not swum seriously. I only dog-paddled until last spring when I learned the crawl. I borrowed my daughter's bike to learn how to ride. My first lesson was getting on and off the bike. When I really want something, I don't give up until I collapse. It takes a lot to get this great-grandma to stop."

In 1980, Norman and Helen traveled to Nepal to trek with a Sherpa guide from Katmandu to the 18,000-foot base camp of Mount Everest. When they hit 17,000 feet, Norm experienced some altitude sickness and the couple returned to 16,000 feet. The next day, the Sherpa suggested taking Norman to the base camp and leaving her behind. He told the couple that he was sure that, because of her age, she would be unable to complete the trek, and that he could not carry both of them back. Norman and Helen stood firm: They would both go or neither would go. So they both successfully completed the trek. "I proved to the Sherpa that you can't say, 'You're too old to do this,'" Helen said.

Three years later, during a tour of Israel, Helen told their guide she planned to jog up to the mountain fortress of Masada. But he insisted she was too old and would hold up the tour. Later, Helen challenged the guide to a three-mile run and finished ten minutes before him. He ended up taking her back to Masada for a sunrise run. "I had no idea you could do that," he said, admitting that he had learned a lesson about not judging anyone by age.

Today, Helen says, "I have such good health that I can do whatever I wish to do. I plan to live a vital life every single year. The key is very, very simple: Eat right and exercise. Apples are my favorite food, plus any fresh fruits, vegetables and all the grains. Before a race, I eat huge amounts of pasta and fruits and vegetables, but only small portions of meat, chicken and fish."

What's the secret of a thirty-year-old's bone density and a svelte figure? Helen runs ten to eighteen miles a day. She retires about 9:30 P.M. and rises at 4:30 A.M. for a cup of coffee, some stretching exercises in a hot tub, then breakfast, the newspaper and a run. "I rest one day each week," she says. "I never overtrain, and I listen to my body. That's why I don't get into trouble. I don't believe in 'no pain, no gain.'" Referring to the ultramarathon endurance events, Helen says, "It may be a little unusual, but with proper training and listening to your body, most dedicated runners could also do these events. It's impossible only if you tell yourself it is."

Here are a couple of other things Helen Klein has learned over the years and miles: "I may be over eighty in age, but I will never be old in mind or spirit... I just like to show what a granny can do. Whenever I'm disappointed, I look at my watch and allow myself exactly ten minutes to feel sorry for myself—to whine and cry and complain. When those ten minutes are over, I put them behind me and move on. I don't have the physical talents, but I have a natural capacity to deal with hardships. We can all develop that capacity... we all have more strength than we think; it comes from doing something you didn't know you could do. I detest driving; if I need to go somewhere and it's less than 100 miles, I run it. Before you decide you're too old to run across mountains, rock-climb in canyons, or take up scuba diving, remember: It's never too late—muscles never lose the ability to improve, no matter how old you are. We are raised with the idea that when you hit fifty, you should relax and take it easy. I think this is a mistake. The more energy you expend, the more you get back. I get more tired sitting all day than when I run fifty miles.

"Ability may put me at the starting line, but heart takes me to the finish. When we carry gratitude in our hearts for what we have, instead of bitterness for what we don't have, the world becomes a place of smiles instead of frowns. And whenever I lace on my shoes, I lace on my smile. I want people to see both. It's great to be living in high gear, but the most significant reward is when I hear somebody say, 'I was going to seed at sixty-five, and you encouraged me to come back to life.'

"Starting out running (or anything else) is like achieving any other goal. Start out slowly. Establish a comfort zone first before you push. There have been times that I have been tired during a long race, and when I am, I don't think about how much farther I have to go. If I do, it can feel overwhelming. I just focus on taking the next step, because I know that I can always do that. Pretty soon, all those little steps taken individually add up to 100 miles."

For Helen Klein, success is not just a race; it's a lifetime: how we live and what we do with our lives. Goals give our life meaning and purpose. "Easy goals," she says, "are not really motivating; they mean little when you achieve them. Large goals are everything, and they can change your life just by going after them. No matter what your goal, keep focused. Do not give your mind a chance to talk you out of something you want.

"I like to inspire others and I don't like the world 'failure.' I don't believe in it. If you try for something and don't get it, that is not failure. That's just a message to keep trying. The greatest gift I can give is encouragement. I hope I can encourage others with my words, but more so by my example."

Running is Helen Klein's passion, but it isn't for everyone. Her four children are all active in sports, but they only run with Mom. None has run a marathon, but as Helen might remind them: "It's never too late."

~Dan Millman
Chicken Soup to Inspire the Body & Soul

87

The Ugly Orchid

We don't receive wisdom;
we must discover it for ourselves.
~Marcel Proust

There it sat, one sad, gangly stem leaning to the left of a plain terra-cotta pot. I peered closer. Tiny brown pods clung weakly to the lackluster plant. I was puzzled. This was the wonderful gift my daughter and son-in-law had sent all the way from their new home in Hanoi?

I picked up the phone, determined not to mention that my new plant looked as forlorn as I felt.

Katie was enthusiastic. "Now, Mom, for a while, you'll have to keep it in a cool, dark place."

No problem there. This plant was not only an eyesore, but it reminded me of what I had lost: family dinners, meeting the school bus, even helping with homework. When my husband, Jim, had died several years ago, I'd gone straight from being Mrs. Jim Ennis to being "Sara and Michael's Nana." That plant with its bare stem reminded me of what I was now: a widow, mother and grandmother with no one left to nurture. It just wasn't fair.

Plunk! I deposited my gift on a junk table in the basement and switched off the light.

Six weeks later, I was lugging boxes to the basement.

There it was: the most beautiful flowering plant I'd ever seen! Creamy white petals draped themselves delicately around the cherry red centers. I stretched out my finger but hesitated to touch. The blossoms were fragile, yet so alive. They looked as though they might fly away.

Back up the stairs I crept, cradling the pot in my arms and trying hard not to breathe on the blossoms. Six weeks alone in the basement had been just what this plant needed!

Suddenly it struck me that what had seemed so ugly and useless only weeks before had now shown itself a treasure.

And what a treasure it was! From its wicker stand, my beautiful orchid shined like a beacon of friendship to passersby. The mail carrier and people I had rarely spoken to waved and even came right up onto the porch, always commenting on "the gorgeous orchid."

"Six weeks ago, it was barely alive," I frequently replied, as I passed iced tea and the orange marmalade cake I was making again after three years. Each day my orchid gave birth to new blossoms, and I renewed old friendships and formed new ones.

Then one morning, Katie called. Ted had accepted a position at a nearby college. They were coming home!

Now, I was the one who was blooming. My once-empty life was filled with joy and friendship. Every day was like a precious blossom waiting to unfold. Time without my family had seemed an ugly and useless thing, but without it, would I ever have begun to live again?

I had been wrong about the ugly orchid and I had been wrong about myself. I wasn't useless or ugly. I wasn't just a widow, a mother or grandmother. I'm all those things and more! I thought gratefully. All I needed was time alone in the darkness to recognize my true potential.

One morning, I grabbed a broom and stepped out onto the front porch. Dried orchid blossoms littered the floor. Why, my orchid was as bare as it was the day it had come! I was still sweeping up when one of my new friends stopped by with an invitation to join her gardening club.

"Oh, dear, it's so sad!" she exclaimed upon seeing the bare stem.

"It'll be okay," I said. "You should have seen me six weeks ago!"

~Shelah Brewer Ogletree
Chicken Soup to Inspire a Woman's Soul

88

Racing for Life

There is no end. There is no beginning.
There is only the infinite passion of life.
~Federico Fellini

Breast cancer. These two words, this cold clinical diagnosis, were to shatter my life, then transform it. The words stirred a cauldron of red-hot emotions: rage, fear, hatred. Now it seems so long ago—literally another century, 1982—when the doctor told me. I remember the day and moment of the dreaded diagnosis as starkly as if it happened yesterday; the taste and smell of fear still lurk just below the surface of my memory.

It's 1982 and I'm forty-seven years old. I run marathons regularly and long ago gave up alcohol, tobacco and red meat. So how could I have breast cancer? Surely it's a mistake. Other people maybe, who don't take care of themselves, but not me, not now. Not fair!

I hate it when I feel sorry for myself. I'm a strong, self-reliant female—the equivalent of a lieutenant colonel in the U.S. Air Force. I shattered the so-called glass ceiling before most people knew what it was. I've raised two dynamic, smart and successful children, largely on my own after the breakup of two tough marriages. I've put myself through college up to and including my doctorate. "I am woman. I am strong. Hear me roar!" In the vernacular, I am one tough broad. Then why am I so frightened? Why am I crying? Tears are for sissies. My value system, my identity, my whole worldview is shaking under the assault of this terrible revelation; everything is turned upside down. And I'm really, really scared. How much time do I have left? I've taken care of myself since I was fourteen years old. I've never asked for anyone's help, nor have I ever needed it. Now I need help. But whom do I ask? And how do I ask?

Anger, rage and self-pity — scalpels of the psyche — cut at my core with deep and vicious slashes, like a monster turned loose inside me. A jumble of confused and ambivalent feelings rise like bile in my belly — the beginnings of an emotional roller coaster ride gone amok. To calm this emotional holocaust, I revert to the clinician in me. As a way of denial, repression, avoidance, I cling to whatever gives me momentary relief from the maelstrom of grief.

Infiltrating Ductal Carcinoma — a moderately fast-metastasizing cancer. The doctors had been following it for the three years since I had first reported a suspicious lump in my right breast. Now it had grown to the size of a golf ball. I know because I saw it. I had insisted on watching the surgery when they removed the large, red, ugly mass of deadly tissue. But because the cancer had spread through the whole breast, the surgeons told me that they needed to perform a modified radical mastectomy. As soon as I recovered from that surgery, they would then have to remove the other breast due to its high risk of being cancerous as well. Worse yet, in the three-year period that the doctors had been "watching" the tumor, it had spread to my bones and left lung.

Devastated, feeling betrayed by the medical system and by my body, I enrolled in a breast cancer research study conducted by author and physician John McDougall. It required me to follow a vegan diet (pure vegetarian with no animal-derived products). I would have tried anything to help save my life. The only catch here was that I could not take chemotherapy or radiation because the challenge was to see if a vegan diet alone could reverse the cancer. I talked to my then-husband. He thought I was crazy to think that diet had anything to do with breast cancer, and he believed I had fallen into the hands of a quack. Furthermore, he said he was surprised I would fall for "such garbage." None of my friends or family knew what to advise. So I decided to set my own course and follow where it led.

Around the time of my diagnosis, I saw a sporting event on television called the "Ironman Triathlon." I was captivated as I watched these superb young athletes race through a 2.4-mile swim, followed immediately by a 112-mile bike ride, then a full 26.2-mile marathon. "I want to do that," I said, then remembered: Hold on, Lady, you're a cancer patient and you're forty-seven years old—way too old to do such an event. But it wasn't just negative self-talk; it was the voice of reason. After all, no woman that old had ever attempted the Ironman. But this idea just wouldn't go away. With my new diet, I could swear I was feeling stronger, lighter, more energetic, faster, healthier and, by God, I decided I was going to do it. I increased my running and added swimming, biking and even weight lifting to my training.

Of course, the doctors thought I was absolutely insane. "You should be resting," they said. "All that stress on your body isn't good for it—running marathons (much less endurance swims and 100-mile bike rides) will depress your immune system." That's when I stopped relying solely on the doctors for advice.

Back in those days, before most people had even heard of triathlons, there was little guidance on how to train for such grueling endurance races. So I just got out there and swam until I couldn't lift my arms, biked until I couldn't pedal anymore, ran until I couldn't run another step and lifted as many pounds as I could without injuring myself. To simulate actual racing conditions, I entered every race I could find. If there were two on the same day, so much the better, because that would force me to race when tired, a condition I knew I'd face doing the Ironman. I entered "The Run to the Sun," a 37-mile run up to the top of Haleakala, a 10,000-foot high mountain on the island of Maui, Hawaii. I remember reaching the twenty-six-mile point and looking back down at the ocean far, far below, not believing that these two legs had already carried me the equivalent of a full marathon — straight uphill. Then I turned back toward the mountaintop, still more than ten miles beyond. My internal response was I don't have it in me; I just can't do it. My next thought was, Listen, Lady, if you think this is rough, just wait until you get in the Ironman! That's what kept me going. If I quit here, how could I face the Ironman? That technique served me well in the coming months. And competing and winning first-place trophies in my age-group events added to the post-race highs.

I found myself getting stronger and developing muscles I never knew I had. I was passing my cancer checkups as well: The hot spots in my bones — once a source of despair because they indicated cancer — were disappearing, and the tumor in my lung stayed the same size, allowing me to avoid chemo and/or radiation, and to stay in the dietary study.

The only real reminder of the cancer were the two postsurgical, angry red gashes, which left a chest that resembled a prepubescent male's. Because of all my training, I was having to shower and change clothes several times a day, so the reminders of the cancer were constant. I wanted so much to have a normal body again. Enter the plastic surgeons, who gave me a fabulous choice: I could now pick my new size. "You want a 'C'?" they said. "We can do that!" I told them I wouldn't be greedy—"Just give me what I had before, a nice, average 'B'." They also gave me something else I never thought possible: breasts that will never sag. I believe you have to look at the positive side of life, and now, at sixty-eight years old, I can really appreciate this benefit.

Today, there's no sign of cancer in my body. I've continued my vegan, low-fat diet now for more than twenty years, and I have never been healthier or more fit in my life. To date I have raced the Ironman Triathlon six times, plus over a hundred shorter triathlons, a total of sixty-seven marathons, plus hundreds of shorter road races. In 1999, I was named one of the Ten Fittest Women in America by *Living Fit* magazine. In February 2000, on a Fitness Age test, my score was equivalent to a fit thirty-two-year-old's. My aerobic capacity score was that of a sixteen-year-old. My bone density has increased throughout my fifties and sixties, which is supposed to be "impossible" since most people are told they will lose bone density as part of the "natural" aging process. My blood pressure runs 90/60; my cholesterol is under 150; I have 15 percent body fat, and my hemoglobin—the test for iron in the blood—is at the top of the charts.

I do not share this information about my physical condition to boast (although I admit I'm proud of it), but to show what can be accomplished through dedication and discipline.

Since I'm a vegan—I eat no flesh or dairy products—I'm "supposed" to be deficient in protein, calcium and iron. Perhaps I'm an anomaly by most medical standards. And maybe a vegan diet and endurance exercise won't be a magical answer for everyone, but I stand as an example of a lifestyle change that might be worth exploring. And I'm not alone. Most people know how Tour de France champion Lance Armstrong also demonstrated the power of racing for life after his own battles with cancer.

When will this awesome journey end? Will I have to slow down gradually, let go, cut back to walking laps around a retirement community? I really can't say. But I know this: I had cancer and it had spread; I might have folded my cards back then, but I chose life, and I'm going to live as long as I can and run the good race. Maybe only a few will take the path I've chosen, but if sharing my story helps a few more to step forward and race for life, it will have been all the more worthwhile.

~Ruth Heidrich, Ph.D.
Chicken Soup to Inspire the Body & Soul

The Next Best Thing

To be upset over what you don't have is to
waste what you do have.
~Ken S. Keyes, Jr.,
Handbook to Higher Consciousness

When my parents reached their seventies and were having difficulty doing the things they had previously done with ease, a quote by test pilot Chuck Yeager became their favorite motto: "Do what you can for as long as you can and when you can't, do the next best thing."

My father in particular was challenged by a weakened muscular system that would cause his legs to sometimes give way without warning. Ever diligent that he might fall, my mother would periodically check to make sure he was still standing as he ambled around outside doing yard work.

One morning, Mom spied him lying flat on his stomach under an apple tree. Alarmed, she scurried out to help. Only when she got closer did she see that he had a trowel in hand and was weeding. Exasperated, she asked, "What are you doing?"

My father replied, "The next best thing."

~Ann Pehl Thomson
Chicken Soup for the Gardener's Soul

New Year's Resolution

The vision must be followed by the venture.
It is not enough to stare up the steps —
we must step up the stairs.
~Vance Havner

Hello Body, I wrote in my journal and listened inwardly for an answer. My belly growled, It's about time you paid some attention to me!

How did my body and I lose rapport? It began in my agonizing year in junior high when I grew eight inches in one year and didn't know what size my feet would be when my lanky form climbed out of bed in the morning. This body, I thought, is way out of control. So I began to pretend that it didn't exist. I fed and clothed it, but hoped if I otherwise ignored it, it might go away.

Determined to heal my mind/body rift, I mustered my courage and marched into a gym near my home, looking for a personal trainer. I had never done any deliberate exercise other than walking, so this was going to be a big stretch.

The bronzed, sculpted woman at the desk could have been a model in a muscle magazine. Gathering my courage, I took a breath, and on the exhale I said, "I'd like a trial session." Clearly bored by the prospect of a midlife client, she put me through an extraordinary number of impossible-for-me exercises, all the while pursing her lips and stealing seductive glances at herself in the mirror.

She could have the mirror. Feeling old and frumpy, I hated every minute on the torture machines, but pride kept me in the game. Muttering this is good for me like a mantra, I signed up for twelve sessions, and paid in advance.

Buyer's remorse descended like a dark cloud when I got home, but I vowed to do it for one month no matter what. The next day I could hardly move; every muscle in my body ached. I canceled my appointment. Still sore two days later, I called and asked for my money back. No one returned my call; the contract's fine print told me no refunds. I'd gotten myself into this pickle and I would have to live with it.

For the next few months, I vented my anger doing exercise videos at home. It's too much trouble to go to a gym, I told myself. I like the privacy of working alone. But these solo sessions at home were inconsistent, and I knew I needed weight training to get results.

One day my psychologist-daughter Lexi told me over lunch that she had begun working out at a gym and raved about the improvement in her body tone, energy level and stamina. Meanwhile, I recounted my hard luck story, getting tired of my whining litany.

Lexi offered to drive across town to join me at my gym, so I bit the bullet and made an appointment with a different trainer. He and Lexi had me laughing all through the session. We clarified my goals and set a schedule of three times a week.

I attended every session, worked at a moderate pace and never suffered the soreness of the original workout again. Sure enough, I began to love the surge of energy and satisfaction that came after each session. When the month was up, I signed up for three more—then three more months after that. By then I found a trainer named Mike Krpan who came right to my house for the same price as the gym, and I've stayed with twice-weekly workouts for almost five years. I realize that not everyone can afford or needs to hire a personal trainer, but that's what works for me.

I'm amazed at how much my formerly ignored body has changed. Even though I weigh only three pounds less than when I began, weight is no longer an issue. Now when I look in a mirror, I purse my lips and smile as I see firm arms and shoulders, a slimmer waist, flatter tummy, taut and toned thighs, and straighter posture. Best of all, I feel years younger.

I was shopping with Lexi the other day, and I tried on a rather revealing dress. "Wow," she said, "guess I'll have to call you 'Buff Mama!'"

The time and effort it took to train these last few years were one of the best investments of my life. Now when I ask my body what it would like me to do, it tells me I'm doing just fine. In the place of anger and frustration is a new sense of teamwork and partnership, my body and soul.

~Diana von Welanetz Wentworth
Chicken Soup to Inspire the Body & Soul

91

Never Too Old to Live Your Dream

In youth we learn; in age we understand.
~Source Unknown

The first day of school, our professor introduced himself to our chemistry class and challenged us to get to know someone we didn't already know. I stood up to look around when a gentle hand touched my shoulder. I turned around to find a wrinkled, little old lady beaming up at me with a smile that lit up her entire being.

She said, "Hi, handsome. My name is Rose. I'm eighty-seven years old. Can I give you a hug?"

I laughed and enthusiastically responded, "Of course you may!" and she gave me a giant squeeze.

"Why are you in college at such a young, innocent age?" I asked.

She jokingly replied, "I'm here to meet a rich husband, get married, have a couple children, and then retire and travel."

"No seriously," I asked. I was curious what may have motivated her to be taking on this challenge at her age.

"I always dreamed of having a college education and now I'm getting one!" she told me.

After class, we walked to the student union building and shared a chocolate milkshake. We became instant friends. Every day for the next three months, we would leave class together and talk nonstop. I was always mesmerized listening to this "time machine" as she shared her wisdom and experience with me.

Over the course of the school year, Rose became a campus icon and easily made friends wherever she went. She loved to dress up and she reveled in the attention bestowed upon her from the other students. She was living it up.

At the end of the semester, we invited Rose to speak at our football banquet and I'll never forget what she taught us. She was introduced and stepped up to the podium. As she began to deliver her prepared speech, she dropped her three-by-five cards on the floor. Frustrated and a bit embarrassed, she leaned into the microphone and simply said, "I'm sorry I'm so jittery. I gave up beer for Lent and this whiskey is killing me! I'll never get my speech back in order so let me just tell you what I know." As we laughed, she cleared her throat and began:

"We do not stop playing because we are old; we grow old because we stop playing. There are only four secrets to staying young, being happy and achieving success.

"You have to laugh and find humor each and every day.

"You've got to have a dream. When you lose your dreams, you die. We have so many people walking around who are dead and they don't even know it!

"There is a giant difference between growing older and growing up. If you are nineteen years old and lie in bed for one full year and don't do one productive thing, you will turn twenty years old. If I am eight-seven years old and stay in bed for a year and never do anything I will turn eighty-eight. Anybody can grow older. That doesn't take any talent or ability. The idea is to grow up by always finding the opportunity in change.

"Have no regrets. The elderly usually don't have regrets for what we did, but rather for things we did not do. The only people who fear death are those with regrets."

She concluded her speech by courageously singing "The Rose." She challenged each of us to study the lyrics and live them out in our daily lives.

At year's end, Rose finished the college degree she had begun all those years ago. One week after graduation, Rose died peacefully in her sleep. Over two thousand college students attended her funeral in tribute to the wonderful woman who taught by example that it's never too late to be all you can possibly be.

~Dan Clark
Chicken Soup for the College Soul

92

Knocked Off the Horse

I am sixty-four years old, soon to be sixty-five. My faith journey has encompassed four-plus decades and has been singularly unspectacular. My journey has been full of ups and downs, times of closeness with the Lord and times of distance, but unlike many of my friends I've never had a lot of dramatic encounters with God. And in my younger life, that worried me. I thought maybe I wasn't paying attention (well, sometimes I probably wasn't!), or God didn't have anything special to say to me. I tried many avenues: daily Mass attendance, Bible study, small faith-sharing groups, even the charismatic movement for a while. Through all of them I met wonderful people, many of whom are still in my life today. They all helped me on my faith journey, but I yearned for a "knocked from my horse" experience. It is only as I look back on my life that I see maybe I'd had them — gently — after all.

As usual, I was at an ordinary Sunday Mass in my early thirties, struggling with all the "stuff" of marriage and two preschool children. But this particular Sunday, as I casually tossed my envelope into the basket, something had changed. I hate to say I "heard" God speak to me, but I really can't explain it any other way. What I heard was, "Jan, I don't want just your money, I want all of you." It was so real and so profound that I found myself still sitting while the rest of the community had risen to their feet, so overwhelming that I remember none of the rest of that Mass. That was the beginning of years of volunteer service that started with preschool, went on to include adult faith development, liturgy, parish council and church committee work and even an advanced degree in theology. While my husband worked at a job that supported our family, I worked thirty-one years at a ministry that supported my faith journey.

Then two years ago a very dear friend of ours died. She and her husband lived about an eight-hour drive from us, in the city where my husband and I had met and married and where we still maintained a wonderful group of friends. Since my husband was retired, I suggested we drive up for the services and make it a mini-vacation. We drove to the services, comforted George and spent a day or so visiting old friends. On our return trip we investigated some of the wonderful areas of our state we had missed on earlier trips. It was October, there was a bit of crispness in the air, most of the tourists were gone and we spent five leisurely days driving home. We had a wonderful time! We rediscovered how well we travel together, how much we enjoy just hangin' out. One evening while enjoying dinner from a candlelit deck overlooking a roaring river somewhere in the Sierra Madres of California, I suggested that we take ourselves on a really long car trip, two or three months, just roam around the Northwest. My husband thought it was a great idea, but said, "How can we do that? You always have commitments at church."

I guess you could say my husband's response was my "knocked off the horse" encounter. How long had I been relegating my husband and our life together to second place behind my commitments at church? He had been retired for ten years. Was it now time for me to retire?

While I was "knocked off the horse," I wasn't blinded. In fact I saw very clearly the Lord's next plan for me. My answer to my husband was, "I can give it up." It came as clearly and simply as anything that has ever been said to me. I knew this was right. I knew this was where God wanted me next, right beside my husband, doing all the things we had been wanting to do — things we hadn't been able to do because of my involvement. As soon as we got home I gave my pastor notice.

We made our two-and-one-half month car trip and loved every beauty-filled moment. We have refreshed ourselves and our relationships with old friends with mini-vacations and retreats. We have been to Eastern Europe to discover an unknown relative of my husband's, and we have wandered the streets of Rome. We see my daughter and grandchildren almost every week now. We have lunch together, we watch baseball together, we cook together, we laugh more, we play more. And, surprisingly enough, my church has gone on just fine without me! Other younger people with fresh ideas have stepped up and taken over the positions I once occupied — positions I thought only I could fill.

I'm happier than I have been in years. I'm less stressed. I have more time to pray.

My increased time with my husband, my family and my friends I count as increased time with my God.

~Jan Kremenik
Chicken Soup for the Christian Soul 2

Older & Wiser

Special Moments

The best things in life are unexpected—
because there were no expectations.
~Eli Khamarov,
Surviving on Planet Reebok

93

Billu the Beauty, Henry the Hero

Of my two cats, I always thought Billu would be the one to make a name for himself. He's the smart one, the orange-and-white calendar cat in the making, the extreme extrovert who flops over for a belly-rub and makes friends with anyone who visits the house. Hi! I'm Billu! That's BEE-lu! Good to see you! Don't I have a beautiful belly? Yet it was his brother, Henry—the "slow" one, the big-pawed, black-lipped tabby—who, in the summer of 2003, saved my life.

I was staying at our summer cabin by a lake in New Hampshire, a place I had been coming to since 1950, the year I was born. One afternoon in late July, I was sitting in the yard reading. The day was sunny; the humidity was low; lake water lapped tranquilly at the shoreline. When I heard Henry's characteristic chirp, I looked up to see him perched in the bathroom window, watching me quite intently. I found that odd—Henry never sat in that window and was rarely, if ever, awake at that time of day. He cried to me several times, and, after I sang out, "Hi, Henry," I continued reading. He kept crying. My right arm and leg, I noticed, were strangely numb, asleep. I decided to get them moving by going for a swim. The lake water did the trick; the numbness disappeared. I said nothing to my husband.

But something was wrong, and Henry knew it. He paced around me all evening long, and, that night, he slept on the pillow next to the left side of my head, something I couldn't remember him ever doing. Usually he stretched out along my side, while Billu draped himself over my ankles. I woke up several times during the night, feeling absolutely awful: nauseated, dizzy and disoriented. You're in for a nasty stomach bug, I thought foggily.

By morning, the nausea was gone, but the numbness had returned. Henry kept butting my shoulder. When I stood up, I fell, but I was able, somehow, to stand again and walk normally. By now, Henry was wailing. Shrill and ceaseless, his message finally got through to me: Something was terribly wrong. I realized I had to get myself to a hospital—after, of course, feeding the cats.

Then I proceeded to make one of the stupidest decisions I've ever made: Since I didn't want to alarm my husband, I didn't wake him and drove myself to the ER—fifteen miles in my stick-shift RAV4. Miraculously, I made the drive without incident, and, some three hours later—after I'd given my insurance information to no fewer than seven people and been ushered into three examining rooms, where I was told to "wait"—I learned what I think Henry had sensed, or perhaps smelled, the day before: Over the past twenty-four hours, I'd had a "gradual" and cumulative stroke.

The ten days that followed remain vague in my memory. After a day or so, I was transferred to Brigham And Women's Hospital in Boston, where I stayed for a week. A clotting disorder, antiphospholipid antibody syndrome, lay at the root of my condition. The doctors assigned to my case seemed genuinely moved by the story I told to them (with a fair bit of mispronunciation and bizarre grammatical constructions) of Henry's warning. "He... him... save I think my life."

Maybe my husband could bring Henry down for a visit, one doctor suggested. But my husband and I agreed: no. He doesn't travel well, and he's too shy; he'd be terrified. I'd see him soon enough.

It's been a year now. As stroke victims go, I have been almost unbelievably lucky: I talk normally; I am writing again. I still get tired daily, but fatigue gives me a good excuse to cuddle and nap with the cats. I think I have a lot of years left. So, I hope, do Henry and Billu, who will both turn five in November. As always, they'll get a party. I'll sing "Happy Birthday" to them and buy them some treats. My guess is that they'll show their love for me the way they do every day: Billu will flop over and show me his beautiful belly, and Henry will chirp, jump into my lap and gaze up at me.

"How did you know?" I ask him sometimes. His purr, low and rumbly, is the only answer I get. But that's all right. As we look into each other's eyes, the difference between us fades away. We sit like that for a while, gazing at each other, no longer a cat and a woman, but simply two creatures who'd do anything for each other, anything in the world.

~Cori Jones
Chicken Soup for the Cat Lover's Soul

94

To Everything
There Is a Season

I think it was the sign that so unhinged me at first. There it was, that impossible-to-miss sign stuck on our front lawn and announcing to the world that an era had ended: Our house was for sale.

For the first few days, I blinked in disbelief at the mere sight of it. Surely, that sign had been plunked down at the wrong address, because we really weren't ready for this. Not yet.

No matter that it had been over a decade since any child had occupied the house with too many bedrooms and bathrooms, the house that suddenly seemed cavernous, silent and a bit forlorn for two late-middle-aged adults.

No matter that from the start, this house, an imperious English Tudor with a will all its own, had been a bit much to handle. Nothing was ever simple in a house where the architectural plans dated back to 1929.

But the weird floor plan, impractical rooms, wide-open spaces? Instead of being annoying, those very "negatives" seemed enormously appealing. Downright charming.

The first time the realtor, a lovely, highly profes-sional woman, brought potential buyers to our door, I felt mounting rage. How dare she? The fact that it was her job, her mission, her mandate mattered not at all. The fact that just a few nights before, we had signed on for this, were future partners in this deed—forgotten. What mattered was that this realtor and the intruders she had in tow were about to judge this place—our place—the house that had enclosed within it everything that had mattered to us for the past twenty-eight years.

Every image of our daughters blowing out birthday candles or going off to proms in pale gauzy dresses, every holiday dinner, every party in the living room, came rushing back as these audacious strangers were overheard remarking that the "flow" was really poor and the kitchen was totally outdated.

I wanted to announce with appropriate disdain and hauteur that the "flow" was just fine for a family that loved every inch of this old place, and that the kitchen had managed to serve up some pretty decent food, to say nothing of joyful memories.

It took a sheer effort of will not to point out the beech tree in the side yard where three daughters had stood as brides on those luminous June days when the concepts "home" and "love" were joined forever.

Instead, I kept my mouth shut and hoped these ingrates wouldn't get to live in our house.

They didn't even make an offer.

Through several very long months, it went on and on, this parade of lookers.

And for that long, I awoke every day with a knot in my stomach. Would there be that phone call announcing that some potential buyers from out-of-state wanted to come in at 2:00 P.M., the precise time I'd planned a finger-painting party with Zay, our gentle four-year-old grandson? Would

I have to rush around cleaning and straightening, hiding all evidence that people actually lived here, and create, instead, a perfect stage set?

Oh, how I hated that illusion!

Occasionally, I rebelled and deliberately left various "exhibits"—a broom, a newspaper, a pair of shoes, towels piled on the dryer—just to be defiant.

Sometimes I tortured myself by staying around and eavesdropping as men and women I'd never met before flung open our closets and saw my shoes, my cosmetics, our dishes. But mostly, I took deep breaths and wondered where we would go, and how we'd ever find a house with a dogwood tree outside our bedroom window that made waking up in spring a gift, or leaded windows that let the afternoon light filter gently into the little den near the front stairs.

My husband and I started a countdown as the contract with the real estate firm entered its final days. And you can bet that just as the calendar was closing in on "the end," along came the lovely couple from Chicago who didn't want to plunk down wall-to-wall carpeting over our fine old wood floors or paint over the mellow chestnut paneling in the foyer. We liked them immediately.

And on a momentous Wednesday morning, after a flurry of faxes and e-mails, inspections and engineers' reports, the deed was done. I signed on the dotted line, then ran into my husband's arms sobbing. That was the morning when we understood fully that a home is so very much more than wood, plaster and stucco. Home is a shelter for the soul, a place where hope and memory collide—a sacred place. But when you're ready to leave a home, you know it.

Yes, to everything, there is a season. And ours for part-ing has come. I'm sure I'll stop weeping soon.

At last, despite the profound attachment to place, my husband and I felt some new stirrings: a sense of optimism that lightened the gloom, the feeling that endings aside, we were in for an adventure as we shifted the center of family gravity from one address to another.

Yes, to everything, there is a season. At last, ours for parting had come.

And on moving day, as we pulled out of the driveway for the last time, neither one of us even looked back.

~Sally Friedman
Chicken Soup to Inspire a Woman's Soul

95

In Search of a Simpler Time

We may look old and wise to the outside world.
But to each other, we are still in junior school.
~Charlotte Gray

We were partners in crime. What started as mischief became a yearly ritual we looked forward to every Christmas.

There were more children than money in our large family, but every year our parents managed to make Christmas a celebration to be remembered.

But one of my fondest Christmas memories is the secret shared only with my older sister, Barbara.

Our crime was committed while shopping for our siblings. Our father would give us a crisp $5 bill with stern instructions that it was to be spent only on presents for our sisters, then drop us at the nearest dime store, with instructions to shop and then wait by the door until he returned. Once our shopping was completed, Barbara and I would sneak to the soda counter, climb up on the tall round stools, plunk down our leftover change and count to see if we had enough. We always did. Grinning, we ordered hot fudge sundaes, then sat there, conspirators in crime, skinny legs dangling as we giggled and licked the thick, gooey chocolate from our spoons.

Fast-forward fifty years. Barbara was diagnosed with incurable cancer. We were told there was no cure, but "palliative therapy" would make her more comfortable. Every day for weeks, particles of energy were bombarded through her brain. Fatigue and nausea became daily companions. Next, chemotherapy, with all its unpleasant side effects. However, with the help of new medications, soon we were pleasantly surprised to find that Barbara no longer experienced nausea. Her appetite even returned. That is when we began our quest. We were determined to find the perfect match of our childhood memory. The ice cream must be the hard kind, the harder the better, since the thick, hot fudge will cause it to melt right away. It had to have a cherry on top and it absolutely must be in a glass dish shaped like a tulip. That was the recipe.

We spent the entire time she was in treatment in search of the absolutely perfect concoction. We didn't tell anyone else what we were doing; once again it was our secret.

Treatment day was always Monday; by evening she could barely keep her eyes open. The week became a blur of growing fatigue, confusion and weakness, but by the weekend, Barbara would begin to rally and by Sunday she was ready.

"You think we will find it this time?" she'd ask. We'd laugh then climb into the car.

We ate a lot of ice cream that year, but it always seemed something was slightly off-kilter. Soft ice cream wasn't the same as the hard-packed we remembered, chocolate syrup didn't give the same sensual delight as the thick goo of our childhood, the cherry on top was missing, or even worse, it was served in a paper container. The exact replica seemed impossible to find. Week after week we searched for the perfect combination. We were on a mission—in search of a childhood memory and a simpler time.

"We didn't find it, did we?" Barbara sighed one morning. I knew exactly what she meant.

"No, but we're not giving up!" I replied. "Are you up for a road trip?"

The next day we took a longer trip than any we had previously attempted.

By the time we arrived at the ice cream parlor bedecked in 1950s décor, she was drained. She needed help just to get out of the car.

As the waitress held out menus, Barbara spoke softly. "We won't need those. We already know what we want—hot fudge sundaes. Do you use hard ice cream?"

"Of course," the waitress replied.

Barbara beamed at me. "I think that we might have found it."

Soon the waitress returned, carrying two tall tulip-shaped glasses filled with cold, hard, vanilla ice cream smothered in rich, thick hot fudge sauce, topped with a squirt of whipped cream and a cherry. "Is this what you wanted?" she asked as she plunked them down on the counter.

I turned toward my sister. Our eyes locked. The silent, secret question hung in the air between us. Was it? Slowly we picked up our spoons, plunged them into the sweet, cold confection and took them to our mouths. As I licked the thick, rich chocolate goo from my lips, I looked toward Barbara and saw she was doing the same. We began to first smile, and then giggle.

Mission accomplished. There we were—not two overweight, middle-aged women enjoying an afternoon dessert with more calories than either needed. We were two giggling little girls, perched on high stools, skinny legs dangling, sharing the precious bond of sisterhood, carried back to a time when life was simple and "palliative treatment," were just words that had no meaning.

~Nancy Harless
Chicken Soup for the Soul Celebrates Sisters

96

Annual Checkup

Laughter heals a lot of hurts.
~Madeleine L'Engle

The call came as expected. It was from Ellen at Davis Clinic. Time for my annual checkup. The tragic time had rolled around again. Spending eight hours being poked, gouged, pitied and X-rayed is no picnic. Have you ever noticed that the nurse always gets in a lead bunker for her protection but leaves your quivering body exposed?

I guess checkups are necessary as we pass through infancy, adolescence, adulthood and over-the-hillhood. After you turn sixty, it's all maintenance, though.

As I entered the clinic, I was met by Ellen with that superior, expectant look. She wanted me to sign a release form so they would not be responsible for anything they did. They wanted to know who would be responsible for the bill if I didn't make it. They also wanted to know where the remains should be sent. She wanted to know if they could use any of my parts that happened to be good. (At that point, I would not need them anymore, she assured me.)

She then handed me a mimeographed list of terrible diseases, and she wanted me to mark the ones I had experienced in the last twelve months. I always mark four or five good ones to give them something to do in the back room. Remember, you are presumed to be senile or you would not be there.

Then a little girl (young enough to be my granddaughter) wanted some additional information. "Dr. Thorn, have you ever shot illegal drugs by needle, even once?" I shook my head. "Tested positive for the AIDS virus?"

"No," I said.

She continued. "Have you given money for sex anytime since 1955?" Then, "Have you had sex with a man? With a prostitute?"

"No, no, no, none of the above." If they are going to give my parts away, they want them without blemish.

She then asked, "Are you married to Jessie Holder Thorn?" I indicated that I was. She said that she wanted to ask me this before, but she did not want to get too personal.

I was then given a sack and ushered into a small dressing room. Being alone, I opened the sack and found the notorious hospital gown. Medical science can give you new joints and organs, but they still have the same gowns they used back in the days of antiquity. One size fits anything—car, chair or table. It is easy to walk into them but impossible to tie the strings in the back. If you can, you have no business being at the doctor's office. If you try and can't, you might have to stay an extra week. I've learned the secret: Just take the gown off, lay it on the floor and tie the strings. Then you can slither into it. This ingenuity shows that the passing of years has not entirely dulled my intellect.

The nurse came in and told me she needed to take my blood pressure. She said, "Have a seat on that metal stool."

The cold stool sent my blood pressure sky high. No one has normal blood pressure in a doctor's office.

With a sneer, she handed me a little jar and informed me that she needed a specimen. When she returned to the room, she noticed that the jar was dry. She cooed, "Now don't you worry, many men your age have this problem."

"My age nothing, I can't get the lid off the jar." The human body is a marvelous contrivance, but it does get a little frayed as time goes on.

There came a stout knock on the door. "Come in," I said. In walked a woman in a white robe. I noticed by the nametag that she was a medical doctor. She informed me that she was here to give me my physical. If they are going to give somebody else my body parts, I guess they wanted to check them out.

She demanded that I take off my robe.

"Doctor, I have never felt this good in my life and everything is working," I whined. Again she demanded that I take off my robe.

"What are you doing?" she screamed.

"Getting down on the floor so I can get out of this gown," I responded.

There I stood with only my clinic identification bracelet, which identified for them that I was a male.

"Do you have any questions before I leave?" questioned the doctor.

"Just one. Why did you knock?"

Apparently, I passed the annual checkup and am still alive with all my parts. You can survive anything except death.

Norman Cousins talked about "that apothecary inside of you," by which he meant the medicine of humor. When this medicine works, muddled thinking clears. Solomon said, "A cheerful heart is good medicine; but a crushed spirit dries up the bones" (Proverbs 17:22).

I believe that the Apostle Paul was more than inspired when he wrote, "A man ought to examine himself...." (1 Corinthians 11:28).

~W. E. "Bill" Thorn
Chicken Soup for the Golden Soul

97

The Worm

I couldn't put the worm on. I prided myself on being a tomboy—I hated Barbies and baths, and loved climbing trees and playing with Tonka trucks—but something about sticking a hook through a wiggling worm gave me the heebie-jeebies. Dad had somehow understood, but how could I tell old Mr. Lyons, who never had any kids? I almost hadn't gone fishing with him because of it, but Mom talked me into it. Then, the closer we got to the river, the more it worried me.

It was nice of Mr. Lyons to take me fishing. Since my dad had died the fall before, it was just my mom and us four girls, and I knew we wouldn't go fishing or camping or canoeing anymore.

I missed my dad and had taken to hanging around Mr. Lyons's yard as he worked on building his houseboat. I loved the smell of sawdust and stain—a scent that was fading from my dad's unused workshop. I think Mr. Lyons liked my company, too. He'd be hammering a nail or planing wood with his eyes squinting in concentration until his dog Brownie would announce my arrival with a bark. When he'd look up and see it was me, he'd set his tools down and scratch his gray, scruffy chin and say he was glad I came by because he needed a break.

Mr. Lyons had finished the houseboat in the spring,

and he'd already taken it down to the river. He pulled the truck up next to the houseboat.

"Well, how's she look?"

"Real nice, Mr. Lyons."

"We'll just fish right off the front bow. It's nice and shady there. The fish'll be keeping cool and waiting for a worm to wiggle on by."

We got the fishing poles out of the bed of the Ford. Mine was just the bamboo pole I had dug out from the camping supplies in the basement. Dad had tried to teach me how to cast his rod and reel but I had tangled the line up something awful. Maybe now that I had turned eleven I'd have better luck.

Mr. Lyons reached back in the truck bed for the tackle box, then reached in again and handed me the Styrofoam container of worms. I followed him down the bank and onto the boat, keeping an eye that the lid stayed on.

Once on the bow, Mr. Lyons started getting everything set up. Any minute now I'd have to admit to him my aversion to worms. Then he'd probably never ask me to go fishing again. He handed me my pole, then set the container between us and fished out a worm for his pole. Then, just when I was ready to confess, Mr. Lyons confessed to me instead.

"Always hate this part," he mumbled as he held the worm in one hand and his hook in the other. "It's silly, but stickin' the poor little guy with a hook makes me feel, I dunno what you'd call it...."

"Like you have the heebie-jeebies?" I offered hopefully.

"That's it exactly. The heebie-jeebies. You get 'em, too?"

"A little," I admitted, relief washing over me.

"Yeah. I guess sometimes we gotta go through the bad to get to the good. Want me to hook your worm for ya?"

There it was. My way out. All I had to say was "yes" and I'd be off the hook and my worm would be on. But I felt bad making Mr. Lyons put the worm on if he hated it as much as me. So I reached into the cool dirt and picked up a fat worm between my fingers. I tried not to think about how slimy it felt as I quickly poked the hook through its middle and wiped my hand on my jeans.

I had done it! It definitely gave me the heebie-jeebies, but I had gotten through it. I looked up at Mr. Lyons. He gave me a wink. I grinned with pride and tossed my line in the water. The bad part was over.

Today, of course, I realize my mom must have shared my problem with Mr. Lyons; I'm fairly certain he didn't have a case of the heebie-jeebies at all. But I also know that he helped me grasp, on a child's level, the principle of persevering through the bad to get to the good. My mom and sisters and I never did fish together again; the days of camping and canoeing died with my father. But we struggled through the grief and, when we got through the bad, we eventually found other good times to enjoy as a family. And I continued to fish with Mr. Lyons... and bait my own hook.

~Julie Long
Chicken Soup for the Fisherman's Soul

98

My Sisters, Myself and the Seasons of Life

*Nothing is more memorable than a smell. One scent can
be unexpected, momentary and fleeting, yet conjure up a
childhood summer beside a lake in the mountains; another, a
moonlit beach; a third, a family dinner of pot roast and sweet
potatoes during a myrtle-mad August in a Midwestern town.
Smells detonate softly in our memory like poignant land mines
hidden under the weedy mass of years.
Hit a tripwire of smell and memories explode all at once.
A complex vision leaps out of the undergrowth.*
~Diane Ackerman,
A Natural History of the Senses

How time changes everything, and too soon we get
caught up in the worrisome trivialities of life. But
one hectic afternoon, the scent of my neighbor's pine
trees—that woodsy-turpentine aroma—took me back many
years to a time and place when life seemed simpler.

With that whiff of pine from my neighbor's trees, I was
suddenly transported back in time to the halcyon days I
spent growing up with my two sisters on our grandparents' farm in Union Grove, Alabama. In my memory, that
265-acre paradise of lush forest, cows, pigs, chickens and

cotton fields remains unchanged, as does the secret place I shared with my sisters.

Our secret place was near a large pond, and we could only approach it in the proper form. We—Mary, Patti and I—would don our flying cloaks (which on ordinary days were bath towels) and race across the pasture, leaping and laughing.

From the pasture we stopped at our clubhouse, which had been used in the farm's earlier days as a place to store corn. Sometimes we slept there on our father's Army cots. It was always fun to see which neighbor's child (or children) would be there, playing; if any were girls, they came along with us.

From there, we ran to our nearest neighbor's house. They were the talk of the county because they had thirteen children. If they were around in the yard, we allowed the girls to join us. What a laughing, squealing bunch we made! We would run together through the woods, crossing the creek where Momma said a silver fox lived. Arriving at the pond, we would set to work on our glorious playhouse.

Our playhouses were architectural, if temporary, wonders, made with whatever was at hand—usually the red, long-dead needles of the pines we found surrounding the pond.

The art to a pine-needle playhouse is first to find at least five trees, grouped to form a circle, more or less. As trees whispered instructions and cicadas sang their praises, we would carefully twine bunches of the sticky, fragrant needles between the trunks of the stubby cedars and pines, working from the bottom up. The needles all stuck together making wonderfully rustic walls.

Our roofless pine needle houses usually wound up being just about five feet tall; we never felt the need to cover the sky. After finishing the playhouse, Mary, Patti and I, plus our friends, would lie on the ground and, facing the sky and encircled by the walls of our house, we would dream.

Within these walls, we planned our futures completely, down to the schools we would attend, the homes and families we would have, the places we would go and the important things we would accomplish. We shared secrets to be told to the wind or only to each other. Breezes would lift off the pond blowing cool perfume over us, laughing with us when we laughed. Those seasons were golden.

Building those pine tree houses taught me many subtle lessons about life. For we, like the trees, were sturdier if we grew close to those we loved. Like our houses built in a circle yet without a roof, our lives grew taller without the confines of a ceiling. That openness, I think, has stayed with each one of us as we've grown up, now with children of our own.

Through the building of our pine-straw playhouses, my sisters and I learned that everything is more worthwhile and more fun when we shared the job, where laughter is shared along with the work. Sharing our dreams helps make them possible. And my "architect" friends showed me the importance of sisters of the heart as well as sisters of the blood.

That was so long ago, and now my sisters—both of the blood and of the heart—and I live several hours apart, and our homes are made of brick, not pine needles, all with snug-fitting roofs.

I hope that when my sisters have rushed days like I do, that when they catch the scent of a pine tree it gives them pause and remember that each season of life, like those golden days we had growing up together, holds promise, and are reminded that living simply and living joyfully hold pleasures that endure long beyond the moment.

~T. Jensen Lacey
Chicken Soup for the Sister's Soul

99

Here with Me

Those who bring sunshine to the lives of others
cannot keep it from themselves.
~James Matthew Barrie

Last weekend marked one of the nicest days so far this spring.

It was warm with a tiny breeze; the sun penetrated through lightweight sweaters to warm the skin; the male choir was warming up, and the graduates were milling around the lawn behind the throng of six-thousand-plus observers.

With all of the parents, sisters, brothers, grandparents, aunts and uncles, the state university was a hub of activity. My nephew was going to receive his bachelor's degree. Who would have guessed that four years would go by so quickly?

As the crowd of freshly polished and scrubbed candidates wandered, joked, hugged and chattered behind the bleachers, I heard several cell phones ring. There were several nonsensical conversations going on with the accompanying giggles of the not-quite-mature students, but then one conversation in particular caught my attention:

"Yes, Grandma, I'm really graduating. I can't believe it, either! I never thought I'd be here today, you know? Really!

Like, I know it! Yup, it's a very special day... Oh, what did the doctor say? He did? I know, Gran... I know you wanted to come... It's okay... No, really, please don't cry... It's a very happy day, you know?

"Hold on, we're lining up... okay, all set... yup, the center aisle... the grass is awesome! Smells really good, too... Oh wow, they've got like a zillion balloons they're going to release! Yes, Kelly's here...Okay, I'll give her your love... here we go! Gran, I'm graduating!

"Love you, too, Gran. I'm so glad you could be here with me!"

And somehow, my initial surprise and disdain at the use of cell phones during such a serious occasion left me. For these little representatives of modern technology had joined a young woman and her doting Gran to share a very special moment in time.

~Gail C. Bracy
Chicken Soup for the Grandparent's Soul

100

Freedom Village

My most vivid memory associated with the American flag flashes back to Korea and a gray, clammy day in early August 1953. The Korean War had come to an end a week earlier, on July 27 at precisely 10 P.M. I remember lying in a rice paddy and suddenly experiencing the thunderous, deafening silence of peace. The Chinese and North Koreans, surely as joyful as I, were singing and raising their flags less than two hundred yards away from where my platoon sergeant and I sat smoking celebratory cigars.

A military spotlight, affectionately referred to as "Moonbeam Charlie," played along the valley floor and crept up the scarred hills, catching the Chinese and North Koreans in spirited dancing around their outpost flagpole. Their flags seemed to mean something to them, and at that time, I wasn't sure what my flag meant to me.

But that changed dramatically a week later, when I was a part of a contingent sent to represent my regiment at "Freedom Village."

"Operation Big Switch" was on. Our prisoners of war were to be returned to American hands, as the Chinese and North Koreans were to be returned to their people. Through the dim half-light of fading memory, I recollect that Freedom Village was in a scooped-out hollow with hills brooding over it from four sides. A few dwellings leaned into the village amid taut canvas hospital tents.

We representatives of the United Nations stood at attention as ambulances and beat-up buses arrived from the north. The UN, American and Korean flags hung limply in the humid August air. Photographers, Army and civilian alike, scurried about for good vantage points.

The Chinese and North Koreans were the first to cross over "Freedom Bridge." They were surly, healthy looking and well fed. Some carried signs decrying capitalism. Members of a Republic of Korea regiment scowled, and one of them sent a spray of saliva in his former opponent's direction. The exchange had a tone of tense and bitter antagonism, and as young as I was, I wondered how long the newly inked truce would last.

When the remaining Chinese and North Koreans had been herded off to their own vehicles, the UN prisoners were ushered from the trucks and buses and sent across the bridge to our side. The UN Honor Guard, combat veterans and observers gasped when they saw the condition of their returning comrades, who struggled, hobbled and staggered, gaunt and emaciated, toward friendly faces.

One after another they came. The next one was in worse condition than the one before. Long lines of dull-eyed soldiers of the "Forgotten War" inched their way to freedom, and out of their number, a gray-faced stick figure of a boy-turned-old-man dragged himself along the bridge. His bony arms were held out like a sleepwalker. He staggered and swayed, and one time fell into the wooden railing. Every eye in that village was suddenly trained on that one figure. Even those on the northern side watched the gallant physical effort of the wasted soldier.

Each tried, inwardly, to help, to urge him on, until

finally, when he lurched forward, an MP major, a giant of a man, came up to help. The soldier waved him off with his skeleton hands and arms.

Looking around at the grim faces, he caught sight of the three color bearers and shuffled toward them. When he reached the American flag bearer, he knelt on trembling knees before the flag as though it were an altar. He reached up and tugged at the flag. The color bearer, either by instinct or by some infinite wisdom, lowered the flag, and the soldier covered his face with it, sobbing and shaking uncontrollably.

Other than the clicks of cameras, the village was cemetery-quiet. Tears streamed from all of us. Cotton replaced saliva in our throats. After several moments, the stillness was broken by the sound of the heavy boots of the MP major, who came crunching across the gravel, his cheeks moist and glistening. He bent down and tenderly scooped the soldier up in his muscular arms and carried him off to a waiting ambulance, much as a father would carry a baby.

There wasn't a dry eye in that silent village, thousands of miles away from Main Street, USA.

~James F. Murphy Jr.
Chicken Soup for the Veteran's Soul

A New
Definition of Health

One day this spring, I went to the pool to swim my usual laps. I arrived during off-hours, had a lane all to myself and immersed myself in the rhythm of the swim as I enjoyed memories of a recent vacation. Then I glanced to my side and found myself sharing the lane with an elderly gentleman. There were other free lanes, but I guess he'd just decided to share this one. I didn't mind and continued my laps. As I swam, I noticed my lane-mate walked rather than swam, exercising his legs. At the end of my swim, I rested at the end of the lane.

My aged companion walked over and introduced himself, and mentioned that he was exercising to strengthen his hip before surgery. We traded names, and I told him that I thought he was smart to keep exercising his hip.

"I'm eighty," he said. "I want to live five more years and I'll do whatever I have to do. I also want to be able to go for morning walks with my lovely wife of sixty years." Then he asked, "What are you here for?"

Usually I avoid the multiple sclerosis (MS) label. I don't want it to become a "thing," and I don't want it to become my identity. Too many people start to make assumptions about the eventual prognosis and wind up adding to my own anxiety. I'd rather they create their own reality, not mine, so I don't bother with the MS label. Plus, I think of myself as healthy and like to affirm that. This time, however, I felt like it really didn't matter what anyone else thought. "Well, I have MS and I'm here to maintain good health."

"Oh, you must know Jim," he replied. "Jim has MS."

Another reason not to use the MS label, I thought. People tend to think it's a club where everyone who has the diagnosis knows one another. After indulging this sarcastic reverie, I turned my attention back to the gentleman. His good heart and intention were clear. "No, I don't know him," I said.

"Jim walks with a cane," he said. "Do you?"

"No, I don't, but I've thought about using one during the tough times."

He grew quiet, turned to face me squarely with his blue eyes and blessed me with his eighty years of wisdom. "Life's too short," he said. "Don't be a hero." With a smile, he turned and continued walking his laps.

I've always believed that what we need to hear will come to us if we're listening. Well, I was paying attention, and that moment was magical. "Don't be a hero." I began to consider my notion of being a hero, and my belief that I couldn't advise other people about wellness if I had to use a cane. I began to think about all the ways we think things should look or be — our images of health and wellness. And I realized something that felt profound and important. Now I have my own inner-directed definition of wellness that can also include not being a hero.

I realized that a cane was a tool I needed to assist me in living my life more fully and joyfully. I figured, if I cut my finger, I'd get a Band-Aid to help it heal. A cane is no different.

I found a cane that fit my needs and bought it. I needed no instruction; my body taught me all I needed to know in order to use it. I only needed to touch it to the ground lightly, as a means of feedback from the earth to me—a way of reassuring myself that the ground is there, ground I sometimes can't feel through the numbness and tingling in my feet. The moment I used the cane in this way, I experienced a renewed sense of ease and freedom. Wow, I thought, now I can take my eyes off the ground and see the trees.

I didn't realize how much I had missed the trees.

Recently, I found another new and visceral understanding of health—in the shower no less. I was washing my body with a scrubbie sponge and foaming soap. As I bent over to lather my right leg, enjoying the sensation of feeling my muscles against the sponge, I also noticed the muscular shape of that leg and how good the lather felt against my skin. When I started lathering my left leg, however, I began comparing it to the right one, thinking, oh, it doesn't look as strong. It won't hold as much weight. Oh, this poor leg.

Then I noticed that I had stopped enjoying the simple experience of lathering my legs—stopped enjoying it at the precise moment when I started judging it. Another thought struck me: What if I love this leg just as it is? What if I honor its weakness? In fact, what if I don't even label it as "weak"? What if I just love the muscles in this leg as they are? What if I love the sensation of scrubbing this leg? What if I love this leg right now? What if I stop waiting until it gets stronger, gets better, gets different? And what if I live my whole life like this—what if I love myself just as I am? What might my life become?

As I experienced this epiphany in the shower, I found myself standing more balanced on both legs than I had in a long time. This new definition of health and of unconditional acceptance has forever changed my life. And whatever challenges or joys I may meet in the future, lessons like these make the journey worthwhile.

~Erica Ross-Krieger
Chicken Soup to Inspire the Body & Soul

Share with Us

We would like to know how these stories affected you and which ones were your favorites. Please e-mail us and let us know.

We also would like to share your stories with future readers. You may be able to help another reader, and become a published author at the same time. Please send us your own stories and poems for our future books. Some of our past contributors have launched writing and speaking careers from the publication of their stories in our books!

Your stories have the best chance of being used if you submit them through our web site, at:

www.chickensoup.com

If you do not have access to the Internet, you may submit your stories by mail or by facsimile. Please do not send us any book manuscripts, unless through a literary agent,
as these will be automatically discarded.

Chicken Soup for the Soul
P.O. Box 700
Cos Cob, CT 06807-0700
Fax 203-861-7194

Chicken Soup for the Soul®

Chicken Soup for the Woman's Soul
1-55874-415-0

A Second Chicken Soup for the Woman's Soul
1-55874-622-6

Chicken Soup for the Golden Soul
1-55874-725-7

Chicken Soup for the Veteran's Soul
1-55874-937-3

Chicken Soup for the Grandparent's Soul
1-55874-974-8

Chicken Soup for the Grieving Soul
1-55874-902-0

Chicken Soup to Inspire a Woman's Soul
0-7573-0210-6

Chicken Soup for the Grandma's Soul
0-7573-0328-5

Check out our great books for

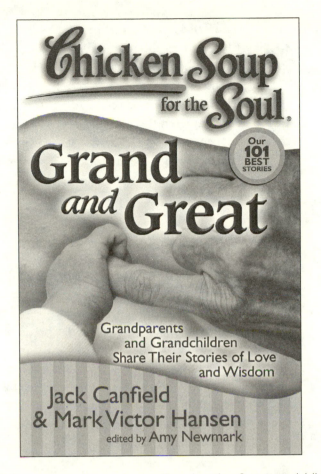

Chicken Soup for the Soul

Our 101 BEST STORIES

Grand *and* Great

Grandparents and Grandchildren Share Their Stories of Love and Wisdom

Jack Canfield
& Mark Victor Hansen
edited by Amy Newmark

A parent becomes a new person the day the first grandchild is born. Formerly serious adults become grandparents who dote on their grandchildren. This new book includes the best stories on being a grandparent from past Chicken soup books, representing a new reading experience for even the most devoted Chicken Soup fan. Everyone can understand the special ties between grandparents and grandchildren—the unlimited love, the mutual admiration and unqualified acceptance.

978-1-935096-09-2

Seniors

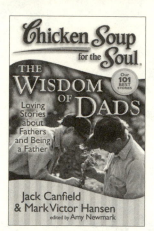

The Wisdom of Dads

Children view their fathers with awe from the day they are born. Fathers are big and strong and seem to know everything, except for a few teenage years when fathers are perceived to know nothing! This book represents a new theme for Chicken Soup — 101 stories selected from 35 past books, all stories focusing on the wisdom of dads. Stories are written by sons and daughters about their fathers, and by fathers relating stories about their children.

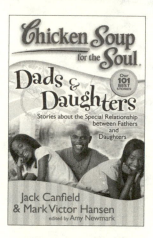

Dads & Daughters

Whether she is ten years old or fifty — she will always be his little girl. And daughters take care of their dads too, whether it is a tea party for two at age five or loving care fifty years later. This wide-ranging exploration of the relationship between fathers and daughters provides an entirely new reading experience for Chicken Soup fans, with selections from forty past Chicken Soup books. Stories were written by fathers about their daughters and by daughters about their fathers, celebrating the special bond between fathers and daughters.

On Being a Parent

Parenting is the hardest and most rewarding job in the world. This upbeat and compelling new book includes the best selections on parenting from Chicken Soup's rich history, with 101 stories carefully selected to appeal to both mothers and fathers. This is a great book for couples to share, whether they are just embarking on their new adventure as parents or reflecting on their lifetime experience.

Check out our great books on

Moms Know Best

"Mom will know where it is…what to say…how to fix it." This Chicken Soup book focuses on the pervasive wisdom of mothers everywhere, and includes the best 101 stories from Chicken Soup's library on our perceptive, understanding, and insightful mothers. These stories celebrate the special bond between mothers and children, our mothers' unerring wisdom about everything from the mundane to the life-changing, and the hard work that goes into being a mother every day.

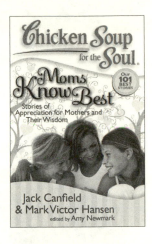

Grand and Great

A parent becomes a new person the day the first grandchild is born. Formerly serious adults become grandparents who dote on their grandchildren. This new book includes the best stories on being a grandparent from past Chicken soup books, representing a new reading experience for even the most devoted Chicken Soup fan. Everyone can understand the special ties between grandparents and grandchildren -- the unlimited love, the mutual admiration and unqualified acceptance.

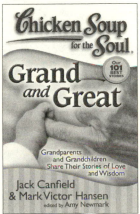

Teens Talk Growing Up

Being a teenager is hard — school is challenging, college and career are looming on the horizon, family issues arise, friends and love come and go, bodies and emotions go through major changes, and many teens experience the loss of a loved one for the first time. This book reminds teenagers that they are not alone, as they read stories written by other teens about the problems and issues they all face every day.

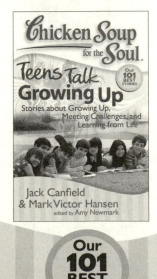

Family

Our 101 BEST STORIES

FAVORITES!

Christmas Cheer
Stories about the Love, Inspiration, and Joy of Christmas
978-1-935096-15-3

Everyone loves Christmas and the holiday season. We reunite scattered family members, watch the wonder in a child's eyes, and feel the joy of giving gifts. The rituals of the holiday season give a rhythm to the years and create a foundation for our lives, as we gather with family, with our communities at church, at school, and even at the mall, to share the special spirit of the season, brightening those long winter days.

Happily Ever After
Fun and Heartwarming Stories about Finding and Enjoying Your Mate
978-1-935096-10-8

Dating and courtship, romance, love, and marriage are favorite Chicken Soup topics. Women, and even men, love to read true stories about how it happened for other people. This book includes the 101 best stories on love and marriage chosen from a wide variety of past Chicken Soup books. These heartwarming stories will inspire and amuse readers, whether they are just starting to date, are newly wed, or are veterans of a long marriage.

Books for Pet Lovers

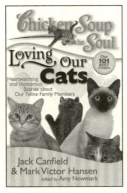

Loving Our Cats

Heartwarming and Humorous Stories about Our Feline Family Members

978-1-935096-08-5

We are all crazy about our mysterious cats. Sometimes they are our best friends; sometimes they are aloof. They are fun to watch and often surprise us. These true stories, the best from Chicken Soup's library, will make readers appreciate their own cats and see them with a new eye. Readers will revel in the heartwarming, amusing, inspirational, and occasionally tearful stories about our best friends and faithful companions — our cats.

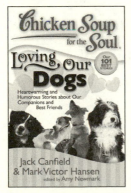

Loving Our Dogs

Heartwarming and Humorous Stories about Our Companions and Best Friends

978-1-935096-05-4

We are all crazy about our dogs and can't read enough about them, whether they're misbehaving and giving us big, innocent looks, or loyally standing by us in times of need. This new book from Chicken Soup for the Soul contains the 101 best dog stories from the company's extensive library. Readers will revel in the heartwarming, amusing, inspirational, and occasionally tearful stories about our best friends and faithful companions — our dogs.

About the Authors
&
Acknowledgments

Who Is
Jack Canfield?

Jack Canfield is the co-creator and editor of the *Chicken Soup for the Soul* series, which *Time* magazine has called "the publishing phenomenon of the decade." Jack is also the co-author of eight other bestselling books including *The Success Principles™: How to Get from Where You Are to Where You Want to Be, Dare to Win, The Aladdin Factor, You've Got to Read This Book*, and *The Power of Focus: How to Hit Your Business and Personal and Financial Targets with Absolute Certainty*.

Jack has recently developed a telephone coaching program and an online coaching program based on his most recent book *The Success Principles*. He also offers a seven-day *Breakthrough to Success* seminar every summer, which attracts 400 people from fifteen countries around the world.

Jack is the CEO of the Canfield Training Group in Santa Barbara, California, and founder of the Foundation for Self-Esteem in Culver City, California. He has conducted intensive personal and professional development seminars on the principles of success for over a million people in twenty-three countries. Jack is a dynamic keynote speaker and he has spoken to hundreds of thousands of others at more than 1,000 corporations, universities, professional conferences and conventions, and has been seen by millions more on national television shows such as *The Today Show, Fox and Friends, Inside Edition, Hard Copy, CNN's Talk*

Back Live, *20/20*, *Eye to Eye*, and the *NBC Nightly News* and the *CBS Evening News*.

Jack is the recipient of many awards and honors, including three honorary doctorates and a *Guinness World Records Certificate* for having seven books from the *Chicken Soup for the Soul* series appearing on the *New York Times* bestseller list on May 24, 1998.

To write to Jack or for inquiries about Jack as a speaker, his coaching programs, trainings or seminars, use the following contact information:

Jack Canfield
The Canfield Companies
P.O. Box 30880 • Santa Barbara, CA 93130
phone: 805-563-2935 • fax: 805-563-2945
E-mail: info@jackcanfield.com
www.jackcanfield.com

Who Is
Mark Victor Hansen?

Mark Victor Hansen is the co-founder of *Chicken Soup for the Soul*, along with Jack Canfield. He is also a sought-after keynote speaker, bestselling author, and marketing maven.

For more than thirty years, Mark has focused solely on helping people from all walks of life reshape their personal vision of what's possible. His powerful messages of possibility, opportunity, and action have created powerful change in thousands of organizations and millions of individuals worldwide.

Mark's credentials include a lifetime of entrepreneurial success. He is a prolific writer with many bestselling books, such as *The One Minute Millionaire, Cracking the Millionaire Code, How to Make the Rest of Your Life the Best of Your Life, The Power of Focus, The Aladdin Factor*, and *Dare to Win*, in addition to the *Chicken Soup for the Soul* series. Mark has had a profound influence in the field of human potential through his library of audios, videos, and articles in the areas of big thinking, sales achievement, wealth building, publishing success, and personal and professional development.

Mark is the founder of the *MEGA Seminar Series. MEGA Book Marketing University* and *Building Your MEGA Speaking Empire* are annual conferences where Mark coaches and teaches new and aspiring authors, speakers, and experts on building lucrative publishing and speaking careers. Other

MEGA events include *MEGA Info-Marketing* and *My MEGA Life*.

He has appeared on *Oprah*, *CNN*, and *The Today Show*. He has been quoted in *Time*, *U.S. News & World Report*, *USA Today*, *New York Times*, and *Entrepreneur* and has had countless radio interviews, assuring our planet's people that "You can easily create the life you deserve."

As a philanthropist and humanitarian, Mark works tirelessly for organizations such as Habitat for Humanity, American Red Cross, March of Dimes, Childhelp USA, and many others. He is the recipient of numerous awards that honor his entrepreneurial spirit, philanthropic heart, and business acumen. He is a lifetime member of the Horatio Alger Association of Distinguished Americans, an organization that honored Mark with the prestigious Horatio Alger Award for his extraordinary life achievements.

Mark Victor Hansen is an enthusiastic crusader of what's possible and is driven to make the world a better place.

Mark Victor Hansen & Associates, Inc.
P.O. Box 7665 • Newport Beach, CA 92658
phone: 949-764-2640 • fax: 949-722-6912
www.markvictorhansen.com

Who Is
Amy Newmark?

Amy Newmark was recently named publisher of Chicken Soup for the Soul, after a thirty-year career as a writer, speaker, financial analyst, and business executive in the worlds of finance and telecommunications.

Amy is a graduate of Harvard College, where she majored in Portuguese, minored in French, and traveled extensively. She is also the mother of two children in college and has two grown stepchildren.

After a long career writing books on telecommunications, voluminous financial reports, business plans, and corporate press releases, Chicken Soup for the Soul is a breath of fresh air for Amy. She has fallen in love with Chicken Soup for the Soul and its life-changing books, and found it a true pleasure to conceptualize, compile, and edit the "101 Best Stories" books for our readers.

The best way to contact Chicken Soup for the Soul is through our web site, at www.chickensoup.com. This will always get the fastest attention.

If you do not have access to the Internet, please contact us by mail or by facsimile.

Chicken Soup for the Soul
P.O. Box 700
Cos Cob, CT 06807-0700
Fax 203-861-7194

Thank You!

Our first thanks go to our loyal readers who have inspired the entire Chicken Soup team for the past fifteen years. Your appreciative letters and e-mails have reminded us why we work so hard on these books.

We owe huge thanks to all of our contributors as well. We know that you pour your hearts and souls into the stories and poems that you share with us, and ultimately with each other. We appreciate your willingness to open up your lives to other Chicken Soup readers.

We can only publish a small percentage of the stories that are submitted, but we read every single one and even the ones that do not appear in a book have an influence on us and on the final manuscripts.

As always, we would like to thank the entire staff of Chicken Soup for the Soul for their help on this project and the 101 Best series in general.

Among our California staff, we would especially like to single out the following people:

- D'ette Corona, who is the heart and soul of the Chicken Soup publishing operation, and who put together the first draft of this manuscript

- Barbara LoMonaco for invaluable assistance in obtaining the fabulous quotations that add depth and meaning to this book

- Patty Hansen for her extra special help with the permissions for these fabulous stories and for her amazing knowledge of the Chicken Soup library and Patti Clement for her help with permissions and other organizational matters.

In our Connecticut office, we would like to thank our able editorial assistants, Valerie Howlett and Madeline Clapps, for their assistance in setting up our new offices, editing, and helping us put together the best possible books.

We would also like to thank our master of design, Creative Director and book producer Brian Taylor at Pneuma Books, LLC, for his brilliant vision for our covers and interiors.

Finally, none of this would be possible without the business and creative leadership of our CEO, Bill Rouhana, and our president, Bob Jacobs.

Chicken Soup

www.chickensoup.com

for the Soul